BETWEEN COMPOSERS

Between Composers

The Letters of Norma Beecroft
and Harry Somers

EDITED BY BRIAN CHERNEY

McGill-Queen's University Press
Montreal & Kingston • London • Chicago

© McGill-Queen's University Press 2024

ISBN 978-0-2280-2274-9 (cloth)
ISBN 978-0-2280-2312-8 (ePDF)
ISBN 978-0-2280-2313-5 (ePUB)

Legal deposit fourth quarter 2024
Bibliothèque nationale du Québec

Printed in Canada on acid-free paper that is 100% ancient forest free (100% post-consumer recycled), processed chlorine free

This book has been published with the help of a grant from the Federation for the Humanities and Social Sciences, through the Awards to Scholarly Publications Program, using funds provided by the Social Sciences and Humanities Research Council of Canada.

We acknowledge the support of the Canada Council for the Arts.
Nous remercions le Conseil des arts du Canada de son soutien.

McGill-Queen's University Press in Montreal is on land which long served as a site of meeting and exchange amongst Indigenous Peoples, including the Haudenosaunee and Anishinabeg nations. In Kingston it is situated on the territory of the Haudenosaunee and Anishinaabek. We acknowledge and thank the diverse Indigenous Peoples whose footsteps have marked these territories on which peoples of the world now gather.

Library and Archives Canada Cataloguing in Publication

Title: Between composers : the letters of Norma Beecroft and Harry Somers / editor, Brian Cherney.
Names: Beecroft, Norma, author. | Somers, Harry, 1925-1999, author. | Cherney, Brian, editor.
Description: Includes bibliographical references and index.
Identifiers: Canadiana (print) 20240395093 | Canadiana (ebook) 20240395379 | ISBN 9780228022749 (hardcover) | ISBN 9780228023128 (ePDF) | ISBN 9780228023135 (ePUB)
Subjects: LCSH: Composers—Canada—Correspondence. | LCSH: Beecroft, Norma Correspondence. | LCSH: Somers, Harry, 1925-1999—Correspondence. | LCSH: Composers—Canada—Biography.
Classification: LCC ML390.B565 2024 | DDC 780.92/2713—dc23

This book was typeset in 10.5/13 Sabon. Copyediting by Gillian Scobie.

In memory of John Beckwith (1927–2022)
composer, Canadian music scholar,
teacher, colleague, and friend

Contents

Acknowledgments   ix

Note on the text   xiii

Introduction   3

Chapter 1: September 1959   34

Chapter 2: October 1959   53

Chapter 3: November 1959   81

Chapter 4: December 1959   147

Chapter 5: January 1960   197

Chapter 6: February 1960   241

Epilogue   260

Notes   267

Index   271

Acknowledgments

First and foremost, I am indebted to Norma Beecroft, who generously allowed me to take this correspondence with me to read when she first showed it to me. (I have described this in more detail in the introduction.) Once I began to assemble the transcribed letters and add footnotes, Norma patiently answered numerous questions concerning people, events, and, above all, her relationship with Harry Somers. As mentioned below, she also helped transcribe many of the letters and became quite enthusiastic about the project.

In the course of preparing the letters for publication, Norma's brother, Charles A.S. Beecroft, has provided me with information of various kinds. He also searched her computer in recent months, when she herself was no longer able to do this, to obtain information related to permission to publish and other matters.

I would like to express my appreciation to Jonathan Crago, editor-in-chief at McGill-Queen's University Press, who met with me during the early part of the COVID-19 pandemic and encouraged me to edit the letters and submit them to be considered for publication. Along the way, he has also given me many valuable suggestions, such as how to deal with the lively writing of Harry Somers, who appears to have had complete disdain for putting apostrophes into possessive forms (never mind other types of punctuation) and had never acquired the habit of spelling correctly, especially the names of people.

Gillian Scobie was the copy editor for the manuscript. She meticulously helped to correct the many oversights and errors in the dozens of footnotes I wrote. Since these letters were written some sixty-five years ago, footnotes are essential, as they identify so many now-forgotten people, places, and events mentioned in the letters.

I also appreciate the help provided by the exceptional staff of the Marvin Duchow Music Library at McGill University, especially that provided by Gabrielle Kern, Melissa Pipe, and David Curtis. All of the staff were extremely helpful but I must single out David Curtis for special thanks. In addition to helping to find esoteric information a number of times, David had a rare talent for tracking down virtually any library item that could not be located by using the usual human faculties to search the stacks of a large library.

My thanks also to my McGill colleague, Professor Christoph Neidhöfer, whose encouragement was so supportive. His research into postwar European serialism intersects with Bruno Maderna's approach to serialism and its influence on Norma Beecroft's early use of this compositional approach. Professor Neidhöfer generously very early music from the 1950s available to me. He also co-hosted with me an extended public interview with Beecroft at McGill on 21 March 2019, when I organized and presented a concert at which actors read excerpts of these letters and music by both Somers and Beecroft was performed.

Several people – David Menzies, Christine Sabbaghian, and Norma Beecroft – helped transcribe these handwritten letters, much of it during those bleak and solitary days early on in the COVID-19 pandemic. They carried out this challenging task with all possible care and accuracy. I could never have completed such a huge undertaking by myself, so I'm all the more grateful for the assistance I received. Any mistakes still remaining in the letters are undoubtedly due to oversight on my part. In such a huge body of correspondence, so detailed, and covering such a wide range of human activity, it would be a miracle if there were not still small errors. The letters have been checked a number of times and I trust that the format and accuracy will contribute to a problem-free reading experience.

I have dedicated this book to the memory of John Beckwith (1927–2022), the eminent composer, Canadian music scholar, and educator, who played such an important role in so many aspects of Canadian music for some seventy-five years. It was because of John that I first started writing about Canadian music – he was the editor of my first book, a monograph on Harry Somers, published in 1975 – and we collaborated on a collection of essays on John Weinzweig, published in 2011. John's example inspired me (and undoubtedly many others) to be curious about Canadian music, to write about it, to try to do everything possible to get people interested in exploring it. I

Acknowledgments

hope that the publication of this unique correspondence between two important Canadian composers will encourage those who read the letters to get curious, to explore their music, and the music of so many others who were their contemporaries. This would be a fitting tribute to John, who cared so passionately about such things.

Brian Cherney
Professor
McGill University

Note on the Text

The letters in this collection were handwritten over a period of five-and-a-half months. Since the calligraphy of both correspondents was very clear and neat, there were few problems (such as illegibility) in transcribing the letters for publication. I tried to keep the format of the transcribed letters as close to the original as possible. Somers generally wrote in short paragraphs, consisting of two or three sentences, whereas Beecroft wrote longer paragraphs. However, they both had some idiosyncratic approaches to punctuation. Beecroft consistently used tildes (~) instead of periods to punctuate sentences. I decided to retain this unusual punctuation in the transcribed letters, since I think it reflected her mental process in writing – a fluidity, one thought flowing into the next.

Somers's letters presented problems other than legibility. His punctuation was cavalier, to say the least, especially when it came to using commas for possessives and in sentences. In addition to this, his spelling was atrocious, not only when it came to people's names but even in ordinary words. If I had left all of these mistakes in the transcribed letters, the "[*sic*]'s" would have been so numerous as to spoil the continuity of the letters. Therefore, I made a compromise: I corrected the numerous errors in possessives and certain other obvious spelling mistakes, but I left the misspellings of people's names as they were (usually correcting these in footnotes). I did not add commas to the text itself, thus hoping to retain as much as possible the character of the letters. Thus, for instance, "your not writing as often as you should ..." was changed to "you're not writing as often as you should ...".

The other problem with Somers's letters was the repetitive nature of his declarations of love for Beecroft, from the end of October 1959 until the middle of February 1960. This was probably due to the somewhat obsessive nature of his feelings for her during this period, but a transcription of his letters in their entirety would have made for tedious reading and would have overwhelmed many other important aspects of his letters. Therefore, I omitted certain sections that contained amorous declarations as well as reassurances (repeated again and again) that he supported Beecroft's ambitions, while leaving enough of such passages to give the reader a good sense of their importance in the letters.

On the other hand, no such extensive omissions were necessary with Beecroft's letters, since they are far more focused on the problems she faced in coming to Rome, such as finding a place to live, getting on with her creative work, meeting people who could provide professional and social support, and (increasingly) writing about her feelings about Somers. However, I made some minor omissions to her letters when I felt that certain passages did not add much of interest for the reader.

B. Cherney

9 Lauderdale Dr.
Jan. 15. 1955.

Dear Norma:

I don't know why, but I feel an urge to write you of my feelings about composition, what it involves etc.

You are beginning. There is so much which is phony around us and in us, a kind of natural part of humankinds make up. In composition any of the self deceptive human traits are absolutely destructive. Ones work is a kind of Portrait of Dorian Gray, for every dishonest flaw is revealed.

All commercial media about us preach the gospel of expediency. It is a death trap to any creative thinking. (I run the risk of sounding like "A Young Girls Guide to Virginal Composition.") But the danger is that an environment can change ones thinking without one knowing it.

2.

If you really mean it, and have something to say, you will survive. If not, it doesn't matter.

In the final analyses one has to find out for ones self — a real platitude, but nevertheless so true — so why am I writing?

Just this — lots of courage and lots of luck.

Harry Somers

Letter of 15 January 1955 from Harry Somers to Norma Beecroft, his first letter to her.

Sunday, September 13 —

Darling,

Let me tell you never to go on an ocean voyage if you are, and have been, emotionally upset and fatigued period — I have been in a state of dizziness, with very weak legs, all day — and am hoping that it will pass by tomorrow — The ocean has been very calm (normal swells) all day — with a hot sun — and the only time I have felt even half human was sitting up in my corner deck chair watching the ocean and the few clouds pass by — Where I was standing when I last saw you on the pier was where I reserved my chair — It is a marvellous spot, and I am talking occasionally with a Catholic priest, taking a sabbatical year to study philosophy in Europe, who sits in the next chair —

Outside of that, it has turned out that I am not alone in my cabin, but have the lower berth — The person occupying the upper berth is an older women (possibly 55 - 65) by the name of Bertha Poncy Jacobson, who is the head of the piano dept. at the University of Washington, in Seattle, a very interesting, but rather strange and strong-willed musician — We have discovered to date friends in common — and she is going to Europe to investigate the contemporary music scene — She has offered to give me some information on libraries in Rome containing old manuscripts — Being only the first day and because of my malady, I haven't desired to talk too much — so more later about her —

I have also met a Mexican criminal lawyer —

NB's first letter to HS, written aboard the SS *Liberté* on 13 September 1959.

4.

Ah ha! Speaking of 'eternal city', the district is to have a glorious addition to its celebrity. As of to-day, Oct 5, what was once known far and wide as the 'Famous Door Tavern', is to be known to the world as 'Jazz City', PRESENTING, LADIES and GENTS ☞ THE *LATEST* AND *GREATEST* IN JAZZ

COVER CHARGE 1.00
weekends 1.50

The line up looks impressive though.

By the way, a chap who styles himself 'Mayor of Motor City' (As you may gather, a used car dealer, to be exact.) has aroused the righteous wrath of our illustrious City of Toronto, mayor of all the people, Mayor Nathan, or 'Nate', Phillips. He claims that this Mayor of Motor City by using the title of the most noble office of our fair city doth detract from the grandeur and dignity of said office. Mayor of M.C. won't budge so that quite a case is developing.

With these important items from this hub of commerce and art to brighten up the dullness of that provincial little town your staying in, I conclude my epistle to the Beecroftian.

With so much love it would crush you to death —

Harry

Letter from HS on 3 October 1959, with his drawing of the announcement of a new jazz club, the "Famous Door Tavern."

BERKSHIRE MUSIC CENTER
CHARLES MUNCH, DIRECTOR
TANGLEWOOD—LENOX, MASSACHUSETTS

COMPOSERS' FORUM

Sunday, July 20, 1958 at 8:30 P.M. - In the Chamber Music Hall

Moderator - Milton Babbitt

THOMAS ARONIS (Indianapolis, Ind.)   Sonata for Violin and Piano

Allegro - Lento espressivo - Presto

DOUGLAS LEEDY (Portland, Oregon)   Variations on a Ground-Bass
for Clarinet and Piano

ROBERT LOMBARDO (Hartford, Conn.) Three Songs for Alto and Piano
Text by Adalaide Crapsey

Triad - November - A Warning

THOMAS PUTSCHE (West Hartford, Conn.)   Two Virgins Contemplate a
Cowboy Who Contemplates In
His Turn

First Virgin - Second Virgin - Cowboy

Conducted by the composer

MARVIN SALZBERG (Ithaca, New York)   String Quartet No. 1
(To be played without pause)

Moderato - Singingly
Slow-gaily-slow-gaily-fast-slow

NORMA BEECROFT (Toronto, Canada)   Study for Woodwinds and Brass

Victor DiBello - Conductor

FROMM FELLOWSHIP PLAYERS

Theodora Mantz - Violin   Herbert Resnick Oboe
Peter Marsh - Violin   Efrain Guigui - Clarinet
R. Scott Nickrenz - Viola   Richard Lottridge - Bassoon
Donald McCall - Violoncello   Paul Ingraham - French Horn
Gerardo Levy - Flute   Robert Miller - Piano
Corinne Curry - Soprano

FROM ORCHESTRAL DEPARTMENT

Homer Lee - Clarinet (Leedy)
Donald McComas and Fred Orkiseski - Trumpet (Beecroft)
Robert Gutter and Ulysses James - Trombone (Beecroft)

BALDWIN PIANO

Tanglewood program for 20 July 1958. NB's *Movement for Woodwinds
and Brass* was performed, although it is titled "Study for Woodwinds and
Brass" on the program. Also performed was a work by Thomas Putsché,
whom Beecroft met again in Rome in 1960. Boston Symphony Archives,
archives.bso.org.

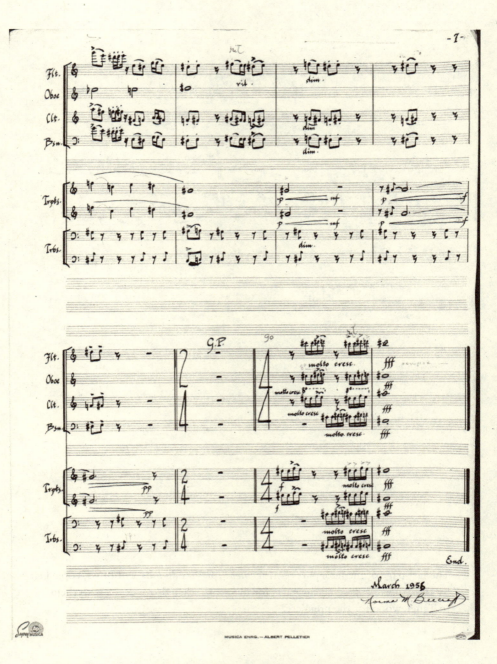

The last page of the autograph score of NB's *Movement for Woodwinds and Brass*, completed in March 1956. Beecroft's music calligraphy already closely resembled that of HS.

The last page of the flute part of *Movement for Woodwinds and Brass*, copied by HS. Somers copied all the parts for this work, then drove down with them to Tanglewood for the premiere.

Composition class at Tanglewood 1958. Front row (*left to right*) includes Thea Musgrave (*second from the left*), then Lukas Foss, Aaron Copland, unknown, and NB. Standing, on the far left, is Mario Davidovsky.

Tanglewood 1958. *Left to right*: Claudio Abbado, Thea Musgrave, Mario Davidofsky, NB.

Kearney, Ontario (?) ca. 1957–58. HS and NB.

Toronto ca. 1958–59. Front row (*left to right*): HS and NB; back row (*left to right*): unidentified, girlfriend of Eric Beecroft, Eric Beecroft.

Kearney, Ontario (?) ca. 1957–58. HS, NB, and John Weinzweig.

Rome 1960. *Left to right*: Aram Babukian, Dr Paul Chevalier, and NB on the balcony of her apartment.

Rome, spring of 1960. Goffredo Petrassi (*on the left*) and some of the students in his composition class: (*left to right*) NB, Will Eisma, and Virtu Maragno.

Darmstadt, Germany, summer 1960 (?). *Left to right*: Severino Gazzelloni, NB, Bruno Maderna, Roman Haubenstock-Ramati, and Signora Gazzelloni.

BETWEEN COMPOSERS

INTRODUCTION

Between Composers: The Letters of Norma Beecroft and Harry Somers

(September 1959 to February 1960)

Some years ago, I began working on a new book on the life and music of Harry Somers. My original book on Somers had been published in 1975, just as Somers turned fifty, and was not only incomplete (he lived until 1999 and produced a good deal more music) but lacking in certain information, which only became available after his death, when his papers were turned over to Library and Archives Canada. Many years earlier, I had heard from someone well acquainted with both Somers and Norma Beecroft that they had been in a relationship during the 1950s. I had not written about this in the earlier book and arranged, therefore, to visit Norma Beecroft and ask her about her relationship with Somers, to see if she could provide me with any insights into the man himself and/or his music.

Thus, one day in 2014, I arrived at the train station in Oshawa (where she lived) and made my way to her house. Once settled in her living room, we proceeded to talk about Harry Somers (with whom she had, indeed, been in a relationship and for much longer than I had realized). As we talked, I noticed an enormous pile of letters sitting on the table between us. She must have sensed my barely contained curiosity about these and eventually explained that these were letters exchanged between her and Harry Somers during the early period of her stay in Rome in 1959 to 1962. As she spoke, I was trying to figure out how I could politely ask whether I could have a look at a few of these, wondering whether it would be too impertinent of me. However, such a request became unnecessary, for, much to my amazement, she *offered* (without any prompting or need for persuasion on my part!) to let me take *all* the letters back to

Montreal on the train. As a veteran of many hours spent at Library and Archives Canada in Ottawa, where I, as a researcher, was under constant surveillance, always under suspicion of attempting to steal a precious document or of taking unauthorized photographs of some page or other of a musical sketch, I nearly fell off my chair when offered such a generous, suspicion-free opportunity. I recovered sufficiently to help her load the letters into a shopping bag to return to the Oshawa train station for my trip back to Montreal.

I will always be grateful to Norma Beecroft for her generosity that day, in letting me borrow those letters, even though she barely knew me at the time. But she trusted me. This correspondence – both Beecroft's letters to Somers and his to her – amounted to about one hundred and twenty letters and had been in her possession all these years. As I read through them on the train that day, and in the days to follow, I became convinced that they should be published. Not only did they provide a detailed glimpse into the lives of the two correspondents at the time – but they also conveyed a vivid sense of the musical and cultural life of Canada in the late 1950s. As far as I know, there is no other such body of extended correspondence between two Canadian composers. Beecroft and Somers both came from the same musical milieu (in Toronto) but were at different stages in their compositional development. For both, the period of the correspondence (from September 1959 until February 1960) represented an important turning point in their respective creative development. In addition, Norma Beecroft was a young woman who was struggling (at the end of the 1950s) to resist the pressure to take on the traditional woman's role of wife and mother in those years, to live independently and fulfill her own creative needs as a composer. As a male, of course, Somers was under no such pressure.

In addition, reading an exchange of so many detailed letters, written over a relatively short period, can be like listening to a conversation. Gone are the pauses and delays of chronological time, the lapses of time between the sending and receiving of letters. The person reading the letters in chronological order can imagine they are eavesdropping on an extended conversation, much as one can "see" the opening of a flower through the technique of time-lapse photography.

The basic trajectory of the letters is as follows: in September 1959, Norma Beecroft, a young composition student, left Toronto and travelled to Rome with the intention of studying with a well-known Italian composer, Goffredo Petrassi. Harry Somers, a somewhat

Introduction

older, and widely recognized, composer in Canada, remained in Toronto to carry on with his writing, intending to visit her in Rome later. By that time, they had been in a romantic relationship for about four years but had made no arrangement to make their relationship permanent, largely, it would seem, because Somers was not willing to commit himself to any such permanence.[1] However, after Beecroft had been gone for some weeks, Somers rather abruptly declared that he loved her passionately and wanted, more than anything, to marry her. Over the next few months, however, she became increasingly dubious about this possibility, coming more and more to value her independence and anxious to proceed with her composition studies in Rome. Somers became more and more insistent about marriage and her returning to Canada. Much of the narrative thread in the correspondence centres around this issue, which became increasingly stressful for her. When he visited her in Rome in mid-February 1960, he angrily challenged what she was doing and this brought their relationship to an end. Somers returned to Toronto almost immediately and continued writing to Beecroft until early May 1960, but as far as she was concerned, their relationship had already ended in February.

NORMA BEECROFT

Born in Oshawa, Ontario, in 1934, Norma Beecroft was the second of the five children of Eleanor Norton (1906–2007), who later became a well-known actress in Toronto, and Julian Balfour Beecroft (1908–2008), a musician, inventor, and machinist. Norma developed an interest in music during her childhood (her father had trained as a pianist but did not encourage her musical interests) and only began formal studies when she moved to Toronto in 1950, after her parents separated. During the 1950s, she studied both piano and flute but, more important, began studying theory and composition in 1952 with the composer and teacher John Weinzweig. Supporting herself in a variety of jobs in her early years in Toronto, she began working for CBC Television in 1954 as a script assistant on music programs. She later wrote that there must have been "something inside" of her that responded "profoundly" to music and that she "wanted to participate in this world of sound in some way."[2] She wrote several pieces in these early years, including a choral work based on some lines from T.S. Eliot's "The Hollow Men" (translated into Latin) and a work for string orchestra, Fantasy for Strings. She also wrote two movements of a piece for woodwinds and brass and two movements of a work for orchestra; the former were given a reading during the summer of 1958 at the Berkshire Music Centre at Tanglewood, where she studied with Lukas Foss. The experience at Tanglewood was of the utmost importance for her future, as she met (among others) the young conductor Claudio Abbado, who suggested that she go to Italy o study with the Italian composer Goffredo Petrassi. Thanks to a modest inheritance from an uncle of her father's, not long after her return from Tanglewood she made plans to travel to Rome to study with Petrassi and left for Europe in September 1959.

The following passage describes, in her own words, how Beecroft, twenty years old, who had just started working as a script assistant for CBC Television in the fall of 1954, came to meet Harry Somers:

> In the late fall of 1954, I was working on a CBC Television production called Canadian General Electric "Showtime," starring vocalist Shirley Harmer and the Howard Cable Orchestra. Rehearsals were taking place in CBC's Studio 7 on Yonge Street, and on one of the morning breaks I wandered down to the studio floor from the control room, and ran into a tall, blond man, unknown to me as a part of the production, who introduce[d] himself to me as Harry Somers. He was delivering parts for Cable's orchestra, which he and others had spent the night copying. I was duly impressed meeting this young man, whose reputation as a highly talented composer was known to me through my teacher John Weinzweig. He was also a very attractive male, with a lanky frame like that of a tennis player, which indeed he was, and a handsome head with a very high forehead and deeply inset probing eyes. I was to learn that Harry Somers, in spite of his stature in the music world, made his living in part by copying parts from another composer's orchestral score, which was a bit of a revelation.[3]

It is important to point out that the thread connecting them, right at the outset of their relationship, was the Toronto composer and teacher John Weinzweig (1913–2006). Weinzweig had been teaching theory, orchestration, and composition at the Royal Conservatory of Music (as it had been called since 1947) since 1940 and had

Introduction 7

been appointed an assistant professor in the Faculty of Music at the University of Toronto in 1952. In these years, he was undoubtedly the leading figure in Canadian new music, both as a composer and a teacher. He was the one of the first composers in Canada to explore twentieth-century musical modernism and the first to explore twelve-tone technique. In 1951, he had co-founded the Canadian League of Composers (along with Somers and Samuel Dolin). Beecroft had gone to the Weinzweigs' home every week since 1952 for theory lessons and considered them a second family. Somers had studied with Weinzweig in the 1940s and still consulted him about compositional matters and considered Weinzweig and his wife Helen to be close friends. Weinzweig is mentioned frequently in the present correspondence, and it was through him that Beecroft already knew who Harry Somers was when she met him at the CBC studio that fall day in 1954. Thanks to her relationship with Weinzweig, she was familiar with other recent developments in new Canadian music.

Beecroft's relationship with Somers began only in January of 1955, however, when he felt the need to write a brief letter to her, warning of the perils of avoiding "expediency" and wishing her luck. This letter is notable for several reasons. First, the handwriting is distinctive. Probably influenced by his friend, the Toronto lawyer and poet Michael Fram (1923–1989), who supplied elegantly written texts for no fewer than eight compositions during the 1950s, Somers had recently started using the distinctive italic script displayed here. At this stage, certain strokes are longer than they later became (with more practice, one assumes), but he wrote all his subsequent correspondence until the 1970s, when he began using a typewriter, in this script. (In later years, even in personal memoranda, thoughts jotted down quickly are similarly written.) In turn, Beecroft herself was inspired by these two men to adapt her own version of this script – this is quite evident in her letters to Somers.

Second, the main message in the letter is that a creative artist has to be true to themselves, has to maintain integrity, regardless of societal or commercial pressures. This remained one of Somers's central artistic concerns throughout his life. Third, he slips in a reference to Oscar Wilde's *The Picture of Dorian Gray* to reinforce this precept: if one isn't honest in one's work, that dishonesty will be revealed in the work of art. For a man who never finished high school, Somers was extremely well read, with enormous intellectual curiosity (even though his spelling was atrocious). His letters to Beecroft and to others over the years are full of references to books he was reading, ranging from authors such as Dostoyevsky to Stravinsky's *Poetics of Music*. And finally, there is the humour – the slightly risqué pun in his expression "A Young Girl's Guide to Virginal Composition" (derived from the title of Benjamin Britten's 1945 work *The Young Person's Guide to the Orchestra*).

The relationship between Somers and Beecroft from 1955 until the fall of 1959, when she left for Europe, can be traced through a series of twenty letters (including the letter above) written to her by Somers during that period. Her letters to him appear not to have been preserved. This letter writing generally occurred when they were separated, either for a holiday on her part (in Muskoka in the summer of 1957), or for professional engagements on his part (a trip to Montreal in late March of 1958 for the premiere of Fantasia for Orchestra by the Montreal Symphony Orchestra and to Vancouver in August 1959 for the première of his String Quartet No. 3). Eight of these letters were written in July 1958 when Norma was at Tanglewood, studying composition with Lukas Foss and hearing a great deal of new music. These letters show that Somers was trying to support her as much as possible as she was struggling with her first experience presenting herself as a young composer to a wider musical community. In addition to copying the parts for her piece and bringing these to Tanglewood for a reading, he also gave her detailed comments about her orchestration and notation, thus giving her the benefit of his considerable experience in such matters.

Somers's music and his ideas about music had a considerable effect on Beecroft's musical development during their relationship in these years:

Meeting Harry Somers in 1955, roughly 3 years into my studies in composition with John Weinzweig, without question hastened my development as a fledgling composer. Harry's life was one-hundred-per-cent music – he was always writing, commissioned or otherwise...Harry's scores were like works of art, with a fine italic script accompanying beautifully and accurately aligned staves. I was so impressed by these works of musical beauty that I tried to emulate his graphic style. I certainly learned a great deal about the importance of making scores not only appealing to the eye, but easily read by practicing musicians who had no time to try and translate the composers' wishes from confusing notation. We spent many happy hours listening and dissecting other composers' music, and I recall being particularly drawn to the work of Charles Ives, with his superimposition of different musical materials one layer over another. Harry's own music conveyed a very linear direction, the long line, which was often absent in music of that period, and that influenced me considerably. I think the passion we both had for music, and the curiosity to explore new ideas, were major factors that kept the relationship alive and stimulated.[4]

The extent of Somers's influence on Beecroft's writing can clearly be seen in her Two Movements for Woodwinds and Brass (1956), *Fantasy for Strings*, completed in the fall of 1958, and Two Movements for Orchestra, the pieces read by an orchestra at Tanglewood in July 1958. Not only do these scores strongly resemble in appearance Somers's scores from that period – the calligraphy of the time signatures, the layout, the actual copying of notes, etc. – but the music itself strongly resembles that of Somers: imitative entries of short, slowly moving chromatic lines, the superimposition of such lines over short rhythmic fragments in another instrument, close motivic connections such as small three- or four-note chromatic figures between various figures, etc. In a sense, Beecroft probably absorbed more about compositional technique and style from Somers than from Weinzweig during the later 1950s. Both she and Somers admired the music of Bartók; certain traits, such as imitative entries and chromatic turning-note figures in both their works, may have been due to Bartók's influence. There is no sign of any influence of Charles Ives.

During the 1950s, music in Canada was quite conservative compared with postwar developments in contemporary music in Europe and the United States. Most of the "new" music Beecroft would have heard in these years would have been performed at concerts organized by the Canadian League of Composers through its concert-giving offshoot, Canadian Music Associates. (Beecroft served as president of this organization in its final year, 1957–58). Between 1952 and 1958, this group of relatives and friends of members of the League (not to mention those who simply believed in new Canadian music) organized six orchestra concerts, an evening of chamber operas, and a series of "film nights" (featuring films with music written by League members). As well, there were some twenty-four concerts featuring chamber music, vocal music, and other music for a few performers. (Many of these concerts took place in centres other than Toronto but much of the repertoire was shar from one centre to another.) The music played at these was quite eclectic in style and approach: in Benita Wolters-Fredlund's words, "serialism, polytonality, chromaticism, and music influenced by folk music."[5] The composers most frequently performed were John Weinzweig, Harry Somers, Jean Papineau-Couture, John Beckwith, Murray Adaskin, and François Morel.[6] Others, such as István Anhalt and Barbara Pentland, were using serial techniques more strictly by the late 1950s than were most of their contemporaries (even Weinzweig) but Beecroft would not have heard a piece such as Pentland's Symphony for Ten Parts, which received its first performance in Vancouver in September 1959, the month she left for Rome. This piece, written in 1957, shows the enormous influence of Webern's music on Pentland – and on the postwar generation of European composers. However, Pentland discovered Webern, not in Canada, but on trips to Europe in the mid-1950s. The only other Canadians to discover Webern in these years, and who also became acquainted with the music of European composers such as Pierre Boulez, Olivier Messiaen, and Karlheinz Stockhausen were the Quebec composers Gilles Tremblay (1932–2017) and Serge Garant (1929–1986), who both spent time studying in Paris during the 1950s.

Thus, Beecroft arrived in Rome in 1959 with little or no knowledge of recent developments in contemporary music in Europe in the years after the war. In a letter to Somers early on in her stay, she wrote that she found the environment in Rome very stimulating but:

> [I] somehow feel perhaps a little bitter that Canada seems to be so backward in its interest in contemporary music ~ I am passionately attached to the country and physical beauty and space, but find the people, in retrospect and not for certain in the long run, so content to sit and wait for leadership from elsewhere, which makes me angry ~ Am I crazy, or is this just a natural reaction ~ Canada produces seemingly passive people to me~[7]

She had already disclosed, in a previous letter, that Weinzweig had never introduced her to twelve-tone technique or the music of the Second Viennese School (strange, since he had been using his own

Introduction

version of twelve-tone pitch organization for some years). She felt, therefore, somewhat at a disadvantage but was also curious to learn more about this approach.[8]

During her first weeks in Rome, however, she was preoccupied with practical matters, such as finding a more suitable apartment, renting a piano, and arranging for flute lessons with Severino Gazzelloni, a well-known flutist associated with the Italian avant-garde. After finally meeting with Goffredo Petrassi on 9 November, she resumed work on some songs she had begun in Toronto (with texts by Michael Fram) and began to develop ideas for a work for chamber orchestra. This project, however, did not get very far, partly because she was attempting to use a five-note series, which Petrassi felt was not suitable; he suggested that she instead write a twelve-tone piece for piano and try to complete the Fram songs for submission to the Accademia Nazionale di Santa Cecilia. This she did, finishing the copying of the first part of the songs on New Year's Eve 1959.

Her correspondence during the months before beginning the class at Santa Cecilia indicates that her lessons with Petrassi constituted only one source of information about recent developments in new music. Through one means and another, she met several young American composers also studying in Rome and they were glad to look at her scores and discuss new ideas. She mentions at least three such people. One of them, a Peter Chrisòfides, had studied with Darius Milhaud and someone in Philadelphia (perhaps George Rochberg?). Another key source of information, someone who gave her information about Darmstadt and the composers associated with Darmstadt, such as Boulez, was her flute teacher, Gazzelloni. Because he was associated to such an extent with new music, her association with him gave her a direct sense of the *idiom* of recent music, especially its rhythmic language. Whenever possible, she also went to concerts; especially noteworthy is the David Tudor concert she mentions in her 10 November letter. Although she liked the sounds created, she felt that these did not communicate "something important," that they were not used "musically."

Another concert, which featured Petrassi's 5th Concerto for Orchestra, left her uncertain as to what she was looking for, what she wanted to express in her music:

But I felt so sad, truly ~ this music is not of our time in a sense, a thought which plagues the hell out of me ~ I can no longer even listen to Bartok very often without getting restless, and perhaps bored even ~ I fear the future ~ I cannot understand the avant-garde music of today as music, and other things written in the past 50 years are not expressing to me what I want to express ~ I wonder sometimes if I really will ever answer securely these enormous, paralysing questions ~ But today we are in a transient stage which is affecting even older generations of artists ~ They, however, are having perhaps a little easier time of it for they have a good 10, 20 or 30 years of solid writing behind them and perhaps cannot be as easily uprooted.[9]

Throughout the letters, one gets a sense of Beecroft's growing confidence and an increasing desire to persevere with her writing. Early on she wrote that even if she was not a composer, she knew that she had "the soul of an artist." After some weeks of sporadic work, due to various health problems of her own and concerns about Somers's state of mind (his ever more ardent letters were urging her to make a commitment to marry him), she gradually became more assured, recognizing that she *wanted* to write music but felt that she needed to focus all of her energy on her writing. She felt that for the first time in her life she had the freedom to achieve something according to her own needs, free of "being caught in emotional explosions."[10]

During the early part of her time in Rome, Beecroft realized that she needed to know more about the twelve-tone approach to pitch organization. Thus, her sketches are full of various kinds of attempts to derive material from a twelve-tone series: permutations of the row (changes in the order of pitches), derived two-and three-note groups, transpositions, etc. But, evidently, she did not feel that she could then apply these various procedures to the actual writing of a piece (and she noted several times in her letters to Somers that she had difficulty writing strictly organized twelve-tone music à la Schoenberg). It was not until the summer of 1960 that she became acquainted with Bruno Maderna's use of certain techniques for the choice of certain parameters that she was finally able to feel confident about working with serialism.

On the strength of part of the Fram songs, in January Beecroft was accepted into Petrassi's class at the Accademia Nazionale di Santa

Cecilia, the "Corso di Perfezionamento," not "as a female" but on the basis of her work (as she wrote to Somers, upon learning of her acceptance).[11] Her confidence in what she was undertaking increased greatly as a result – she felt that there was "a certain path" she must take and that every day she became "more committed to composition," more "surely finding Norma Beecroft."[12] Once classes got underway, she completed the second part of Fram's songs and began working on the third part. As well, she began working on some songs for flute, piano, and contralto voice on texts by W.B. Yeats but did not proceed very far with this.

Her compositional breakthrough came during the summer of 1960, some months after the relationship with Somers was finished. She attended contemporary music gatherings/festivals in Darmstadt (Germany) and Dartington (England), where she met a variety of composers, most important, Bruno Maderna, who introduced to her his method of organizing material using what he called "magic squares." This approach she used in her first "mature" work of this period, Tre Pezzi Brevi for flute and harp, which were performed in Darmstadt the following summer with considerable critical success, and subsequently published by the leading publisher of new music, Universal Edition of Vienna. In 1960–61, she successfully completed the "Corso di Perfezionamento" (under Petrassi), having written a large work for flute and orchestra, Improvvisazioni Concertanti No. 1. For this second year, she was successful in obtaining a grant from the Canada Council, so was not under the kind of financial restraint she mentioned so often in her letters to Somers. She then spent a third year in Italy thanks to a scholarship from the Italian Ministry of Foreign Affairs, before returning to Toronto in the summer of 1962.

Therefore, if we take a long-range view of her time in Italy, her correspondence with Harry Somers took place during a kind of prelude to the central activity of her time in Italy, the course with Petrassi at the Accademia Nazionale di Santa Cecilia. By the time she returned to Canada in 1962 and resumed work at the CBC, she had evolved from a person who had taken some tentative first steps as a rather insular composer, uncertain of her compositional personality, to a composer who had developed a sophisticated compositional language, one that reflected the world of international contemporary music, and who was confident and independent as a person.

HARRY SOMERS

By the time Beecroft met Harry Somers in the fall of 1954, he was considered one of the leading young composers in Canada. This was at a time when, it seems in retrospect, there was considerable interest in Canada, on the part of the press and especially in the CBC, in the younger generation of composers who were breaking away from the late-nineteenth language that had dominated concert music in Canada until the late 1940s. From that time until the time of these letters (the late 1950s), several important institutions came into being that encouraged the creation of new Canadian music. These were: 1) a Canadian branch of the American performing rights organization BMI (Broadcast Music, Inc.) in Toronto in 1948, resulting in the promotion and publication of scores of its Canadian members (including Somers); 2) the Canadian League of Composers in 1951 (of which Somers was a founding member) and its presentation of Canadian music in concerts during a good part of the 1950s; 3) the CBC Symphony Orchestra in 1952 (which performed much of the new Canadian orchestral repertoire for broadcast, including Somers's 1951 Symphony); 4) the Canada Council in 1958 (providing support to both Somers and Beecroft in 1960); and 5) the Canadian Music Centre in 1959, which made scores and recordings of Canadian music widely available.

Born in 1925 in Toronto, Somers had studied piano with Reginald Godden for a year (1942–43) and theory and composition with John Weinzweig at the Royal Conservatory of Music from 1942 until the late 1940s, except for a period of training in the armed forces in 1944–45. In the late 1940s, in his early twenties, he gained considerable recognition for several works which were performed in concerts and broadcast on the CBC, including the Piano Sonata No.1 (entitled "Testament of Youth") and *North Country*, an astonishingly original and evocative work for string orchestra, commissioned by the CBC. He wrote quite prolifically during these years, including piano music, chamber music, and a piano concerto. In 1949, he was able to go to Paris for a year to study composition, thanks to winning a $2000 scholarship awarded by the Canadian Amateur Hockey Association. Shortly before leaving, he married a young woman he had known since high school, Catherine Mackie (1927–63), and they spent a full year in Paris in 1949–50. He had intended to study with Arthur Honegger but ended up instead in a

Introduction 15

class with Darius Milhaud. Returning to Toronto in the fall of 1950, he chose to not try to teach or find some other way to earn a regular income but found that he could earn enough through copying music commercially (for well-known Toronto arrangers) to cover his basic expenses. The largest work he completed at this time was his Symphony, begun in Paris but completed in Toronto, probably the most mature and accomplished piece he wrote during these early years. Other important works of the 1950s included Passacaglia and Fugue for Orchestra, the chamber opera *The Fool*, *Five Songs for Dark Voice* (commissioned for Maureen Forester and premiered at the Stratford Festival in 1956), and the Piano Concerto No. 2.

What his letter of January 1955 to Norma Beecroft does not reveal is that by this time Somers was no longer living with his wife, Cathy. At some point between March 1953 and July 1954, they separated and were no longer living together. A letter to Cathy written in March 1953 from Montreal indicates that they were still together. (He was in Montreal attending the production of a short National Film Board film showing a rehearsal of his Suite for Harp and Chamber Orchestra.)[13] He had probably been drinking earlier in the evening before writing:

I love you, you wonderful bitch!! You understand! You know my insanity!! I'm stark raving mad! I love life and the sensitive perceptions to such a degree that I die from their god damned beauty – from their sacred and profane beauty. Cathy this is a 'night' letter and the day would see it sober, but not differently. How I need woman, desire her, must drive my beauty and my body through her!!! – and <u>you</u> are woman! Do not deceive me for the knife has a saw-toothed edge that rips my insides out!! There is no woman such as you!!

This does not appear to be the letter of a man who is about to leave his wife.

Yet, by July of 1954, another letter to Cathy reveals that they were not longer together and that he hopes that she "will find some measure of fulfilment and happiness in the future to balance your loneliness and hurt in the past." There is no direct explanation here or anywhere else in Somers's correspondence or other written documents as to why they had separated. The closest he comes to an explanation is the following sentence: "I want to apologize, Cathy, for being very petty and mean and cruel in the past and ask only that you understand it as a part of pride that was hurt." There is no indication here of how his pride might have been hurt but one suspects that this is a ruse or, at least, a face-saving and meaningless attempt to remove some of his responsibility for the break-up. (Six years later, in February 1960, when the relationship with Norma Beecroft was ending, he again claimed "hurt pride" as an excuse for his emotional and angry behaviour when they met in Rome.) It is likely (judging by his later inability to remain faithful to one woman, be it his wife, or a woman, like Norma Beecroft, to whom he was not married) that he had had an extramarital relationship (or perhaps several) at some point around 1953 or 1954 and that this was the reason his marriage to Cathy broke up.

THE RELATIONSHIP BETWEEN
BEECROFT AND SOMERS

After January 1955 (when he first contacted Norma Beecroft by letter), their relationship developed rather quickly and endured until Norma left for Europe in September of 1959. It seems that the relationship was not without its ups and downs. In the main correspondence published here, there are references to "battles" and arguments between them during these years. As well, among the twenty letters from Somers to Beecroft between January 1955 and September 1959, three (dated 9 August 1956, 25 January 1959, and 27 January 1959) indicate that Somers considered the relationship finished, but it wasn't. The second letter (25 January 1959) is especially significant with respect to the present correspondence, because it contains a preview of how he later describes his past behaviour to her. After declaring that she is "one of the most wonderful women" he has ever met, he goes on to write the following:

> There is one real reason why I behaved so strangely, erratically, treated you so harshly and often badly – that is because you meant something very important to me and I loved you and I was afraid of anyone becoming so important to me and my loving them.[14]

This particular rationalization for his bad behaviour – not a very credible one – is repeated throughout the present correspondence; Somers explains that he treated Norma badly because he was afraid

Introduction 17

that the relationship would become too important, that he would be terribly disappointed if it didn't work out. In a letter to her mother, Eleanor, during the early weeks of her stay in Rome, Norma confirms that during their relationship in Toronto Somers had made it clear that they could never be married ("I have been told for so long it was impossible for the two of us") and that since leaving Toronto she had tried to "reconcile" herself to "a new life without him."[15] He also explains that he has always had trouble expressing his emotions and feelings since youth and is only capable of doing so when he has had a good deal to drink.

The fact that Somers was still married and had never divorced his wife clouded his relationship with Norma Beecroft and this also *may* account (in part) for the fact that he was never willing to commit to a permanent relationship with her. She recalls that during the four years of her relationship with Somers, Cathy was always in the background, so to speak, even making suicide threats. This situation is mentioned here because it has a direct bearing on what one encounters in the correspondence: as the weeks and months went by in Rome, Norma was more and more inclined to reject his belated wishes to marry her; at the same time, the more ardent became his desire to marry her (while admitting that he had been unwilling to commit to any permanent arrangement such as marriage during their years together in Toronto). The fact that he resumed a relationship with Cathy only a few months after his relationship with Norma ended indicates that there was a certain ambivalence in his mind about Cathy during the years they were separated (c. 1954–60).

Early in the present correspondence, Norma told him that what she really wanted was the security that marriage offers:

I am becoming convinced through absence, that most of what
I desire at this time in my life is a situation of security, in other
words, marriage ~ I also realize that my desire to write music
could be lessened by the idea of marriage becoming an obsession,
or lessened, by marriage in actual fact, whether temporarily or
not. All this sounds very confused, but I find these things very
difficult to express ~ In other words, I suppose I want to know
how you are reacting to our separation, as it is, and has been,
fairly obvious that any further decision has to be taken by you ~
I never wanted to come to Europe alone, and I do not know if

I have the strength to stay here alone ~ and yet, should I even consider the possibility of returning to Canada with no hope of future with you.[16]

Initially, Somers's reaction to this appeal in his next letter was anger – he thought that she was looking to marriage to provide answers to what she was seeking – but on the evening of 27 October he telephoned her. This conversation appears to have been a major turning point in their relationship. Subsequent letters indicate that during this conversation they must have discussed the possibility of his coming to Rome quite soon for a while. More important, however, either the conversation itself or a sudden epiphany on his part beforehand made him believe that he truly loved her and was in danger of losing her, that he wanted to spend the rest of his life with her. Until this point in the correspondence, his letters had been chatty and full of news but free of any declarations of love. At the end of October, this changed drastically and suddenly:

Monday [November 2nd] – I am enveloped in my love for you so that the sky, wind, the air is the sight and the touch of you. You'll be sorry that I love you so completely for I shall overwhelm you with the rush of my feelings into extravagant phrases which seek to touch and probe every part of your body and mind and heart, to arouse you with my caressing to the joy and pain of loving, to leave you exhausted with my intensity.[17]

Extravagant declarations of love poured forth from the Somers pen over the next few months, to the point where they became obsessive, dominating the letters to the exclusion of almost everything else except descriptions of his writing projects and of the limited social life he had. Although he frequently declared that he supported Norma's desire to study composition and that she need not fear his interference, he also became increasingly desperate to be with her and suspicious that she may have formed a relationship with someone else. The latter concern comes up in the same letter to her as his initial declaration of love (at the end of October): Is she in love with someone else? Is she living with that person? In these letters, he seems to be playing the role of the tormented lover, desperately regretting his past treatment of her and even asking her whether she will come back to him "now,"

Introduction 19

live with him "now" (and this is early November –at this point she has not even begun to write anything and is still waiting to meet Petrassi). She confirms that she wants to live with him and even marry him but challenges the urgency of his appeal ("What does 'now' mean?").[18]

At the time of the telephone conversation (27 October 1959) and for some weeks thereafter, they seem to have felt the same way about each other. She was still open to considering marriage, although she was still trying to sort out her feelings:

> Harry this is the first time in my life that I begin to feel as though I am loved by someone, by you ~ I am extraordinarily happy ~ and yet so sad to be a long way away ~ I am frightened of my own self as well ~ you know how I have pushed you time and time again, like the drowning man clutching at a straw ~ The straw has become a solid piece of wood now, and I am desperately trying to know whether I have been submerged completely by too much frantic struggling or whether my feelings are real and not just obsessions for a desire to have what I need ~ I believe sincerely and truthfully that I love you, maybe this is all I can hope to know.[19]

But in a letter to her mother, written the day after the telephone conversation (and cited earlier), Norma's confusion about this sudden turn-about on Somers's part is expressed just as strongly, to the point of saying that she is not just upset by this change but "terrified." Nevertheless, for some time after this she seems to be entertaining the possibility of marriage. In a letter to Eleanor Beecroft at the end of November, she says that if Harry gets a divorce and their finances allow it, "we will probably get married some day ~ What a pleasant feeling."[20] Her letters to Somers during November indicate that she misses him terribly and wants to be with him but cannot figure out a practical way of bringing this about, lack of money being the main impediment. The letters frequently contain information about the high cost of living in Rome and the difficulty of getting further access to the inheritance left to her.

Once she actually met Petrassi and began working with him (and composing), her perspective on Somers and her own aspirations began to change. Not only did she begin writing, but she rented a piano (which arrived on 18 November), bought scores to study, attended concerts, and made it her business to meet other young composers (Americans) with whom she could discuss her music and even contemporary music in general. She even began to think about attending the important contemporary music festival in Darmstadt during the coming summer to acquaint herself with the music of composers such as Pierre Boulez and proposed that Somers might also attend. Although she experienced periods of depression and loneliness, during which she was unable to write much, she persevered through this period.

By mid-December, even though her writing was not going well, she was coming to realize that she now had the freedom to live independently:

> nothing is very clear to me right now except this knowledge that I can't return ~ I feel freedom to breathe here, freedom from family, freedom from gossip, freedom to move alone when I wish ~ otherwise freedom to live independently ~ This is the first time in my life I have felt freedom (I am not saying it doesn't have its enormous disadvantages) but at this time I don't want to feel as though anyone is chaining me to anything ~ I alone chain myself, I know, and that is enough to cope with.[21]

Not only that, she was more determined than ever to write music:

> All I know now, is that I can depend only on one thing ~ myself ~ and I intend to do my damndest to write music which cannot change ~ that the expression of myself is positive will last, and is only dependent on me, and I on it.[22]

By this time, she was hoping to enter Petrassi's composition class at the Accademia Nazionale di Santa Cecilia in the new year; this goal made her all the more determined to get on with her writing so she could submit her work for admission. Toward the end of December, she expressed a growing sense of security:

> ...for the first time in my life I feel freedom, I am not bound by anything but myself ~ and I am growing inside into a very secure female, slowly though ~ I can speak with my friends and acquaintances as an individual, and am respected for my intelligence and individuality and personality This is important to me

Introduction   21

to think independently for a while ~ I am also not foolish enough
to think that my admirers like me only for the way I think
either ~ the males, I mean ~ but like me because I am a woman,
but they are not aggressive ~ so, OK![23]

In the same letter, she reiterated her desire to concentrate her energy
on her composition and not be distracted by emotional matters:

> I am <u>afraid</u>, if you can imagine, of repeating or being caught in
> emotional explosions again at this time for I am trying to direct
> my energy to writing music, and I fear if I don't succeed this time
> in accomplishing self-discipline, I shall not be able to try again
> easily ~ You see, I <u>want</u> to write music, but somehow have man-
> aged to let my will be led astray.[24]

(Ironically, there was an emotional explosion when Somers arrived
in Rome on 17 February 1960. The explosion came from him, and
its emotional effect made it impossible for her to work for several
weeks. Nevertheless, she did not allow herself to be "led astray" and
managed to resume writing by the beginning of March.)

At the same time, determined as she was to write music and be
admitted to Petrassi's course, she was clearly having doubts about
taking on a "domestic life:"

> However, I have had some disturbing thoughts lately about 'my
> other life' ~ The more deeply involved I become in music, the less
> I wish for a domestic life ~ This is rather shattering for one who
> so loved to cook and look after a man called Harry ~ Maybe this
> is pure reaction, but it worries me a little, not for me entirely,
> but how do you feel?[25]

In early January she was still struggling with feelings of loneliness
and emotional tensions. She realized that she needed to overcome
these and arrive at some "real inner strength" before she could face
any decision about marriage. She realized, as well, that she could
not give up and return home; if she did so she would feel that she
had left something "uncompleted." On 25 January 1960, she was
able to write that she had been accepted into Petrassi's class at the
Accademia Nazionale di Santa Cecilia and that the class would
begin in two days. She was especially proud of the fact that she had

been accepted purely on the basis of her work, not because she was a female – the admission committee did not actually see or interview the candidates.

Her letters to Somers in the remaining weeks before his arrival in Rome on 17 February show an underlying exasperation with him – she no longer wants to "sort out feelings by letter" and does not want to "face anything but problems pertaining to [her] work." In her second last letter in the collection, dated 8 February 1960, she asked him whether he understood what she was saying in her letters and went on to tell him that he was making her feel "guilty and trapped" and that she frankly couldn't stand it. Yet, she expresses these sentiments rather mildly to Somers himself. Two letters to her mother in the days before his arrival in Rome contain even stronger expressions of concern about Harry's intentions. In the first letter, she writes that she "refuses to be put in a cage now"-and even feels "instinctively" that Somers should not come to Rome now, that "he may be disappointed in what he finds."[26] In her last letter to Eleanor Beecroft before Somers's arrival, she again expresses doubts about whether Somers should make the trip: "Over the weekend I spent two nightmarish days trying to decide whether I should telephone and tell Harry not to come here." She decides finally not to stop him from coming but makes it clear that she must be honest with him about their future:

> But dear Mother, realizing all you have said, my own sacrifices for a future which is relatively secure in spite of economic situations, etc., if I <u>know</u> that I no longer have enough feeling to live with H., I must summon up all my strength and tell him that I cannot ~ I think I would sooner die a slow death alone, than marry someone I didn't love ~ All this is hell for me of course ~ this negative side is the worst thing I know to contemplate, but I must be honest ~ I can live no other way ~ if one can't give, well don't pretend ~ I shall still bloody well hang on to my ideal, and die with it ... It is all so incredibly difficult that I would just as soon forget that I ever existed sometimes ~ If I were able to work at the same time while fighting these things, I would be much happier. But alas ~ I am afraid that I am tied to the earth as all women are and am constantly reminded of it by that thing of horror and beauty called the menstrual period ~ I guess, woman first, woman the creator, and composer second.[27]

Introduction

This excerpt and, indeed, Norma's letters of January and February show the confluence of various strands of concerns and considerations: her doubts about a possible permanent relationship with Somers, her need to be free to concentrate on her writing, and the implications for her as a woman in rejecting a traditional life – marriage, children, looking after someone else's needs, etc. In Canada, by the late 1950s, only three women had gained prominence as composers: Jean Coulthard, Violet Archer, and Barbara Pentland. In the early years of her career, Barbara Pentland had to struggle against her family's wishes and expectations. Thus, there were few, if any, role models to guide Beecroft's decisions. At this point, she was driven by a desire to study composition and to write music and over the months of this correspondence, what was only a vague notion at first became a serious ambition. In following this path, she became one of the pioneering figures in contemporary Canadian music – both because she established an important career as a composer (one of the first women to do so during those years) and because she was one of the pioneers in the development of electronic music in Canada.

In separating herself personally from Somers, Beecroft was also separating herself musically from his influence. The music she wrote in Italy in the early 1960s was highly influenced by the European (and specifically Italian) avant-garde in many ways – in serial organization of pitch structure, rhythmic language, more angular and fragmented instrumental writing, and contrasts of texture. This was a major turning point for her as a young composer. For Somers as well, 1960 was an important turning point. As evident in his letters of December 1959 and January 1960, while writing the music for the film *Saguenay*, he became far more interested in instrumental colour. He acquired a considerable amount of information about certain jazz techniques from his jazz composer friend Norm Symonds, especially for percussion and brass instruments. This experience significantly affected on his writing in works such as *Five Concepts for Orchestra* (1961) and *Stereophony* (1963) and beyond. Furthermore, the influence of recent European music – Boulez, for one – begins to be heard. This can be heard in certain sections of *Stereophony* (especially when the percussion first enters in the second half of the piece) and even in the *Twelve Miniatures* for soprano, recorder, viola da gamba, and spinet, written in 1964.

SOMERS'S LETTERS TO BEECROFT

The letters from Somers in this correspondence are multidimensional and voluminous, therefore difficult to easily summarize (although many are obsessively focused on his love for Beecroft). They provide various "snapshots" of certain aspects of daily life in Toronto at the end of the 1950s but they also provide the reader with a vivid sense of what sort of person Somers was and how he lived: his frequent melancholy moods, as opposed to the elation he expressed after recording the music for *Saguenay*; his sense of humour; his keen awareness, described so often, of the quality of light and sound in his immediate environment (especially at all hours of the night); his living arrangements during these years (a rather Spartan existence, living from one copying job or commission to the next); the people he knew and socialized with (mostly from the worlds of theatre and art); his relationships with various women; and, of course, his approach to composition (especially the music for *Saguenay*). Of course, a good part of his correspondence is devoted to expressions of love for Norma and attempts to persuade her that his love is genuine and that he wants nothing less than a permanent relationship with her.

A great feeling of "sadness" is mentioned early in the correspondence, seemingly associated in part with the autumnal dead leaves and mists but such sentiments occur throughout his life, going back to his time in training in the army in the spring of 1945, and appear frequently in various written notes and memoranda in the later years, especially in the 1990s. Sometimes this seems to arise from an inner sense of futility and despair, not necessarily from external events:

> It has been one of those days during which I've felt an overpowering sadness. Paralysing melancholy. Only dead leaves, mists, night and nothing. Oh well, I've learned by now just to let go to the depression so that it will sooner pass. Footsteps, footsteps – silence.[28]

This suggests that he was accustomed to periods of depression. He makes another reference to a period of depression just after the telephone conversation of 27 October, mentioned earlier. Again, he appears to confirm that he suffers from periods of depression:

Introduction
25

I feel a sadness I've rarely known before. I don't feel like eating, I can't sleep, in fact all the symptoms of those who require something like Carters Little Liver Pills. Perhaps I should try to write some 'happy' music like Dixie. Right now it's just the 'blues'. Ole Somers Blues. A pocket full of darkness. There's really too much for me to do. This is no time for one of my depressive periods.[29]

On the other hand, the letter written on 2 February after the recording session for the music for *Saguenay* conveys a sense of elation bordering on mania:

Girl – I'm a God damn genius!! <u>Anything</u> I can conceive in my head I can realize on paper!! Such a feeling – such rarified air to breathe! From now on I'm really taking off! – such things to write!! I feel that everything up to now is just training for what's to come!! But then that's one's whole life! The sun sings in my veins, the sky streams from my eyes and I have worlds to tell of in my music...I'm strong, I can sing with the Gods, I <u>know</u> you are my love and I am happy. You can't protest – it's like stemming the St. Lawrence River or the ocean tide – even King someone or other couldn't do <u>that</u>!!![30]

The mood of this resembles the letter he wrote to Cathy from Montreal in March 1953, during the filming of *Rehearsal*.[31] In both these cases, the sense of elation (in this case, the feeling of omnipotence) seems to arise from a feeling that, such are his abilities, he can achieve whatever he wants. In the letter to Cathy, the sense of omnipotence is transformed into raw sexual energy.

Despite his seemingly frequent bouts of "sadness," he had a lively sense of humour, often carrying seemingly ordinary names or situations into absurd humour.

After hearing that Beecroft's cabin companion on the voyage to England was a pianist named Berthe Poncy Jacobson, he wrote that, with a name like that, she should, instead, be the name of a piano, recommended by no less an artist than Artur Rubinstein: "Rubinstein says – 'I only perform on a Berthe Poncy Jacobson. You may too for as little as $350.00."[32] The name of a new snack bar on Church Street, near his apartment building, drew the following comments:

Correction!! – the new snack bar across the corner is called 'Adams' Snack Bar.' <u>Adams'</u>. Isn't that significant! The beginning, garden of Eden, Eve and all that! It has poetry – Adam back to feed the world as penance. God's short order cook! What marvels are witnessed here on <u>Church St</u>. Isn't that extraordinary?! Adams' Snack Bar on Church St. An evangelist could make a song out of it! "I'm in the mood for pie, – simply because God made it, – I'm going down to Adams', – Snack Bar on Chuhurch Street." (Copyright Hellish Harry Somers, Pub. member of H.O.R.S.E.S.H.I.T. MMMMMMMXIV.)[33]

Many of his letters "set the scene" by describing, quite vividly, the quality of light and the sounds he is hearing (or has just experienced) as he writes:

It is noon. Sunlight filters through slight overcast. Leaves of dark and light dance to the breeze. The traffic sounds lessen allowing children's voices to scream their joy or momentary anger. Sounds approaching – disappearing. Poor sad bus heaves great sighs as it stops then moves on, occasionally emitting more vulgar sounds.[34]

Another letter, early in the correspondence, shows how vividly he could capture in words the sounds of a late Saturday night in downtown Toronto:

2 am. A still wet fall night. I've just been for a walk along the weekend streets of couples, of drunks singing, yelling and even crying. Two girls, perhaps late teens, fleeing a house and the strange sound of a man crying almost hysterically. The jazz and laughter and noise and silence. A wild party up the street. Trumpet, yells, womans' voice piercing laughter. Cars roaring, screeching. High heels on pavement. By the '1st Floor Club. Young people feigning many things ~ being high, bored, interested etc. Back along the street. Singing group. Lone people. Car radio. Moments of emptiness. All the while the leaves are dying to a wailing saxophone. But these are only weekend people. The night people shy away and hide 'till the night is theirs again.[35]

This soundscape is so multilayered and varied that Charles Ives (or R. Murray Schafer, for that matter) would have loved it. Somers's

Introduction

later interest in musical textures comprising several layers of material moving at different speeds (as in *Kyrie*) may have sprung not so much from his early interest in Ives but from actual experiences such as this. His acute sensitivity to his physical surroundings seems to have begun in childhood (when he would leave his house at night and wander around the neighbourhood) and later had a direct connection with his musical creativity – transforming sensual impressions into sounds (which frequently involved the physical qualities of a landscape, as was the case in his early work for string orchestra, *North Country*).[36] The opening of a letter to Norma Beecroft, written before the present correspondence, provides some confirmation of this but also shows that he was acutely aware of the inevitable cessation of sensuous experience in death. It may have been this juxtaposition of the richness of sensory experience and the "inescapable" end to all this that was the source of his darkness of spirit at times:

> All the warm sensuous moisture of spring overwhelms my senses so that I feel the deep ache of growth of life of longing. All things conspire to deceive us into thinking there is only eternal birth, colour, light, sound ~ vibrant, rythmic [*sic*] like the great pulse of creation. But outside of life is eternal death ~ black, soundless, void, final. The wonderful riotous comedy held in tragic hands ~ inescapable.[37]

Somers's letters reveal that his living arrangements and financial situation in these years were not likely to help encourage a cheerful outlook on life. He lived in a small apartment in downtown Toronto on Church Street a few blocks north of Wellesley Street, not exactly one of Toronto's upscale neighbourhoods. Outside of paid commissions, he relied on music copying for various Toronto arrangers for his basic sustenance, since he chose not to teach or take on other regular employment, as did most Canadian composers of that era. Thus, travelling to Europe to visit Norma Beecroft was a major expense that he could afford only by using part of the commission of $1,000.00 he received from Crawley Films for writing the music for *Saguenay*. He mentions the expense of $300.00 as a reason why he cannot go ahead with a divorce from Cathy, his first wife (but there may have been reasons other than financial ones for not proceeding with this, as already suggested). In one letter he describes the humiliation of being turned down for a small loan unless he had a guarantor.[38]

However, I suspect that he *needed* to see himself as the struggling artist, living alone, renouncing the possibility of a comfortable life. In the July 1954 letter to Cathy (bidding her farewell), he portrays himself (with considerable self-pity and even misrepresentation) as the complicated creative artist, implying that the world that he inhabits does not permit him a normal relationship with others – it sets him apart:

> I – live in the fantastic world of the creative artist. The monkish world seeking salvation, being driven, tormented, exalted, torn spat at, laughed at, revered, despised, ignored, loved and scorned, seeing the universe in a page of music, living and dying for nothing and for everything, twisted, torn, always seeking, talking about 'craft,' crazy creatures who are dreadful bores and sometimes really happy, not knowing but sensing, arguing endlessly, creating thousands of heaven and hells of their own invention, preoccupied to the world yet needing the world so desperately, creatures doomed like figures in Greek tragedy by their very natures and their only freedom being to realize it. Not belonging. Don Quixote.[39]

This kind of self-portrayal – as the struggling, solitary artist – surfaces again at the end of his relationship with Norma Beecroft in May 1960. In a lengthy "farewell – live well!" letter to her, he sets himself apart as the solitary artist, who must forego the luxuries of life (whereas Norma, he claims, cannot do without them).[40] Therefore, they would never be able to live together.

> I work so much alone, yet am not alone. From the length of my solitude I draw my inner strength. For twenty-one years I've been writing music in endless solitude peopled with countless struggles, ideas, – the silent sounds. I think perhaps I might be fortunate in time to write something of real and lasting worth. If not, then it is not to be. If so, then it is to be.[41]

Beyond this stance of himself as the struggling, solitary composer, however, these letters provide considerable insight into the special experience for him of creating sounds, of communicating in this manner with others:

It's curious the love I have for the shaping of sound. It would be a great pity should composers, like insurance companies, only use computers and gadgets. Nothing can equal the thrill of writing a dot on paper which is translated into vibrations through an instrument set in motion by another human being who will always vary it, humans being so variable. It is the human element – the communion of people performing and listening – which is the greatness of music. I know the beauty of music listened to over a radio or in solitude. But even if there are only a few listening and performing the air can be transformed. It is that moment of truth that exists in no other way. But I so love sound! Chamber music was one of my first loves. The infinite subtlety of solo instruments in concert – all the quartet literature, Lieder, woodwind, Mozart violin sonatas etc. How can one explain it? One can't, it's foolish to try. It just is, like the comprehension of beauty, of subtlety, sense of taste. So few in this world possess it, but those that do possess the treasures of this world. 'What is beauty?' It's an empty question, for like jazz, if you know what it is you don't ask, you just know.[42]

Readers of these letters will no doubt be surprised by the number of references to various people involved in Canadian theatre in these years, as well as to artists such as Jack Nichols and Graham Coughtry and a number of musicians. Somers may have become acquainted with the theatre people through being around the CBC, copying music for variety shows, or through Norma Beecroft and her mother, Eleanor, an actress who was involved with various productions in Toronto theatres and at the CBC. In any case, the list of actors and directors mentioned in the letters reads like a "Who's Who" of Canadian theatre in these years: Harvey Hart, Len Casey, Robert Gill, George McCowan, George Luscombe, Hugh Webster, Powys Thomas, Bruno Gerussi, Ted Follows, Joan and Antony Ferry, to name only a few. Somers's interest in Canadian theatre went beyond fraternizing with actors and directors. In the letters, he describes various theatre productions he attended during these months, including James Reaney's first play, *The Killdeer*. Some thirty years later, Somers wrote the music for an opera entitled *Serinette* with a libretto by Reaney, first performed at the Temple of Peace in Sharon, Ontario. Considering his keen interest in theatre in these years, it seems somehow appropriate that his second wife was the actress Barbara Chilcott, who, with her brothers, Donald and Murray Davis, founded and operated Toronto's Crest Theatre from 1954 until 1966.

Others mentioned in the letters include musicians such as Mario Bernardi, Maureen Forrester, Jean Beaudet, Eli Kassner, Paul Scherman, Julian Bream, Norman Symonds, John Weinzweig, and Ron Collier. All of these are identified in the footnotes to the letters. As well, Somers mentions the National Ballet choreographer Grant Strate (for whom he had written two ballet scores by 1959) and the filmmaker Christopher Chapman, who was responsible for *Saguenay*, the film for which Somers wrote the music in late 1959 and early 1960. Thus, he was keenly aware of what was going on in the arts in Canada, writing to Norma in early December 1960 that since she had left he had discovered that "Canada under the surface is in quite an exciting ferment – composers, poets, painters, writers, theatre, etc. The whole thing will explode to the surface one day not so far away."[43]

There are also frequent references to jazz, including performers, repertoire, and jazz venues in Toronto. In the early 1950s, Somers had become seriously interested in jazz; his closest friend during the 1950s was probably the composer Norman Symonds, who had come from a jazz background. One of the people mentioned frequently in the letters is the jazz columnist Helen McNamara, who had been writing her column, "McNamara's Bandwagon," in the *Toronto Telegram* since 1949; the letters provide a glimpse of this pioneering figure's personal life in the late 1950s.

Finally, however, Somers's letters provide a fascinating portrait of a complex, enormously creative individual, flawed (by his own admission), mercurial (given to sudden "emotional explosions" as he described them, at other times tightly sealed emotionally), a man capable of great love and generosity but tending to push people away when they tried to get too close. This was a person who was enormously curious about the nature of human existence, continuously struggling to understand it, and who left extensive and articulate testimony to this struggle in his correspondence and other written documents. He was single-mindedly devoted to his work as a composer, refusing to take on anything that would interfere with this powerful need to be completely absorbed in creative work.

As the correspondence shows, he was also a man whose relationships with women were an essential part of his daily existence. The

Introduction

physical aspect was a powerful *need* on his part, as is evident from the correspondence, but it would appear that he was incapable of being faithful to one woman, probably from the early 1950s on. It is clear from Norma Beecroft's letters that during their four-year relationship in Toronto, she suspected that he was involved with other women. Whatever the nature of these relationships, they were seriously detrimental to their relationship, and once Norma had gone to Rome she clearly felt that she could not trust him to remain faithful (and probably not before that, either), despite his ardent protestations that she was the only woman he loved. (In one of his letters, he goes to considerable pains, even listing all the women he knows, to assure her that he is not involved with anyone else). Perhaps the most puzzling development in their relationship is his apparently sudden realization in late October 1959 that he deeply loved her after all and wanted to marry her, a possibility that he had not been willing to consider before she left for Europe. After this, his letters are obsessively focused on his love for her, as if he needed to make up for lost time. The manner in which their relationship ended (i.e., the meeting in Rome in mid-February, described in the epilogue) is equally puzzling. After so many letters professing great love, why would he then sabotage the relationship by aggressively attacking his beloved's life and aspirations?

Perhaps even more puzzling is the fact that once he realized that the relationship with Norma Beecroft was over, Somers reconnected with his wife Cathy, whom he had not divorced, with whom he had not been living since about 1954. Puzzling all the more because in the present correspondence, he not only declares that Norma is the first woman he has asked to marry him – does this mean that he never actually proposed to Catherine Mackie? – but at least *twice* in the correspondence declares that she is the first woman he has really loved.[44] Understandably, one might wonder why a man who states so unequivocally that he has only truly loved a woman *other than* his wife would then return to that wife at the end of the current affair. Yet, by the summer of 1960, when he was in residence in Stratford, Ontario, having written incidental music for *A Midsummer Night's Dream* and performing as a guitarist in the production, Cathy was receiving loving notes similar to the ones he had written to Norma Beecroft only months earlier. And in the fall of 1960, the two of them went off to Paris for a year. All of this suggests that Somers was, at the very least, an unreliable lover, perhaps also an unreliable witness – when it came to his emotions and his feelings about the women in his life. But that is another story, for another time.

Be that as it may, Harry Somers was undoubtedly one of the major creative figures in Canada in the second half of the twentieth century. In the 1960s, he wrote a number of works that remain outstanding in their particular genres – for instance, the orchestra piece *Stereophony* (1963) and the opera, *Louis Riel*, commissioned to be performed in 1967, Canada's centennial year. *Louis Riel* is widely regarded as the most important and successful opera yet written in Canada and it has been revived several times. Somers went on to write several more operas, as well as orchestral music, experimental works for voices and instruments, such as *Kyrie* and *Chura-churum*, and concertos for violin, guitar, and piano. The period of his correspondence with Norma Beecroft, especially in the fall and winter of 1959–60, was an important turning point in his life and in his creative work, marking not only the end of an important personal relationship and the neoclassical phase of his writing,[45] but the beginning of his maturity as a composer, during which he responded far more than previously to international developments, such as the use of indeterminacy,[46] and during which such parameters as colour and texture took on far more importance. As well, a new preoccupation arose, that of working with various layers of sound simultaneously.

After returning to Canada in 1962, Norma Beecroft rapidly became one of the leading figures in the development of contemporary Canadian music. After becoming interested in electronic music, she was one of the Canadian pioneers in this field working in New York at the Columbia-Princeton Electronic Music Center with Mario Davidovsky (whom she had met at Tanglewood in 1958) and for many years in Toronto at the University of Toronto's Electronic Music Studio. During the following years, she produced a number of commissioned works using tape, such as *From Dreams of Brass* (1963–64), *Elegy, Two Went to Sleep* (1967), *Piece for Bob* (1975), *Jeu II* (1985), and Amplified String Quartet (1992), as well as works for orchestra and ensembles (including some electronic music for productions at the Stratford Festival). She also returned to the CBC and was active for many years as a producer and host (*Music of Today*) and later produced a number of documentaries on Canadian composers. In addition to these activities, in 1971 she co-founded New Music Concerts, with flautist and composer

Introduction

Robert Aitken, and remained president until 1989. In 2018, her series of interviews with composers who had worked in the field of electronic music, originally undertaken in the late 1970s, was published in book form as *Conversations with Post World War II Pioneers of Electronic Music.*

CHAPTER ONE

September 1959

[Norma Beecroft sailed from New York to Plymouth
on board the SS Liberté on Saturday, 12 September 1959,
arriving on Friday morning, 18 September]

NB to HS
Sunday, September 13/59 ~
Darling,
Let me tell you never to go on an ocean voyage if you are, and have
been, emotionally upset and fatigued ~ I have been in a state of dizziness, with very weak legs, all day ~ and am hoping that it will pass
by tomorrow ~ The ocean has been very calm (normal swells) all
day ~ with a hot sun ~ and the only time I have felt even half human
was sitting up in my corner deck chair watching the ocean and the
few clouds pass by ~ Where I was standing when I last saw you in
the pier was where I reserved my chair ~ It is a marvellous spot, and
I am talking occasionally with a Catholic priest, taking a Sabbatical
year to study philosophy in Europe, who sits in the next chair ~

Outside of that, it has turned out that I am not alone in my
cabin, but have the lower berth ~ The person occupying the
upper berth is an older woman (possibly 55–65) by the name of
Bertha Poncy Jacobson, who is the head of the piano dept. at the
University of Washington, in Seattle, a very interesting, but rather
strange and strong willed musician[1] ~ We have discovered to date
friends in common ~ and she is going to Europe to investigate

1 Berthe Poncy Jacobson (1894–1975) was a Swiss-born concert pianist and teacher,
who taught at the Cornish School in Seattle (today the Cornish College of the Arts) and
at the University of Washington. She had concertized extensively on the West Coast. She
was the widow of Myron Jacobson (1883–1934), a Russian-born composer and pianist
who had studied with Rimsky-Korsakov.

the contemporary music scene ~ She has offered to give me some information on libraries in Rome containing old manuscripts ~ Being only the first day and because of my malady, I haven't desired to talk too much ~ so more later about her ~

I have also met a Mexican criminal lawyer ~ who gave me an opportunity to practice my Italian, French, and a few words of Spanish all at the same time ~ A New York art dealer, Viennese-American, who showed me the luxurious lounges and decks of the First Class ~ I do think it would have been worth while to pay the extra money to have the quietness and space to move around ~ and be by yourself, especially if you are not feeling too well ~ I know!! it is all inside, darling ~ it may take me quite a while to discover the secret of how to relax ~

Undoubtedly, there are many interesting people on board ~ I have not been too interested as yet, for I am constantly thinking of how much the scenery (the sea, horizon, cloud formations, sunsets, etc.) would interest you ~ you are very much there, so I know you are here with me....

... Today the sky is overcast and the sea a grey-black ~ I shall never cease to be fascinated by the space and distance here in the middle of nowhere (supposedly) ~ Yesterday evening, with my lousy head, I found the most magnificent spot on the ship up in First Class quarters ~ the very front, almost top-deck but below the bridge, and there I stood by myself enraptured by the stillness and the moon's reflections across the water ~ There were no sounds of people ~ just a little salt spray, the moon, and me thinking how much you would enjoy this ~ I think the extreme front and back of the ship is probably where I shall spend most of my time ~

The blotches on the page are because it started to rain ~

More later, darling ~

7:30 PM

Darling, you will be pleased to know that the sea is commencing to agree with me ~

This afternoon I went to see a movie, even ~ a new version, and very poor, of the 'Blue Angel'[2] ~ no Marlene Dietrich, just a typical

---

2 *The Blue Angel* was a 1959 American film directed by Edward Dmytryk, starring

36 Between Composers

Hollywood-type blonde, and as her agent, none other than Theodor Bickel ~ He seemed rather self-conscious in this role, but would seem to have the necessary qualities of a good actor ~

Love, you would enjoy this boat ~ one has all the advantages of a good hotel, but you don't (seemingly) have to pay much extra....

... We have a simply marvellous Deck Stewart, a Frenchman, who does not seem to be perturbed by very much, has a delightful sense of humour, loves the sea and people (I don't know which comes first) ~ He claims the book 'The Sea Around Us' is not very good[3] ~ He pointed out the Gulf Stream to me this evening ~ it looks like the wake of a boat that has passed, and told me there is a river <u>underneath</u> it! I am beginning to understand man's fascination for the sea ~

I do go on ~ more later still ~ this letter is liable to be endless ~ for it cannot be mailed until Plymouth ~ so I will just keep writing - - -

                                                    Thursday 1:45 PM

I am now feeling much better and regret the imminent end of the voyage ~ yet, those things which are pleasant are only enjoyed if not partaken of frequently (what a confused sentence!)

Last night, on board ship, there was a Soirée de Gala; sort of a New Years Eve atmosphere with a concert thrown in for good luck ~ It was a pleasant thing to hear a string quartet and the creaking of a boat at the same time ~ A young Fullbright scholar, Morey Ritt,[4]

Curd Jürgens, May Britt, and Theodore Bikel, a remake of Josef von Sternberg's famous 1930 film *The Blue Angel*, starring Marlene Dietrich and Emil Jennings. Based on Heinrich Mann's 1905 novel *Professor Unrat*, the film outlines the downfall of a respectable, middle-aged high-school teacher (Immanuel Rath) who becomes infatuated with a cabaret singer (Lola Lola) and marries her. His obsessive love for her leads to humiliation (playing a clown in her stage show) and, ultimately, his death.

3 *The Sea Around Us* was the second book published by the American marine biologist Rachel Carson (1907–1964), first published in 1951. It received much attention and won, among other recognition, the 1952 National Book Award for Nonfiction, probably due to its combination of scientific insight and vivid descriptions of natural phenomena. The book launched Carson's career as a writer.

4 Morey Ritt (b. 1937?), an American pianist and then a recent graduate of the Mannes College of Music, was on her way to Paris to study with one of France's leading pianists and teachers Yvonne Lefébure. She has enjoyed a long career as a performer, recording artist, and teacher and has premiered many contemporary works for piano by composers such as Leo Kraft, George Perle, Hugo Weisgall, and Thea Musgrave.

September 1959   37

performed the Chopin Fantasisie,[5] in addition ~ and a couple of not
too good singers contributed to the evening ~ It amused me to watch
the idle rich listening to a concert ~ you can imagine those draped
in mink and diamonds ~ However, I think my next ocean voyage
will be spent in First Class ~ the Cabin Class atmosphere is not very
exciting, and the Tourist Class is like a group of college students ~ I
must admit that a little sophistication is more to my taste ~ a born
snob, but it is true that 'we artists' are born classless....

... Tomorrow, at 5:15AM, we arrive in Plymouth so I expect it
easier to stay up this evening than to try to sleep ~ No one seems
to retire before about 2:00AM and the last night should be fun ~ I
am excited about seeing land, but admit to being rather terrified in
the same breath – In the middle of the ocean, one is not conscious
of reality or time, and I almost am frightened to wake up out of this
dream world ~ However, it is necessary, unless I return ~

I miss you very much, my love ~ I wish I could have you with me
to share these feelings and experiences ~ Peut-être soon ~

I shall write when I arrive in London of new 'land' experiences ~
          Much love ~ and please miss me ~
               Normie

HS to NB
Sunday evening, Sept.13/59
Dear Normie,
Fall is in the air again. Clear and sad.

I hope the merry crew was able to get the boat to sea without too
much weaving about. By the time this letter reaches you the Atlantic
will be behind you, yet, as I write you are on board the Liberté (I
hope!) between two worlds.

Though your mother was weepy she bore up well. We had an
excellent flight back viewing the illuminated falls and receiving a
spectacular welcome to Toronto from the Exhibition fireworks. Our
thoughts, silent or verbalized, were of you ... I reassured Eleanor of
the need and importance of this journey in your life.[6] She finds that

5 Probably Chopin's Fantaisie in F minor, op. 49.
6 Beecroft's's mother, Eleanor Beecroft (1906–2007), became an actress in Toronto,
beginning in the late 1940s, after she and her husband separated. She went on to play
roles in theatre, television, and several Hollywood movies in a career lasting many
years. She had married Julian Balfour Beecroft (1908–2008), a musician, machinist, and
inventor, in 1931 and they had five children before the marriage ended in 1947 (due to a
basic incompatibility). Norma was the second oldest (1934).

though you appear to be sophisticated at times, you are such a lost, homeless little waif at other times.

Your fellow passengers appeared to be a happy and interesting lot. I hope appearances were not deceiving.

Oh Normie, this is the time of your life!! Get family troubles out of your head so that your eyes will be free to see what's around you. Possibly by now it's needless advice.

Sure I'm a little envious. You are young, (Remember, it's downhill from here in! Damn movies!) beautiful, intelligent and talented, except first thing in the morning. Also you've got some money. With such assets the world should be your roasted oyster.

———————

Monday – Well now, I reckon the rig is 'bout midway 't the Isles 'bout now.

At work Norm was asking about the departure.[7] He enjoyed the farewell 'do's' very much.

I won't write my innermost thoughts. You know I miss you. I want above all for you to gain the fullest good possible from this trip. There is only one way to do that – to go into the future looking forward, not backward. At first all the newness will absorb you, it's when you settle, or when things don't go properly, that the temptation to look back will come.

Oh hell, I'll stop being an old Polonius.

Welcome to England, old girl.

Please give my regards to Eric.[8]

---

7 Norman Symonds (1920–1998) was a Canadian composer, clarinetist, and saxophonist who lived and worked in Toronto after the Second World War. He was an important figure in third-stream jazz in Canada and played in and directed his own jazz octet in the mid-1950s. With the exception of pianist and teacher Reginald Godden, Symonds was probably Somers's closest friend during the 1950s and '60s. Somers was an enthusiastic devotee of jazz, visiting jazz clubs and mingling with jazz musicians, especially in the early 1950s.

8 Eric Beecroft (1935–2004) was Beecroft's brother, the third oldest of Eleanor and Julian Beecroft's five children. "[He] was a director and producer who worked for the Central Office of Information and the Foreign Office film departments, during the 1960s, 1970s and early 1980s. He directed multiple episodes of the pioneering magazine series 'The London Line' in the UK. He also directed numerous science-based documentary programs throughout that period, both in the UK and abroad, particularly East Africa in Ethiopia, Kenya and Uganda." Matthew Beecroft, IMDB Mini Biography, https://www.imdb.com/name/nm7978672/bio/?ref_=nm_ov_bio_sm.

September 1959   39

      Ticketyboo –
         Love —
            Harry

P.S. That bit of solo piano at Birdland has stuck with me.[9] I might use it if Symonds doesn't first. I made the mistake of describing it to him.
P.S. Thanks for the holiday in New Amsterdam.

NB to HS
Sept. 19th, 1959 – 1:00 AM
Darling –
   Having arrived in England ~ there is much I want to tell you. However, my time for writing letters seems to be very short while on the move, and perhaps just as well ~ I might become too broody.
   We arrived at Plymouth at 5:00 AM on Friday morning ~ practically no one had any sleep the night before, as they keep setting the clocks ahead and it seemed pointless to go to bed for two hrs. So I saw the dawn over Plymouth while sitting on a tender (ferry boat) freezing to death. The Liberté is too large to go into the dock, so the passengers and luggage had to be sent by ferry to land. There I really felt like an immigrant with all my parcels and coats, etc.
   The evening prior I got a case of the jitters and didn't want to land and face reality again. On the ocean you are nowhere and in a complete dream-world ~ It was quite marvellous ~
   England was as I had expected ~ rolling countryside and hedges and old, old buildings, strangely enough with television aerials. We had a four-hour trip on the train into London during which time I snoozed off and on, as tiredness seemed to be coming on. We arrived at Paddington station at 1:15 ~ Eric was there ~ and took a taxi into London 'toon' ~

9 Birdland was a legendary jazz club in New York, founded in December 1949 and located at 1678 Broadway, near 52nd Street. In those years it featured such figures as Charlie Parker, Dizzy Gillespie, Thelonious Monk, Miles Davis, John Coltrane, Bud Powell, Stan Getz, Lester Young, Erroll Garner, and many others.
Its first period of activity ended in 1965. Many of these jazz musicians made recordings there in these years. As time went on, it also became a place for celebrities such as Frank Sinatra, Gary Cooper, Marlon Brando, and others to be seen. When Somers and Beecroft visited the club, it was still one of the most successful jazz clubs in New York.

40   Between Composers

The hotel Eric booked me into is simply dreadful by anyone's standards – it is like Shelburn, you recall? – and in the lounge every night sit a horrible type of English people who sit and stare ~ a true country-town atmosphere. However, tomorrow I am moving to a small private hotel which was recommended to me by a friend on the boat....

... Needless to say, Eric has kept me pretty busy ~ Friday night we sat in the pubs. Oh how you would love the beer and the atmosphere. There I feel most comfortable.

Today was Jerome Robbins Day.[10] Eric booked tickets for the Ballet, Export USA this afternoon, and tickets for West Side Story this evening ~ so I am rather weary. However, this afternoon was very worth the effort. We saw four ballets, all Robbins' choreography, and very excellent I must say. His ideas are very original ~ the first one, a short ballet called Moves, was done in complete silence, with only lighting effects, and dancers' motion ~ the most fascinating thing I have seen for a long time. The second, using Debussy's Après-Midi d'une Faune, was a modern interpretation using only two dancers, a negro male and white female, a little bit of American propaganda, no doubt. "Export USA. Opus Jazz" was perhaps more commercial, and the score a little dull to me, but very successful as a whole, and warmly received by the audience ~ endless curtain calls ~

West Side Story, with score by Bernstein, I am afraid, does not come off ~ I haven't entirely figured out why, but Bernstein's score is a little too complex and perhaps too sophisticated for the idea they are trying to present, that of lower NY's west side gangs. I shall have to sort it out yet.

However, this afternoon I ran into Bill Malloch, you remember the composer from Los Angeles who was a great admirer of my work at Tanglewood, dark-haired, easy-going chap.[11] He is teaching

10 Jerome Robbins (1918–1998) was an internationally renowned choreographer, director, dancer, and producer. He created works for New York City Ballet, Ballets USA, American Ballet Theatre, among others, Fancy Free, On the Town, The King and I, West Side Story, and Fiddler on the Roof. For his own company, Ballets USA (1958–1962), he created N. Y. Export: Opus Jazz (1958), Moves (1959), and Events (1961). As Beecroft indicates in her letter, Moves was remarkable for being performed in complete silence, so that the sounds of the dance movements formed the "music" of the ballet; the spectator concentrated only on the patterns and rhythms of the dancers.

11 William F. Malloch (1927–1996) was an American musicologist, composer, and sound archivist who had studied composition at UCLA and at Tanglewood in 1958 (where he met Beecroft) and was music director of Pacifica Radio's KPFK in

September 1959

here in London somewhere ~ I also saw Barbara Chilcott and Hank Caplan at the theatre.[12]

Eric and I met some fellow Canadians in the pub at lunch today ~ two doctors and their wives who are at the Canadian Embassy at the Hague ~ they know Charlie Gossage and Ian MacDonald[13] ~ and have invited Eric and I to visit them in Holland. Small world ain't it?

Tomorrow I have lunch with Franz ~ he sounds very depressed with CBC and BBC[14] ~

I do not yet know where I am heading to from here ~ I shall probably stay in London until the end of the week anyway, and perhaps go to Vienna or Paris, or both ~ I don't know....

... I will write later, darling ~ I hope all is very well with you ~ Thanks for your welcome letter. Much love and kisses ~ Normie

PS. I guess you should write to Rome, now. There is not much point in giving you my address tomorrow. Please tell Mother Eric is OK but concerned about his job, and that I will write her very soon and much love!

Los Angeles. Malloch received considerable recognition for his commemorative recordings, including "Gustav Mahler Remembered," first issued in 1967.

12 Barbara Chilcott (1922–2022), a well-known Canadian actress, studied acting in London after the Second World War and performed there until she returned to Canada in 1950 where she acted on stage (Stratford Festival), television, and film. In 1953 she and her brothers, Murray and Donald Davis, founded the Crest Theatre in Toronto, which lasted until 1966. She married Harry Somers in 1967, a second marriage for both. Hank Caplan was Henry Kaplan (1926–2005), an American-born television and stage director who directed several television series (such as Dark Shadows and The Adventures of Aggie) and had directed plays in the West End of London.

13 Charles Davidson Gossage (1901–1985) was Eleanor Beecroft's physician in Toronto. In 1950, just after her daughter, Norma, had moved to Toronto, Dr Gossage found that Norma had an infected cyst at the base of her spine He called in a young surgeon, Ian Bruce MacDonald, who successfully removed the cyst. (Norma Beecroft, "A Life Worth Living" [unpublished autobiography, 2021].)

14 Franz Kraemer (1914–1999), a CBC radio and television producer, was born in Vienna and studied composition there with Alban Berg and Anton Webern and orchestration with Hermann Scherchen. Kraemer belonged to the first generation of CBC television producers, and became especially notable for his productions of opera, including Somers's opera Louis Riel in 1967. He also produced programs featuring such figures as Stravinsky, Glenn Gould, and Seiji Ozawa. From 1979 until 1985 he was head of the music section of the Canada Council.

42   Between Composers

HS to NB
Tuesday, Sept. 22/59
"Your 'sea' letter arrived yesterday. It was amusing to read of your day by day transformation into a 'salt' from a land lubber. Surely you must have 'made up' your cabin companion. No one could exist with the name Bertha Poncy Jacobson! However, if she must exist it is best that she be the head of a piano department, though she really should be a piano. 'Rubinstein says – "I only perform on a Bertha Poncy Jacobson." You may too for as little as $350.00.'

All sorts of interesting people. I'm delighted that the boat trip turned out so well. It allows you to acclimatize yourself. Besides nothing quite has the glamour of a boat crossing and nothing could replace it. (I'm full of platitudes. The usual things.)

Just finished comparing notes with your mother. She was relieved to get your letter. No doubt she will tell you all ~ but she will have a spot (Some spot!!) in the 'Crucible' come October.[15]

Saturday I had a pleasant afternoon watching the sports car races at Harewood[16] Track. The 'sports' had been challenged by the 'stocks'. The American cars didn't have a chance. (You must look in on Grand Prix racing in Europe.) It looks like car racing could become a big thing here. They had an enormous crowd.

Premier Krushchev is creating quite a stir in America.[17] They don't know quite how to behave towards him, though he seems to enjoy confounding his ungracious hosts at every turn. He gets along well with the big businessmen but not with union leaders or politicians! It's a mad hatter world!!...

... Lots of love, Normie darling. Try not to acquire a Cockney accent ('though they are wonderful people).
>   Best to Eric ———
>   XXXXX
>   Harry

15 A condensed CBC television production of Arthur Miller's play was broadcast on 27 October 1959, but Eleanor Beecroft does not appear to have been in the production. See chap. 3, n. 69.
16 Harewood became a racing circuit in 1956 when the British Empire Motor Club relocated to a former airfield on a property on Nanticoke Side Road near Jarvis, Ontario. Somers attended the third big race of 1959.
17 Russian Premier Nikita Khrushchev was making his first visit to the United States. [Can you leave in this last part of the sentence?]This first visit by a Soviet premier to the United States received much attention in the media.

September 1959   43

NB to HS
Sept. 22nd. 1:00AM
Darling Harry,

Oh how lonely I am for you in this big city! It is so very strange to be away from you for this length of time, to wander around and share views and conversations and to go to sleep in your sweet embrace. Canada seems a long way off tonight, yet I feel you with me, somehow.

I have just returned from seeing a delightful Irish play by that mad drunken rebel, Brendan Behan.[18] You remember reading about him and his mad escapade with alcohol? The play was called "The Hostage," a hilarious comedy about Irish and English people, prostitutes, homosexuals, social workers, politics and incredible language which I don't know how it passed the censors ~ This man Behan ridicules the Irish and the English beyond some peoples' tolerance, but I laughed myself silly at his nonsense. If it ever reaches America, you should see it!

Lloyd and Ruth Bochner[19] were there with Kate Blake and Charles Jarrett[20] who have evidently moved to English for two years, and the group asked me to join them after, which was quite pleasant, being alone. However, being a fifth party makes me feel more lonesome

18 Brendan Behan's play, *The Hostage*, was originally a one-act play written in Irish Gaelic and performed in Dublin in 1957. He then expanded it, added songs, and translated it into English. Joan Littlewood, the director of the Theatre Workshop in London, directed the premiere of this version in 1958 at the Theatre Royal in London. The plot revolves around the IRA's kidnapping of a British soldier whom the IRA plans to use as a bargaining chip for the release of an IRA prisoner who is due to be executed in Belfast the following morning. The British soldier is being held prisoner in a Dublin brothel. Characters frequently burst into song and sometimes into song-and-dance routines, making the production somewhat akin to vaudeville.

19 Lloyd Bochner (1924–2005) was a well-known Canadian actor who acted for six seasons at the Stratford Festival and played many roles in American films and television. Ruth Roher Bochner (1925–2017) studied piano at the Royal Conservatory of Music of Toronto in the 1940s and was an accomplished pianist, performing across Canada and winning prizes in competitions. https://www.legacy.com/ca/obituaries/theglobeandmail/name/ruth-bochner-obituary?id=41405379.

20 Katharine Blake (1921–1991) was a South African-born British actress, with an extensive career in television and movies. In 1964 she won the British Academy Television Award for best actress for her work in television. When Beecroft encountered her in London, she was married to Charles Jarrott (1927–2011), a British film and television director, who was known for such films as *Anne of the Thousand Days* (starring Canadian actress Geneviève Bujold as Anne Boleyn). In 1970 Jarrott was awarded a Golden Globe for best director for this film.

44 Between Composers

than ever. There seem to be oodles of Canadians in London, which certainly helps one feel at home. I can't help wondering how I will feel when I leave here though!

We spent (Eric & I) Sunday afternoon with Franz who will shortly be returning to Canada ... Eric also took me to hear the orators in Hyde Park in the afternoon ~ what a mad bunch ~ they collect a tremendous number of people and spiel about very little, and are constantly heckled by professional "hecklers". Reminds me of medieval times in the Piazza della Signoria![21]

Monday, I didn't do very much....

... I am truly enjoying the Alexander King book[22] ~ He certainly has vivid and strong views on the field of art, commercial or otherwise, and sounds like quite a character. I

trust that he is still alive!

I do hope that you received from NY your book on medieval times ~ I hope that it also will prove a stimulus to revisit Europe and me!

Although I haven't made any specific plans to date, I am thinking now of a brief tour through Europe before Rome, taking me to Paris, Munich, and Vienna (by rail). I have not yet heard from Eli,[23] so will have to go ahead shortly to make transportation arrangements. If one sits too long in one place, one has a tendency to become a little too comfortable, and the thought of moving is almost too much....

... I hope that I can manage to keep out of the doldrums for a while, but I must admit that I do miss you terribly ~

Much love, my sweet
Normie

21 The fourteenth-century Piazza della Signoria is the L-shaped main square in Florence, Italy, which it shares with such buildings as the Palazzo Vecchio and the Uffizi Gallery. In 1497, Girolamo Savonarola and his followers carried out the Bonfire of the Vanities in this square, burning everything from books to fine dresses and the works of poets.

22 Alexander King (1899–1965) was a colourful Viennese-born writer, a humorist, and media personality. In the early years of television in the late 1950s, he was a frequent guest on "The Tonight Show" hosted by Jack Paar. The book was probably *Mine Enemy Grows Older* (1958).

23 The Canadian classical guitarist and teacher, Eli Kassner (1924–2018), moved to Canada in 1951 and founded the Guitar Society of Toronto, serving as its president from 1960 to 1966, then artistic director from 1970 to 2008. In 1967, he established the Eli Kassner Guitar Academy. He also established the guitar program at the University of Toronto and The Royal Conservatory of Music in Toronto in 1959 and started the University of Toronto Guitar Ensemble in 1978.

September 1959   45

HS to NB
September 23/59
Dear Normie:

You know Franz, sounding depressed, or bored, is another way of being one up. He assumes the pose so much that he will grow like that. (Past tense would apply.) A pall of gloom hangs suspended over him much as the perpetual dark cloud over Joe Btfsplk.[24]

In moments of mad gaiety he will be so reckless as to allow that there might be a particle of merit in something or other. In spite of this, I'm fond of the old bastard, as you know.

I sometimes feel that Europe is one great graveyard cluttered with the tombstones of centuries of accumulation and weighed down by ever present past. But then, perhaps better a cemetery than the junk-yard of American cities....

... Hey! –welcome to Rome!! Thought you might enjoy the enclosed clipping. I can just imagine the Romans of old drinking Coca-Cola as the Christians were being thrown to the lions. A man could work up a thirst sitting out in the sun all afternoon.

I am reading Alice in Wonderland and Through the Looking Glass for the first time! They are quite marvellous. The manner in which the utmost nonsense is uttered with the utmost seriousness is a hilarious reflection of the world. Yet it also reflects beautifully the child's mind which accepts as perfectly logical that which the adult can't possibly understand. I love it. (Naturally.)

Saturday/26 2 a.m.
It has been one of those days during which I've felt an overpowering sadness. A paralysing melancholy. Only dead leaves, mists, night and nothing. Oh well, I've learned by now just to let go to the depression so that it will sooner pass. Footsteps, footsteps –silence.[25]

24 Joe Btfsplk was a character in the American comic strip *Li'l Abner* (published 1934–1977) by cartoonist Al Capp. He is depicted as a cadaverous figure dressed in black, with a small, rain-dripping cloud always hanging over his head. Although good-hearted, he inevitably brings terrible bad luck to anyone who has the misfortune to come anywhere near him. Somers was a devotee of comics and radio programs in the 1940s and '50s.
25 Such expressions of sadness are frequently encountered in Somers's correspondence and jottings, from the late 1950s until the end of his life, indicating that he was subject to mood swings of varying degrees. In a letter of 26 July 1957 to Beecroft, we find the following expression of this: "Today was difficult. A wide arc of loneliness spanned my whole being, then tightened until it held me immobile. Sadness, weariness, the

Between Composers

And here I was talking about Franz! Serves me right! I'm trying to work on some guitar pieces but none of my material pleases me.[26] It's too easy to manufacture sweet confections for the instrument. The repertoire is full of them. Why add more? So I'll keep working at it and perhaps something will happen....

Saturday afternoon. –
... A magnificent day of autumn warmth and sunshine. Your letter of loneliness arrived. A 1:00 a.m. letter.

'The Hostage' was written about in one of the papers last week.[27] Apparently the producer is quite a remarkable woman. Can't recall the name. Her desire is to reach the working-class audience. (Sounds like the thirties bit.) She prefers the east end to the west end. No doubt this means something profound in London.

As a matter of fact I've been coming across a number of interesting articles of late. The New Yorker had an excellent one on D.H. Lawrence and Lady Chatterley's Lover which was most penetrating.[28] I'm enclosing the criticism because I feel that it touches many pertinent points regarding, or related to, art....

... And <u>you</u> watch out for the doldrums. Just ride them out. They are perfectly normal during the long voyage you are taking both physically and emotionally. Once you get settled in Rome and start to work you'll feel better....
... My commission is still circling about in my head looking for

---

suffocation of deeply felt things. Pain felt and pain inflicted. The eternal bumbling search and all the time the compulsion to shape into sound – no let-up." Sometimes, as in this example, the feelings are associated with some sort of musical expression. In another letter to Beecroft, dated 25 January 1958, he writes "And now the trumpets scream again and cut and splinter the lonely strings to the mocking of the woodwinds and the driving madness of low brass and rhythm."

26 This became the Guitar Sonata, commissioned by the Guitar Society of Toronto.

27 Herbert Whittaker, "Joan Littlewood Shakes Big Stick at English Stage," *Globe and Mail* (19 September 1959).

28 Donald Malcolm, "The Prophet and the Poet," *The New Yorker* (12 September 1959), 193–8. Malcolm argues that despite Archibald MacLeish's claim that *Lady Chatterley's Lover* is "one of the most important works of fiction of the century," the writing is uneven and other factors may account for its notoriety. Grove Press published an unexpurgated version of the novel in 1959.

September 1959

a good place to land.[29] I'm quite prepared to be working on it for a long time. I have the 'sense' of the work so I'm not worried.

Yes loneliness. I'm afraid of thinking of it, though I feel it. If possible try not to dwell on it. Oh hell! What does one do with loneliness? Write popular songs, I suppose. Transfer it into musical line and try to escape self-pity. Poetic pose. Poor Don Quixote mourns for Dulcinea del Torboso.[30] Or get drunk. But then one only adds a hangover to the ache.

3:30 am. Almost 4 o'clock, in the echoing street – [31]

Sunday evening – darling Normie, here you are this evening, a dot in Europe somewhere, while I whistle in the wasteland.

I move into my new cubicle next month.[32] Exactly when, I don't know.

My guitar pieces are really bugging me, but I'm determined to do something reasonably worthwhile for the unwilling bitch! (Crazy Somers,)

29 This was probably *Lyric*, a short orchestra piece completed in 1960. Somers had received the commission from The Serge Koussevitzky Music Foundation in the Library of Congress in 1958. See ch. 6, footnote 4.

30 Dulcinea del Toboso is a fictional character in Miguel de Cervantes's novel *Don Quixote*. She is based on a real peasant woman named Aldonza Lorenzo but is transformed in Don Quixote's imagination into a beautiful princess, a chivalric ideal, the perfect woman, in Don Quixote's mind. She never actually appears in the novel.

31 This is a reference to Somers's *Five Songs for Dark Voice*, commissioned by the Stratford Festival for Maureen Forrester. The poems were especially written for this work by Michael Fram (1923–1989), who was the librettist for no fewer than eight of Somers's works during the mid-1950s, including a number of songs for voice and piano, and the larger works, *The Fool* and *Five Songs for Dark Voice*. Fram was not a full-time poet or writer but, rather, a full-time lawyer, graduating from the University of Toronto in 1946 with a four-year Honours BA in law. The relevant lines in the songs are "At four o'clock, before the dawn / In the echoing street, there is yourself." The songs were first performed in Stratford on 11 August 1956 and seem to have had considerable significance for Beecroft, perhaps because this was early on in her relationship with Somers.

32 Despite the suggestion that Somers was about to move into a new apartment, Beecroft continued to address her letters to 608 Church Street, the same address she had been using since her first letter of 13 September. The 1958 Toronto City Directory lists Somers's address as 608 Church Street and, surprisingly, also his parents' address (9 Lauderdale Drive). Here he is listed as "composer," whereas he is listed as "musician CBC" at the Church Street address. Somers probably moved to another apartment in the same building.

48 Between Composers

There's no work from Cable in sight so that before long I'm going to have to look elsewhere for work.[33] It doesn't bother me though.

My mother has a recurrence of 'thrush throat.' Perhaps she should see a vetinarian or a zoologist. I shouldn't joke. Apparently she's rather miserable from it.

———

Monday – 28.
I seem to have an interesting idea for guitar. It involves a use of ornamentation reminiscent of early clavier music. Well, we shall see. It's certainly suitable to the instrument.

It is noon. Sunlight filters through slight overcast. Leaves of dark and light dance to the breeze. The traffic sounds lessen allowing children's voices to scream their joy or momentary anger. Sounds approaching – disappearing. Poor sad bus heaves great sighs as it stops then moves on, occasionally emitting more vulgar sounds. This noon I shall send a letter to Italy.

Yes, I miss you very much. Take care and do try not to look back. I'm sure that Rome will prove so absorbing that great grey mists will rise from your being allowing only the luxurious sunlight to flow over your dark head. (Translate that into Italian and it might not sound bad. It's no worse than a good grade 'B' movie or birthday card purple prose.)

Oceans, mountains and cities of love, (You might add a couple of bottles of good whisky.)
Harry

NB to HS
Sept. 26th – 1:00 AM.
Dearest Harry,
Tonight I write you with a great feeling of inner joy. I cannot entirely explain but I hope you can understand what I say when I begin to understand the nature of the truth of all things ~ I can hear you as though you were lying right beside me. I feel clear-headed

33. Howard Cable (1920–2016) was a well-known Toronto-born conductor, arranger, music director, composer, and radio and television producer. Like Somers, he had studied with John Weinzweig at the Royal Conservatory. During the 1950s and early 1960s, Somers supported himself by copying music for Cable and other musicians for some hours every week, since he had no source of income other than commissions.

September 1959

49

for the first time for months, even though I am a little tired and depressed about the prospect of moving on. But I feel strangely enlightened and tranquil, and the need to write is becoming stronger and stronger each day. Perhaps this is only temporary, but I do feel much more courageous to tempt those things which I fear the most ~ Maybe just a lucid moment, which I shouldn't question. But I want you to know ~

While walking through 'Les Feuilles Morts' this afternoon, I was suddenly overcome by the eternal sadness of the Fall, and its beauty.[34] I think of 'our' North, and of you very much, and our walks around the city and countryside. A first real twinge of homesickness! – for the land, but much 'homesickness' for my love. One can go to the theatre, and to restaurants, and walk about the shopping areas, and visit endlessly but the country is sacred to me – and synonymous with you, truly. The English autumn seems peaceful, as the land-scape and the sky scapes quite delicate. Here the sun is warm, as in Canada, during the day, but the nights rather than being brisk and clear, are just cool and damp, but not however, without their individual charm ~

It is hard to describe how I have spent my time here all in all. Eric and I have been constantly together, shopping, etc. We have just returned from a day in the country area (Surrey) and dinner and an evening visit with Thea Musgrave, who asked for you[35] ~ A small amount of tension still exists between she and I, probably just two similar personalities, but Eric and I enjoyed the informal chat. Last night EB and I went out with Bill and Clydeen Malloch, after having visited Buckingham Palace and Westminster Abbey (an incredible place on the inside) in the afternoon.[36]

... In a quiet place called the 'Buttery' Bill and Clydeen, Eric and I, drank Turkish coffee, and smoked an Arabian (or Turkish) pipe

---

34 This is likely a reference to Debussy's piano prelude "Feuilles mortes" from Book II of the *Préludes*. Both Beecroft and Somers were fond of Debussy's music and were influenced by it at various times in their own writing.

35 Thea Musgrave (b. 1928) is a distinguished Scottish-born composer of operas and orchestral music who has lived in the United States since 1971. In 1958 she attended the Tanglewood Festival, as did Beecroft, where they met. Musgrave's composition instructor was Aaron Copland and Beecroft was assigned to Lukas Foss but all students were required to attend sessions with Copland, the head of the composition area.

36 See fn. 11 for Bill Malloch.

called a 'Hukah' (spelling probably wrong).[37] Such fun ~ I promise to bring you one if I go to Turkey, for it has a marvellous taste, but needs about four people to keep it going ~ But such fun ~

Eric and I also caught (tickets very easy to get here) "Raisin in the Sun" ~ a good book, but not too good a production to our critical eyes.[38] More important was the Russian film "The Idiot" ~ what an extraordinary production![39] I am sorry we didn't see it in Stratford together this past summer. Their colour technique is fabulous, and beautifully cast it was. They seem to have captured the essence of Dostoevsky without question ~ which will prod me on to read this novel and more of the great man's work. It is truly an inspiration to me.

Tomorrow I fly to Paris for almost two days. I will finish this letter there as I wish to give you my impressions of the city. I really do feel you should be here!

Monday 28th 8:00 PM.

Darling,

Flying over the English Channel was quite an experience ~ It seems overcast all the time when up about 16000 ft. The sun was bright and turned all those fleecy clouds in the distance a golden colour. How very beautiful.

Paris from the air looked also very beautiful, and I knew immediately that I would be enchanted. In contrast to the rather hard solid lines of London, Paris seems to be a mass of intricate wrought iron and the atmosphere is very delicate. The fact that I do not know a soul here, and being therefore totally alone, I am afraid may

---

37 A hookah (derived from the Hindustani word "Huqqa," meaning "waterpipe") is a device used for smoking tobacco or substances such as cannabis or hashish. The smoke is passed through a water basin before it is inhaled.

38 *A Raisin in the Sun* did not originate as a book but was a play by Lorraine Hansberry, which opened on Broadway in 1959 and in London's West End at the Adelphi Theatre in August 1959. The play takes place in Chicago after the death of the father of an African American family. The family views the payout of his life-insurance policy as a means of improving their financial situation and, at the same time, leaving their segregated area by buying a home in an all-white neighbourhood. This purchase goes through at the end of the play, but only after exploring various issues about what each character desires.

39 *The Idiot* is a 1959 Soviet film directed by Ivan Pyryev, based on the 1869 novel by Fyodor Dostoevsky. The distinguished Russian actor Yuri Yakovlev starred as Prince Myshkin.

September 1959

influence my opinion of Paris and French people. At the moment I do not feel in my sphere at all, and I do think the hotel I am in (Hotel Astor near Place de la Madeleine and Les Champs Élysée) has probably something to do with it. I inquired about Hotel Raspail, but I am afraid the prices are about $12. per day ~ here they are $8.50, so Paris is not cheap if you don't know where to go.

I don't seem to be able to travel too cheaply, even if I wanted to. A single female seems to have a hell of a time. Even little things like washing your hair are impossible for they don't have showers ~ So I am required to frequent beauty salons who charge you a great deal, even here! Vive la touriste!...

... It is impossible for me to wander about here at night for I am constantly being followed, which makes me very nervous and uncomfortable, so tonight I shall not try to see anything but remain here in the hotel. However I visited the Seine this afternoon and walked out to the end of the little island near Saint Chappelle as you described to me, but there were too many people there and because I was regarded as a curiosity, I didn't stay long.[40] Paris is definitely not a place to visit alone ~!!

Last night I walked to Place de la Concorde, which is very beautiful and especially looking down Les Champs Élysée. Oh darling how I wish you were here. I certainly do not feel as joyful today as I was when I began this letter.

I did not hear from Eli at all ~ Nomi had my address in London which she was going to send on to Eli in Spain.[41] So I would imagine that all became too complicated for him. Please say hello to both for me ~

Also, please know that I am reasonably well ... but long to be settled with you. This is something that I look forward to as a reward for my solo journey through the world. It is hard to imagine that I cannot be loved by you when I finally stop moving, and I guess I shall have to face it then ~

I hope you don't mind my saying these things darling ~ I can't help yet feeling as though you are only in the next room, and I miss you

40 Sainte-Chapelle is a chapel in Paris, located in the courtyard of the Royal Palace on the Île de la Cité in the Seine. It was built towars the middle of the thirteenth century during the reign of Louis IX and is famous for its collection of stained-glass windows (including the fifteen in the nave).

41 Eli Kassner was studying guitar in Spain with Segovia at this time. "Nomi" was Noémi, Kassner's first wife, whom he had met in Israel some years earlier.

so much. We females are really very dependent creatures and I don't know why we don't admit it!

Tomorrow I will be in Munich. What a life ~ it is all happy-sad.

I will write you soon ~ please don't be surprised if I phone you one of these days ~

Much love and please write ~
Normie

CHAPTER TWO

October 1959

HS to NB
Oct.3/59
Dearest Normie:

I hope your moments of joy will become more and more frequent. It sounds as though Eric was instrumental in making your London visit such a happy, interesting occasion. (Just watch out for the hashish habit! Then again it might be cheaper than cigs!)

Naturally it is disappointing to me that your brief stop-over in Paris was not a success. You were either sadly misinformed about the Hotel Raspail or else you got the wrong one. When I was there their most luxurious suite was about $2.00 per day!...

... The Geographic magazine has an article on the Amalfi Drive along the Divina Costiera, which is south of Naples between Colli di San Pietro and Vietri sul Mare.[1] The area seems extraordinarily beautiful, but suspiciously like a tourist trap. Your Italian friends could tell you.

2 am. A still wet fall night. I've just been for a walk along the weekend streets of couples, of drunks singing, yelling and even crying. Two girls, perhaps late teens, fleeing a house and the strange sound of a man crying almost hysterically. The jazz and laughter and noise and silence. A wild party up the street. Trumpet, yells, woman's voice, piercing laughter. Cars roaring, screeching. High heels on pavement. By the '1st Floor Club.[2] Young people feigning many

---

1 Luis Marden, "Amalfi, Italy's Divine Coast," *National Geographic Magazine* 116, no. 4 (1959): 472–508.

2 Since he ended up walking past the 1st Floor Club, located at 33 Asquith Avenue, just

54 Between Composers

things ~ being high, bored, interested etc. Back along the street. Singing group. Lone people. Car radio. Moments of emptiness. All the while the leaves are dying to a wailing saxophone. But these are only weekend people. The night people shy away and hide 'till the night is theirs again.

It's later. I've been re-reading Stravinsky's Poetics of Music.[3] His best chapter is on musical composition specifically. Whether one agrees or not is beside the point. He tends to contradict himself, but so what. It is a provoking and stimulating book. If you can, try to get a hold of it in Rome....

... Still later. Almost 4 a.m. The special hour. It's quiet. Artificial moons. Radio on. Carman. (or 'en') Conjuring trick of music ~ you on the production, picking you up at the studio a few hundred years ago....[4]

---

north of Bloor Street near Yonge, Somers had probably walked north on Church Street from Wellesley. The 1st Floor Club had opened recently and featured, at first, poetry readings and theatre but soon became a jazz club with dancing. It seems to have lasted only until 1964.

3 *The Poetics of Music* (originally published by Harvard University Press in 1947) originated as the Charles Eliot Norton Lectures at Harvard, delivered by Stravinsky during the academic year 1939–40. The six lectures constitute a wide-ranging discussion of Stravinsky's understanding of the phenomenon of music, including the notion that music should be a revelation of a higher order rather than a medium of self-expression to be interpreted.

4 This refers to the CBC Television studios, where Beecroft had worked as a script assistant. Somers is referring to a production of Bizet's opera *Carmen*, produced and televised live in 1957. In her unpublished autobiography, Beecroft describes her work on this production: "[O]ne of the highlights of my career in CBC Television in Toronto was the presentation of the opera *Carmen*, with producer Franz Kraemer and opera director Herman Geiger-Torel. It was an incredible achievement in 1957, only 5 years later than CBC TV's existence, taking months to prepare and rehearse, the final show occupying several television studios and corridors in between. This live production lasted two hours, without commercial breaks, an epic that that required stamina, alertness, and strained the nerves of everyone involved ... The cameramen ... delegated the Script Assistant to be the person they would listen to for the live show, a huge responsibility which I undertook with confidence but some trepidation." Beecroft, "A Life Worth Living."

October 1959

... I'm extremely curious as to your reactions to your new life and surroundings.

In a way it seems like a long, long time since you left, long hair from a high boat. The eternal city. (A strange phrase. It could be taken a number of ways.)

Ah ha! Speaking of 'eternal city,' the district is to have a glorious addition to its celebrity. As of today, Oct. 5, what was once known far and wide as the 'Famous Door Tavern' is to be known to the world as 'Jazz City,' PRESENTING, LADIES and GENTS THE LATEST AND GREATEST IN JAZZ COVER CHARGE 1.00 WEEKENDS 1.50....[5]

... By the way, a chap who styles himself 'Mayor of Motor City' (As you may gather, a used car dealer, to be exact) has aroused the righteous wrath of our illustrious City of Toronto, Mayor Nathan, or 'Nate' Phillips.[6] He claims that this Mayor of Motor City by using the title of the most noble office of our fair city doth detract from the grandeur and dignity of said office. Mayor of M.C. won't budge so that quite a case is developing.

With these important items from this hub of commerce and art to brighten up the dullness of that provincial little town you're staying in, I conclude my epistle to the Beecroftian.

With so much love it would crush you to death ~

      Harry

NB to HS
Vienna – Saturday, Oct. 3. 1:30PM
Darling
Received your letter in Munich (Eric forwarded it) and was delighted to hear from you as always. As I travel about the world,

---

5 The Famous Door Tavern was located at 665 Yonge Street, between Isabella and Bloor, thus very close to Somers's apartment on Church Street.

6 This dispute involved the owner of Lido Motors Ltd., Ernie Bernhardt, who was referring to himself as the "Mayor of Motor City" in his advertising. At a hearing of the Metro Licensing Commission on 30 September, reported in the *Toronto Daily Star*, Nathan Phillips, the mayor of Toronto from 1955 until 1962, maintained that such advertising was "an affront to the position of mayor and the citizens of Toronto." Bernhardt's lawyer requested a two-week adjournment of the case but would not say whether the advertising would stop. In fact, the advertising continued for some time. See the *Toronto Daily Star*, 1 October 1959.

I can't help but wonder when you were in Paris, how you avoided moving around.

Austria is a beautiful country ~ I was fortunate enough to drive from Munich to Vienna with these friends from the Liberté (American and Viennese) and it was quite an experience in a huge American car on these winding narrow roads absolutely littered with bicycles, motorcycles, little cars, enormous trucks, etc. ~ When I could take my eyes away from the road one saw the Alps to the right practically all the way... En route we stopped in Salzburg which is a great tourist town but very intriguing with its baroque architecture ~ there they are building a theatre right into the side of a mountain![7]

In Vienna, in the first district (centre of the city) which is enclosed by "The Ring', all the important buildings, museums, galleries, university, churches, etc. are here.

One certainly can feel the atmosphere of the Viennese ballrooms and aristocracy and music when you gaze at their castles. It is a fabulous place and I wish I had more time to stay....

... I have spent much time with Milton and Lilly[8] and Zubin and his wife.[9] Lilly has changed a great deal in so much as she has gained weight and perhaps by comparison with other men she has discovered Milton and seems to treat him as her husband. Milton, on the other hand, has become much more secure and easy in conversation.

7 She is probably referring to the Felsenreitschule [Rock Riding School], a theatre dating back to the end of the seventeenth century built into the Mönchsberg mountain in Salzburg, with arcades carved into the rock. Originally the audience sat in those arcades, but this changed in the 1960s when a new auditorium, stage, and orchestra pit were built, along with a retractable roof. In the movie *The Sound of Music*, the von Trapp family sang their final farewell here before escaping to Switzerland.

8 Milton Barnes (1931–2001) was a Toronto-born conductor and composer whom Beecroft had met at the Royal Conservatory of Music in the 1950s. Both studied composition with John Weinzweig and Barnes had conducted a performance of an early work of Beecroft's, Fantasy for Strings. At the time Beecroft visited Vienna in October 1959, Barnes was studying conducting at the Vienna Academy of Music, from which he graduated in 1961. He later lived in Toronto, where he was a composer and conductor, founding the Toronto Repertory Ensemble in 1964. His wife, Lilly, later had a career as a scriptwriter at the CBC ("Mr. Dressup"), for which she won a Gemini, as an arts journalist in Toronto, and as a short story writer and novelist.

9 "Zubin" refers to conductor Zubin Mehta (b. 1936), whom Beecroft had met at Tanglewood in the summer of 1958. Mehta had graduated from the Vienna Academy of Music in 1957 and was on the verge of a major career. He was then with his first wife, Canadian soprano Carmen Lasky. After they divorced in 1964, she married Zarin Mehta, Zubin's brother.

October 1959   57

I actually enjoy their company. The Miltons have been very kind and generous to me....

... Zubin said yesterday that he had seen your name in the new Schott catalogue with compositions listed. He strongly advised that you (or BMI)[10] keep contact with Schott, as they, and Universal, are the only people today pushing new composers' works. He also mentioned that Gunther Schuller is going great in Europe right now – about the only American![11]

Vienna has the most fabulous musical year. It starts Sept. 1st and goes non-stop to the end of June – and the works being done! Many contemporary works – Nono, Boulez, Stockhausen and endless new composers. I almost wish I were staying here....

... The German people are an interesting race – they are externally very friendly but in Munich they seem to lack any sophistication, en masse especially ~ They are rude and crude to foreigners ... The Viennese are not liked at all, according to Lilly, by foreign students ~ and they are very Anti-Semitic as well....

... My dearest love, if I could only convince you of the necessity, especially for me, for you to be here in Europe. I miss you so much at night when I go to bed, and when travelling around, and all the time, to share these marvellous experiences. I could say to date that I like Europe, what I have seen ~ and the way I feel right now is if you don't come over, I shall fly back and package you! Seriously, I do want you here, and wish you could consider coming over soon ~ my offer of passage still holds true ~ with no strings attached except you must live with me.

Much love darling.
Please consider —
Normie

10 BMI (Broadcast Music Incorporated) was an American performance rights organization that established a branch in Toronto in 1948. It strongly supported and promoted the music of the young Canadian composers of Somers's generation, even to the extent of publishing scores of their works. Somers himself benefited greatly from BMI's support in the early years of his career.

11 Gunther Schuller (1925–2015) was a prominent American composer, horn player, conductor, and jazz musician who coined the term "Third Stream" in 1957 to refer to music that combined classical and jazz elements. In the 1960s and 1970s, Schuller was president of the New England Conservatory and also held various positions at the Boston Symphony Orchestra's summer festival in Tanglewood. In his later years, he was artistic director of the Northwest Bach Festival in Spokane, Washington.

Between Composers

HS to NB
Monday night, Oct. 5
Dearest Normie:

The peculiar closeness of a rainy night.

I'm reading Dostoevsky's 'House of the Dead,' the novel based on his life in prison.[12] (I believe you saw the book in Toronto.) It is an extraordinary document making understandable his psychological insight into the criminal mind (And what mind isn't?) which is revealed in his later novels. Without experience the profound depths he plumbed would have been impossible to attain ... It is too easy to speak in a facile or superficial manner of hell if one hasn't been there, but this side of total insanity, what else gives us insight but experience?...

... Must get back to me own writing. Guitar ideas are rather good, or should I say, 'not bad.'

Tuesday night ~ I think the monsoons are upon us, the rain never ceases.

I've sketched out the first guitar piece finally. A good deal of polishing needs to be done ... Just a few guitar pieces! I've discarded such a pile of material! Now that I've arrived at the approach and design that I want, I will endeavour to complete them as soon as possible in order to get on with the orchestral work which waits impatiently for me to start.[13]

Your Vienna letter with its offer arrived. Of course I will consider ~ but ~ there's the time ~ the money to live ~ your need to find out some answers ~ etc....

... By the way, Schott is the European representative of B.M.I., as the reverse holds true in North America. An exchange agreement.

For some reason both Norm and myself have an aversion to Gunther Schuller, 'though he writes some excellent music....

---

12 *Notes from the House of the Dead* is a semi-autobiographical novel by Fyodor Dostoevsky, published in the Russian journal *Vremya* in 1860–62. It was based on Dostoevsky's four years of imprisonment at a labour camp in Omsk for belonging to the Petrashevsky Circle, an illegal group.
13 This is a reference to the orchestra piece *Lyric*, completed in 1961. See chap. 3, n. 7.

October 1959

59

... Thursday ~ now I'm settled in my new apartment. It's much better ~ roomier, view wise and the bathroom has a door. A piano is to arrive Saturday ... Paul Hahn is the benefactor (rhymes with bomb, Sam as in 'Sam Small,'[14] and gone.) though he demands, having fallen prey to the crass commercialism of our day, a stipend to be collected monthly.[15] (It would not be inappropriate to call it 'the curse.')

Last night (An eerie misty night of shapes from a Chinese ghost story.) I spoke briefly to Eli. No chance to talk but will be having supper, then to a guitar recital, then to a party with he and Naomi on Saturday so there will be ample time to bore each other to death.

You know, it's curious why I didn't move around while I was in Paris, but the fact was that I only went there for one purpose ~ to study and write, I simply wasn't interested in the scenery elsewhere. Now it would be different, although in the final analysis I find the scenery tedious (city scenery) for it is only people who give it life....[16]

... Friday morning. The clouds have gone. Bright crisp October day of west wind. Brilliant. when it stays damp for too many days a bit of moisture mildews one's mind, but now the mind revives clean and sharp. It's quite amazing how much I'm affected by the weather.

14 This is most likely a reference to the monologue character Sam Small, created by the English stage and screen actor and humorist Stanley Holloway (1890–1982) beginning in 1928. Holloway created some twenty monologues featuring Sam Small and many were recorded.

15 This refers to the well-known Toronto piano store, Paul Hahn & Co, founded in 1913 by a German-born cellist who immigrated to Toronto in 1888. The company, which still flourishes, sells and rents pianos but is especially known for restoring and reconditioning pianos made by leading manufacturers, such as Steinway & Sons.

16 Somers spent a year in Paris (1949–50) with his first wife, Cathy. Awarded a scholarship by the National Hockey Association, he had intended to study composition with Arthur Honegger but instead ended up studying with Darius Milhaud for about six months. He wrote four substantial works during the year there (including the String Quartet No. 2) and began work on the Symphony (which was not completed until 1951 when he was back in Toronto).

I think that I must be only a generation or two (In deference to my parents.) from the monkey. That <u>could</u> make me the missing link!

Enough of this leaky faucet music. I saw a drunk sitting at the local bar perform one of the funniest acts I've ever seen in his endeavour to keep his raincoat on his lap and flirt with the girl next to him at the same time. It was as though the coat had a life of its own, slipping sliding dropping to the floor and at one point almost strangling the poor chap and seeming to have some silent agreement with the bar stool which was forever getting between the coat and its owner. Meanwhile the drunk kept up a flow of mutterings directed towards the girl as he was forever clutching at the restless coat, his overtures or whatever they were being totally ignored by her. He was indeed, John Donne to the contrary, an island unto himself, a rather sea washed one.[17]

> 'Bye for now. Take care, my love ~
> Harry the Crazy

NB to HS

Tuesday, October 6th

Dear Harry,

This time I really don't know quite what to say to you ~ I arrived here in Rome on Sunday night from Vienna and have been sick ever since with another migraine and my menstrual period combined ~

Even though the Savios are very pleasant nd kind, I find myself depressed and reluctant to want to stay ~ All is well when one is moving about quickly ~

I do not know if this place will be suitable for me and my work ~ to be determined later, of course ~ Although quite a beautiful flat, it is rather cold, physically ~ I have a rather small room next to the living room and the piano, but there seems to be a little confusion here as there are two other girls living here as well, and I find a lack of privacy[18] ~

---

17 A reference to the well-known line from John Donne's *Devotions Upon Emergent Occasions*, Meditation XVII (1624): "No man is an island entire of itself; every man is a piece of the continent, a part of the main."

18 The apartment was owned by the Savio family. Beecroft remembers that it was in an old building, and that the floors were marble, which was very cold, especially when she arrived. She was given a small room with a bed, and had her meals with the family, but the room had a glass door and there was little privacy. The apartment had been recommended to her by a colleague at the CBC who had stayed there. She recalls that

October 1959

However, when one is sick, one is depressed ~

Your letter was very welcome when I arrived ~ but I felt terribly upset by your sadness and loneliness ~ Needless to say, I share your feelings ~

Perhaps it would be better if I continue this later ~

Wednesday ~ 10:30 PM.

Darling:

Tonight I feel a little better ~ the headache has disappeared, and I have managed to put in a full day though not very fruitfully....

... I walked over to the Academia (about 20 minutes from here) and set eyes on historic spots including the ancient Tiber ~ Rome is very beautiful indeed ~ a combination of very artistic antiquity and extreme modernism. Somehow they don't jar! One can see the remnants all over of an ancient civilization ~ pieces of walls just sitting there! The Italians seem to be a rather happy bunch from what I can observe ~ and so far I haven't been bothered at all! The weather here is very mild ~ hot almost in the day time, cooling a little at night ~

This evening I attempted to make an appointment with Petrassi, and am very disappointed to report that he will not be in Rome until the end of October![19] Although it annoys me a little (an understatement), I suppose I can put myself to good use by studying the language and generally getting adjusted with perhaps a little work....

... The language problem is a great one, believe me, and I really feel left alone here ~ I have almost decided to look for another place soon ~ The diet here, etc., I don't think will prove too satisfactory ~ and on top of that, it is very costly, I understand –

I received a letter from the lawyers in the US. who also informed me that I would probably not receive any further monies for six months to one year, so I am forced to consider my budget ~ C'est la vie....[20]

---

the Savios were very hospitable and kind "but it was not the environment conducive for working or even physical warmth." (email message to the editor, 14 November 2020.)

19 Goffredo Petrassi (1904–2003) was a prominent and influential Italian composer, conductor, and teacher. He began teaching at the Accademia Nazionale di Santa Cecilia [National Academy of St Cecilia] in Rome in 1959; his students included Franco Donatoni, Aldo Clementi, Cornelius Cardew, Mario Bertoncini, Eric Salzman, Peter Maxwell Davies, and Richard Teitelbaum. His best-known works are the Eight Concerti for Orchestra, written between the late 1930s and the late 1970s. *Coro Dei Morti*, a "dramatic madrigal," written in 1941–42, based on Giacomo Leopardi's "Dialogue of Frederick Ruysch with the Mummies" from the *Operette Morali*, is also widelyadmired.

20 The five Beecroft children had been left an inheritance by their father's uncle: "[A] distant uncle of mine had died and left a portion of his estate to the five Beecroft

62   Between Composers

… Darling, I do not know what more I can say to you now ~ I have lost a bit of the excitement now that I am here, as you can see, and outside of trying to know Italian and Rome, anything further that I can say can only be more depressing ~

I do hope that your move to the new apartment went well and that you are settling into your work ~ Please tell me how you feel after a month away from me, if you can and will, and send me news of Toronto ~

Life seems rather tough sometimes, don't it?

> Much love
> Normie ~

NB to HS
Friday, October 9th
9:30 PM.
Darling,

How happy I was to receive your letter this morning ~ you cannot imagine how one waits for the mail delivery every day, and the importance of letters from home. I am especially happy to know that you love me and miss me ~ You say so little in letters, and in person, that I place, and I hope not too much, emphasis on one little line….

… I would imagine that the fact that I bought two dresses today has also lifted my spirits ~ Shopping does marvellous things for women, you know.

To date I have been very good about spending money on clothing, etc., and I wanted to do a little shopping especially in Rome. The fashion houses are marvellous here ~ to my taste exactly.

You will love these elegant clothes ~ one a pale blue – fine wool – casual sheath dress, and the other, an extremely elegant sheath (also wool bouclé) with a Grecian line in a strange, almost olive-coloured, green ~ To your taste even though we both prefer black ~ I thought of you very much while trying clothes on – for different reasons.

My other purchases to date have been: a white fox fur stole (why I don't know) in London – nothing in Paris, – a large soft leather bag in Munich – nothing in Vienna – and my dresses today. Don't you think I have done pretty well?

---

children. This was in fact my father's uncle, Charles Smith, who for many years had been confined to a veteran's hospital in the USA. Someone I didn't know." Beecroft, "A Life Worth Living."

October 1959   63

All these details I am sure will interest you ~ but really Rome has some beautiful shops, completely unlike New York ~ but I have done my shopping for the year I am afraid....

...Yes, darling, I have informed the Savios of my intentions to look for a place to live ~ It is very strange, but as I expected, ~ living in a family circumstance is very uncomfortable ~ you get too involved with all their problems outside of being obligated to be here for meals. I do not enjoy the food here too much ~ they eat so much pasta (all kinds of spaghetti) and fried foods ~ nothing simple and naturally, it does not agree with my system at all – Signora Savio is extremely kind in helping me with my Italian, and very patient and sensitive and perceptive ~ I do hope to maintain a relationship with her after I leave ... Carla, on the other hand is very sweet, but almost too sweet, and the worst driver I have ever been with – she never stops at intersections – and I just refuse to be in her car now....

... I am rapidly learning to understand the language when spoken clearly and rapidly – but more slowly am learning to speak it. I am rather pleased with my progress to date –

I do hope that you will somehow consider coming over here – I think you would love Rome, and the climate especially – Musically, I wonder if it is very active –

Darling, please write often – Home, and you, are a long way away.

Love, love and more

Normie

HS to NB

[11–13 October 1959]   Sunday night

Darling Normie:

Such a fierce wonderful October day. Windy, cold and a cloud-scape which was wild and foreboding set in relief by rifts which permitted the hard brilliant sunlight to dazzle the earth. At night great dark shapes flee across the sky under the light of the moon. Always the flurry and rustle of parchment leaves.

The great west wind blows life into tired spirits making them soar to such freedom....

...2 a.m. Tuesday. I've just finished 'House of the Dead.' This journal of Dostoevsky's has agitated my thoughts concerning confinement, freedom, crime, law, society and so much else.

64 Between Composers

In short, the substance of his novels.

His prison experience must have been for him horrifying beyond all ability to describe it. One must weigh his words and read between the lines for he is not one to disembowel himself in public as is the wont of contemporary writers. Though he gives an inkling of his own suffering he dwells at greater length on his fellow prisoners, their crimes, behaviour, effect of internment on them, their revelation as humanity. His psychological insight was gained from personal experience. His ability to be detached in his observation of his fellow men, yet compassionate in his feelings towards them are, to me, those attributes which make for a great writer....

———

Tuesday Oct. 13.

... Stick it out Normie dear. Your first reactions are those of most students in a new place. Mine were pretty similar. The language isolates you, the environment is strange and you're trying to get settled to work, all of which is frustrating as the devil. Little by little those frustrations are conquered until you are 'at home.' Perhaps the language is first....

... Do not feel so sorry for yourself that you miss what is around you. A lot of people would like to be sad in Rome.

It's positively miraculous what new clothes do for women! The sunlight shone out of your report of 'shopping expedition # 1.'

As to the local scene ~ Oct. 25 I will be attending Ron Collier's wedding having received an invitation.[21] What a racket! One must send a present whether one goes or not! It's like paying for that bloody domestic champagne they usually have. However, it should be amusing.

21 Ron Collier (1930–2003) studied music in Toronto with Gordon Delamont and in New York in the early 1960s. His Jazz Quartet performed widely in the 1950s and early 1960s (at the Stratford Festival and on CBC Television) and he collaborated with Duke Ellington on the 1969 album *North of the Border in Canada*. Collier also contributed arrangements for many of Ellington's concerts and recordings. Collier was one of the musicians/arrangers for whom Somers copied music on a regular basis to earn a living during these years.

October 1959

I haven't seen Gwen since you left and Norm only once.[22] Helen has called me a couple of times.[23] She is so 'blue' poor thing, so I cheer her up by talking of murder and torture. One day I'll drop by and talk about Jelly Roll Morton.

Last Saturday evening the Guitar Society evening[24] was given over to a recital by a young Mexican – something Lopez.[25] First half of serious music was badly performed but the second part of the Mexican folk tunes was quite delightful but musically so shallow that I asked Ken Young 'when the floor show started?'[26] All the regulars were there including Jack N.[27]

The party afterwards was quite gay. The Mexican proved to be an unassuming, slightly wistful, slightly melancholy but friendly little chap who recited Spanish poetry when he was high. I ended up on the floor, as usual, reciting my Dylan Thomas gobbledygook of 'Whither wist dooly down trodden sender worst wore I o'er whale prolipthian depths, etc.' which Lopez found quite moving, though he

---

22 Gwen was Norman Symonds's girl friend at the time. Beecroft was unable to recall her last name but remembered her as a tall, slim woman. A later letter of Somers indicates that she was probably a dancer but Beecroft did not remember her being in any of the CBC Television productions of the late 1950s with which she was involved.

23 Helen McNamara (1919–2007) was a pioneering jazz columnist, author, artist, and broadcaster who began writing a regular column on jazz, "McNamara's Bandwagon," in the Toronto *Telegram* in 1949. Her book, *The Bands Canadians Danced To*, was published in 1973.

24 The Toronto Guitar Society was founded in the mid–1950s by Eli Kassner and a group of guitar enthusiasts – many of them his students – to promote the classical guitar through concerts featuring the Society's own members as well as international artists. They also published a monthly newsletter, the *Guitar Toronto Bulletin*. Eventually, the Society commissioned many new works for the guitar, including the piece Somers was working on in the fall of 1959 (which became his four-movement Sonata), the Society's first commission.

25 The guitarist was the Mexican-born Gustavo Lopez (1938–2016), who had been playing with a Mexican "bolero trio," and who had moved to the United States in the early 1970s. The concert took place on 10 October and included music by Bach, Scarlatti, Handel, Villa-Lobos, Ponce, and Robert de Visée.

26 Ken Young had studied guitar with Eli Kassner and became the secretary of the Guitar Society in its early years. In his article "The Guitar Society of Toronto," Kassner described Ken Young as "a lover of the guitar, and an enthusiastic and capable organizer," *Guitar Canada* 2, no. 4. (Spring 1989). Later, the Ken Young Scholarship Fund was established in his memory

27 Jack Nichols (1921–2009) was a Montreal-born artist who served as an official war artist from April 1944 to August 1945. Most of his paintings depict the landing operations at Normandy and destroyer movements off Brest. Lithographs by Nichols, along with works by other artists, represented Canada at the 1958 Venice Biennale.

66 Between Composers

professed he couldn't understand it! Jack and some girl jitterbugged to a couple of guitars playing very effective Django Rhinehardt late 'thirties' kind of guitar. The evening shook with song, dance, talk, and Lopez and my poetry all in a great stew of sound. Marguerite Young found I had lost some weight, looked pale and a bit sad....

... All evening I spoke but a few words to Eli! ... Naomi says that this coming summer he wants to go to Sienna in Italy to study with Segovia then to Santiago again in the month of September taking Naomi and Annie with him (to both places).[28] He looks extremely well, bulging in fact like a gopher after an enormous meal, and quite brimming over with life ... I must say all his application and work is deserving of it....

... You may place a great deal of emphasis on 'one little line' Normie dear.

When I say I miss you and that I love you it is an understatement. As you know I dislike revealing too much of certain feelings because I find it almost unbearably painful. It is a way of keeping control in order to write and to live.

I kiss your lips and press their warmth –
I love you very much –
Harry

NB to HS
Tuesday, October 13th
9:00 PM.
Dear Harry,

Received your letter this afternoon with mixed feelings ~ I am always happy to receive your letters and to hear news of Toronto and your movements and thoughts, but sometimes find myself very exasperated trying to read between the lines ~

You must realize how lonely I feel here with no close friends and just temporary acquaintances in the house here ~ And you know that part of my reason for leaving Toronto was to get a perspective on our relationship ~ I often, and more often, think that perhaps my departure was slightly mad, as I am becoming convinced through

28 See chap. 1, n. 23 for information on Kassner. He had received a Canada Council grant to study with Segovia in Santiago de Compostella in Spain. Soon after the founding of the Toronto Guitar Society in 1956, Segovia had agreed to become its honorary president; he had met Kassner on previous visits to Toronto while on tour. "Naomi" was Kassner's first wife, Noémi, and "Annie" was their daughter, Annick.

October 1959   67

absence, that most of what I desire at this time in my life is a situation of security, in other words, marriage ~ I also realize that my desire to write music could be lessened by the idea of marriage becoming an obsession, ...

... In other words, I suppose I want to know how you are reacting to our separation, as it is, and has been, fairly obvious that any further decision has to be taken by you ~ I never wanted to come to Europe alone, and I do not know if I have the strength to stay here alone....

1:00 AM.

... My letter was interrupted, and perhaps just as well, for reading this first page over I realize perhaps I sound a little ungrateful and angry ~ Maybe these questions which I want answered, I also will have to answer ... I still find it difficult to understand why I must wait for you and what is the actual problem ~ Why can we not be together?...

... I hope your party with Eli and Nomi finds them well ~ I am most anxious to hear how Eli made out in Spain ~ Mother sent me some clippings on Eli's appointment to the Conservatory staff,[29] and an article about the publication of your 12 x 12,[30] so I am being kept up to date more or less ~ I wish I could go with you to the party ~ ~ ~ ~

Last Saturday I visited the Accademia Americana in Roma,[31] the place which Alan Jarvis recommended to me to visit[32] ~ All the Prix

---

29 This appointment was announced in the *Toronto Daily Star* (7 October 1959) and the *Globe and Mail* (3 October 1959).

30 This is a set of 12 twelve-tone fugues by Somers, written in 1951 and published by BMI in 1959.

31 The American Academy in Rome has existed since 1894. The founders thought that the richness and power of Rome's artistic and cultural legacy would stimulate creative thinking among scholars and artists. Each year the Rome Prize is awarded to a select group of artists and scholars in various fields such as medieval and renaissance studies, early-modern studies, architecture, landscape architecture and musical composition. The recipients of the Prize are invited to Rome to pursue their work in an atmosphere conducive to intellectual and artistic freedom.

32 Alan Jarvis (1915–1972) became director of the National Gallery in Ottawa in 1955, after holding a number of positions in England during and after the Second World War. In August 1959, he was forced to resign as director of the National Gallery by the recently elected Diefenbaker government over the purchase of a Breughel painting.

68 Between Composers

de Rome winners live there, or other fellowship artists ~ What a set-up! I went to get information on living accommodation, and walked into this spacious Roman building with an inner piazza, and was shown around by a fellow composer from Pennsylvania on his first year Prix de Rome.

The main building has enormous rooms, one of which is specifically for composers and contains a fantastic collection of records and tapes, and three enormous tables for copying, undoubtedly ~ Each composer, outside of having living quarters, has a private studio with piano in another villa a short distance ~

This composer, John Eaton by name, visited Tanglewood the year I was there, and studied with Sessions and Babbitt[33] ~ It was rather comforting to chat with an American composer, and we discovered friends in common....

... In order to occupy myself until Petrassi returns, I have returned to practicing the piano and flute, and with great pleasure too ~ I am going to take a few flute lessons with a very famous flautist, Gazzelloni, (do you know of him?)[34] Music lessons are very costly here ~ 1 hr. with this man for 5000 Lire which is approx. $8.00 ~ Maestro Petrassi will be much higher, I am told ~ Evidently, the situation for musicians and teachers is pretty bad in Rome, financially....

... I have not yet started to feel much like writing, but it will come....

... Many things are expensive here in Rome ~ Kleenex is about .80 cents a box, cigarettes run between .55 to .75 cents per package

33 John Eaton (1935–2015) earned both a bachelor's and master's degree from Princeton, studying there with two eminent American composers, Milton Babbitt and Roger Sessions, before spending more than a decade in Rome, supported by three Prix de Rome fellowships and concert tours with his quartet, the American Jazz Ensemble. He went on to receive international recognition for his operas, making extensive use of electronic and microtonal resources. It was in Rome, during the mid-1960s, that he began to explore the possibilities of microtonal writing (such as in the 1965 work for two pianos tuned a quartertone apart, Microtonal Fantasy). He later taught at Indiana University and at the University of Chicago.
34 Severino Gazzelloni (1919–1992) was a world-renowned Italian flutist and teacher who was principal flautist with the RAI National Symphony Orchestra in Turin for some thirty years. Many leading composers, including Berio, Boulez, Maderna, and Stravinsky wrote pieces for him. Berio's Sequenza I for solo flute (1958), dedicated to him, is a testament to the influential role Gazzelloni played in innovative writing for the flute.

October 1959   69

... The day I arrived the taxi driver-charged me <u>over double</u> the fare, and you have no argument with them...

... Rome, nevertheless, has incredible weather. It is truly sunny Italy and no wonder the Italians are molti contenti...

Wednesday AM.

Another bright day, but slowly turning a little cooler ~ I often think of how beautiful it must be in Canada right now, and get terribly nostalgic and homesick for the sweet smell of fall ~

I am sitting here in front of your picture ~ how magnificent you look to me ~ I get terribly envious to think you could be in the hands of another female ~ It is so peculiar that I have such an obsession to know of your personal life when I know so well that you think 90% of the time only about your work and this is what you write to me about ~ Perhaps that is why ~

I have finished reading the 'Woman of Rome'[35] ~ I do not entirely comprehend why you were so concerned about me living here as a result of your reading the book, unless you are drawing a parallel with the after effects on me of our relationship....

... I am also perusing the 'Letters to a Young Poet' again, and find Rilke says so much about the artist that is a reflection of your entire personality[36] ~ It is a sort of bible to me ~

Needless to say, over and over again I miss you I do hope you will find me here soon, for I am still waiting ~

> Much love, dearest Harry
> Normie

---

35 *The Woman of Rome* [*La romana*] is a novel by Alberto Moravia, published in 1947. It portrays the lives of a number of characters during the time of Mussolini's dictatorship, including a young prostitute named Adriana, a university student who is interrogated by fascist officers and betrays his associates, and an officer in the secret police, Astarita, who is also one of Adriana's clients. The novel was made into a movie in 1954, directed by Luigi Zampa, and starring Gina Lollobrigida.

36 After reading Rilke's poetry, Franz Xaver Kappus (1883–1966), while a student in 1902 at Theresian Military Academy in Austria, learned that Rilke had earlier been a pupil at the academy's lower school at Sankt Pölten. He wrote to Rilke asking for advice about becoming a writer and Rilke replied by considering various issues, such as the nature of art, religious belief, and the choice of career. In 1929, after Rilke's death, Kappus compiled ten of Rilke's letters that he had received from 1902 to 1908 and published them under the title *Briefe an einen jungen Dichter* ("Letters to a Young Poet").

70   Between Composers

HS to NB
Thursday, Oct. 15.
Dearest Normie:

Last night I took up the prelude of my Suite for Guitar up to Eli's. I think I'm on a good vein for the guitar. The compositional technics are relatively simple and the tonal organization isn't too far removed from the diatonic. Perhaps it would be closer to say that it is closer to modal methods. At any rate, it should be effective for the instrument.

As far as I'm concerned the guitar is ideal for the exploitation of the most 'far out' dodecaphonic ideas. The only drawback is that even though the guitar is ready the guitarist is not.

Eli spoke at length of his summer both up north and abroad. After his initial disappointment with the classes he found them to be extremely interesting, stimulating and informative. Segovia only reveals his secrets to the keen eye and ear and to the advanced student. Eli discovered many new things, for the technic of the instrument is still being evolved.

We discussed at length my beef about the guitarist ~ the drivel so dear to their hearts called 'repertoire.' Mind you, only the composer can change this. Their catalogue after Bach is filled with the most inconsequential mishmash of candy floss to please the superficial taste....

—————

Sunday – 18th – Just finished a heavy session of copying for Ted Sh. which started Friday.[37] Such are the fortunes of war that Ted is doing most of the arranging for the Joan Fairfax Show as well as handling the copying.[38] It's up and down according to what producer is in power. At present Len Casey, who likes Ted's work, is producer.[39]

37 "Ted Sh." was Ted Shadbolt, an arranger/copyist for various CBC variety programs during the 1950s. No further information about him could be found.
38 Joan Fairfax (1926–2010) was an English-born singer and accordionist who was a frequent performer in the early years of CBC Television, culminating in "The Joan Fairfax Show" (1959–60). She had trained as a coloratura soprano for several years at the Royal Conservatory in Toronto. In the early 1960s, she moved to the US to pursue a career there.
39 Len Casey (1925–?) was a prominent producer of variety programs such as *The Barris Beat, Showtime,* and *Live a Borrowed Life* during the 1950s. He had trained as a musician (violin and clarinet) but later occupied a number of positions in the CBC and

Casey won't have anything to do with Cable now since Cable tried a power play over his head to the sponsors of Showtime last year. The C.B.C. brass didn't like it either so that Cable cut his own throat ... So Ted's idol has fallen. Cable must be terribly galled, to top it all Jack Kane is on top of the arranging heap now and Ted could possibly become quite successful.[40]

... To-night there's a stag party for Ron Collier but I'm not going. All they do is get too drunk and become completely incoherent. What's the point? At least when I'm drunk I may be incoherent, but I articulate every word clearly, even though it doesn't mean anything.

It's cold and wintery outside and I feel a bit sad about it. About 5 a.m. I went for a walk. The streets had the melancholy of an amusement park late at night when everyone's left. Old newspapers scraping to a mournful breeze, which cut to the marrow. Deserted streets echoing to strange footsteps, your own.[41] Silence of a city sleeping. It could be a dead city, an ancient ghost.

To-day the fierce northern wind howled its conquest of summer. Across the great treed land from Arctic space, unhindered, strong, touching the most remote isolation and the most familiar peopled places. Such proud music. It's strange that so many Canadians are so without character, definition, decisiveness, without 'profile' when these are the characteristics of the physical environment.

---

elsewhere: head of Sports Broadcasting (beginning in 1964), head of Variety (in the early 1970s), and director of programming at Ontario Place. Producers appear to have had a good deal of authority in the early years of television broadcasting. Alex Barris is quoted as saying that Casey "constantly and often successfully tried to impose his own vision of the show." See Paul Rutherford, *When Television Was Young: Primetime Canada 1952–67* (Toronto: University of Toronto Press, 1990), 215.

40 Jack Kane (1924–1961) was a prominent English-born arranger, conductor, clarinettist, and composer in Toronto who became one of the main figures in CBC variety programs in the 1950s. He performed with various CBC orchestras during the war but then studied composition with John Weinzweig for two years (1946–48), at the same time as Somers; therefore, they were likely acquainted. In the late 1950s, he had his own orchestra, which performed on The Jack Kane Show and other programs, and made a number of excellent recordings. Kane died tragically young of cancer at the age of thirty-six.

41 This is another reference to Somers's *Five Songs for Dark Voice*: "At four o'clock, before the dawn / In the echoing street, there is yourself."

Monday ~

Your 'angry young woman' letter arrived today. Try as I may not to, I find myself very annoyed. I feel that I should rip up what I've written in this letter because it must be so boring to you since it doesn't dwell on our personal relationship. What is the point of writing to you if what I have to say is only exasperating to you?! You aren't stupid, surely writing to you of the things I feel speaks for itself! Do I have to spell everything out?!

So you want to get 'married,' the magic word that's supposed to solve all your problems. So you '<u>never</u>' wanted to go to Europe alone. The obvious question is then why did you?!...

... How do I react to our separation? "as it is, and has been, fairly obvious that any further decision has to be taken by you." unquote! I'm at a point of knowing how I react to our separation then I get a letter like that and I'm not so sure. Perfect timing. God damn it, do I know you at all? Is everyone only a figment of our imagination?

I better take time to cool off or else I will say things I will be sorry for.

Love —
Harry

NB to HS

[n.d. (20 October?)]

Dear Harry,

This morning I received your reply to my angry letter, and as you probably know, it upsets me as much as my original letter upsets me in retrospect [~]

Perhaps this letter of mine, or any letters of mine are not thought out clearly, which makes me wonder whether I should write anything on-paper at all ~ However, I trust that you understand these things that bother me to a certain extent, and I suppose perhaps I expect you to read between the lines ~ I do not wish to hurt, but it is incomprehensible to me in the long run, how you cannot have known your feelings or know them now, even though we seem to be constantly contradicting them....

... I do not for one moment believe that 'the magic word 'marriage" is the word to solve all my problems ~ Perhaps I could even be more afraid of it than you, I don't know ~ but I do not feel that a) I was

October 1959 73

made to exist in solitude nor do I think it is desirable; and b) I have spent almost four years with you, and have honestly been constantly frustrated by the fact that it was leading nowhere....

... Harry, I suppose this is where our age and experience differ ~ I am sorry ~ but please look from my point of view if you can ~ That by the way may partially answer your question 'why did I come to Europe' ~ to find, if possible, answers for some things as to what I am, and what I can give, and what I desire ~ Perhaps it will take a lifetime ...

my feelings for you have at certain times overcome my reason, and therefore I may be a little irrational ~ On top of that, I am lonely, and loneliness seems to breed bitterness in me ~

I love you, please understand

Normie ~

[continuation of the same letter]
Wednesday, Oct. 21 [1959]
Dearest Harry,

I received your letter with the cartoon, and perhaps have felt a little guilty as the last note I wrote to you was full of accusations and bitterness, and it crossed perhaps one of your warmest letters in the mail

~

I am delighted to hear of all the news of Toronto, but must say very frankly that I am starting to feel very relieved to be out of the rut that I was in ... after a while it seems necessary to create a new environment for oneself....

... If possible, you might try to get a copy of a very strange book called 'The Unquiet Grave' by Palinurus (a Harper edition)[42] ~ I am presently engrossed in this, and Stendahl's

---

42 *The Unquiet Grave*, published in 1944 under the pseudonym Palinurus, is a collection of aphorisms, quotes, and reflections by the English literary critic and writer Cyril Connolly (1903–1974). Palinurus was the navigator of Aeneas's ship in the *Aeneid* and was sacrificed by the gods to guarantee safe passage for the Trojans. Aeneas encountered Palinurus in the underworld but Palinurus could not cross over Cocytus into Hades because he was unburied after death. Connolly uses this framework to explore his feelings and review his situation as he approaches the age of forty, presenting a very pessimistic and self-deprecating account. Into this he brings quotes from some of his favourite authors: Pascal, De Quincey, Chamfort, and Flaubert et al. (e.g., "Approaching forty, sense of total failure; not a writer but a ham actor whose performance is clotted with egotism; dust and ashes; "brilliant" – that is, not worth doing. Never will I make that extra effort to live according to reality which alone makes good writing possible: hence the manic-depressiveness of my work, – which is either bright,

74   Between Composers

'The Charterhouse of Parma'[43] ~

I find reading a little easier, and very helpful to take one's mind off oneself ~

Last night, of all things, I went to an American jazz concert at the Teatro Sistina,[44] and who appeared but Jimmy Rushing[45] with Buck Clayton's octet (?)[46] and Dizzy Gillespie's quintet ~ Strangely enough, Rome doesn't seem like Rome with American jazz! Although, the house was not good, in both ways, I am told that the Italians are very interested in Jazz, but please inform Norm that there is very little activity here in this world (contrary to what he mentioned) … Unfortunately, the concert was conducted in English, and all Gillespie's remarks were in English, so enthusiasm was limited ~ I enjoyed the concert nonetheless ~

I don't remember if I told you that while in a London pub on the Haymarket, Eric and I met two Canadian doctors and their wives who are with the Canadian Embassy at the Hague ~ One of these doctors suggested that I contact his counterpart in Rome, an ex-Canadian who would show me around Rome, and help me with my problems of shopping, living, etc ~ After two weeks here, I got in

cruel and superficial; or pessimistic; moth-eaten with self-pity." *The Unquiet Grave* (London: Hamish Hamilton, 1945), 85–6.

43 *The Charterhouse of Parma [La Chartreuse de Parme]* is a novel by Stendhal published in 1839. It relates the adventures of a young Italian nobleman, Fabrice del Dongo, during the Napoleonic era and later. Greatly admired by writers such as Balzac, Tolstoy, André Gide, di Lampedusa, and Henry James, it has in recent years been adapted for opera, film, and television.

44 *Il Sistina*, a large theatre hall in Rome designed by Marcello Piacentini, was built on the former site of the Pontifical Ecclesiastical Polish Institute. It was inaugurated as a cinema in December 1949, but by the time Beecroft came to Rome it was being used mostly for theatrical and cabaret presentations.

45 James Andrew Rushing (1901–1972) was a highly esteemed and influential blues and jazz singer and pianist from Oklahoma City, Oklahoma. Over the years he performed with many of the great jazz artists: Jelly Roll Morton, Billy King, Count Basie (he was the featured vocalist of Count Basie's Orchestra from 1935 to 1948), Humphrey Lyttleton, and Muddy Waters. In 1959 he recorded an album with Duke Ellington.

46 Wilbur Dorsey "Buck" Clayton (1911–1991) was an American jazz trumpet player who was a leading member of Count Basie's "Old Testament" Orchestra and a leader of mainstream-oriented jam session recordings for Columbia Records in the 1950s. Clayton's career took him all over the world – to Shanghai in the 1930s as leader of the "Harlem Gentlemen" at the Canidrome Ballroom, back to New York in 1937 as a member of the Count Basie Orchestra, and many times to Europe, where he toured annually, beginning in 1959.

October 1959

75

touch with this doctor, who has turned out to be extremely obliging[47] ~ I have been helped in many ways, and it is surprising how much difference it makes to have an English-speaking friend who has lived in Rome for 10 years and knows the ropes of Rome thoroughly ~

I have begun to search for an apartment here, which is proving very difficult ...So perhaps in a couple of weeks, I shall really be on my own!...

... Monday morning I started flute lessons with Gazzelloni, and got a bad cold at the same time, so have not been able to practice ~ He is changing my whole technique of flute playing, ie. posture, etc., so it will be interesting to observe the results ~ I have been given a rather severe schedule of practice, including an introduction to double-tonguing, and more work on vibrato ~ and I hope this dirty cold will clear soon! The lesson was very amusing, as he doesn't speak English ~ I am at the point now where I can understand most of what is being said, but forming sentences [is] difficult....

... I await and am terrified of Petrassi's return to Rome ~ I don't have an idea in my head musically ~ Dear Harry, I sometimes think I will end up as predicted by so many, and what keeps me going in the direction of music is sometimes a mystery ~ I know one shouldn't question so much, but I know that to write I must, of necessity, be alone ... So many things to know and sort out!
Please write soon ~

       Much love
       Normie

NB to HS
[29 October]
Thursday AM ~
Dear Harry,

Needless to say I was left rather speechless by your telephone call on Tuesday night, and have been rather speechless ever since ~ I am sorry I did not have more to say to you on the telephone ...

---

47 This was Dr Paul Chevalier, who was also instrumental in having Beecroft treated for a severe reaction to a headache tablet that she was taking toward the end of her time in Italy. Dr Chevalier found a doctor who successfully treated her and she stayed in his apartment for a time after she was released from hospital. Some doctors Beecroft had met in a pub in London before going to Rome had suggested that she look him up once she got to Rome, as he worked in the emigration section of the Canadian Embassy there. He turned out to be very helpful, also introducing her to various people.

76 Between Composers

... However, after the initial shock of hearing your voice and what you said to me, I am still rather speechless ~ When I left Canada, as you know, I truly thought that this was the end of our relationship ~ and the best thing for me to do was to reconcile myself to that fact once and for all, and try to make a life for myself here in Rome with my music ~ I have been trying to break with past memories and desires for I felt that I couldn't afford to continue in a dream that would never come to fruition ...You have told me to make a life for myself for three years, and I have battled all the way ~ for I loved you very much and was convinced that we were right for each other whether you believed it or not....

... Please let me say a few things about living here in Rome ~ It is very expensive without question, and probably what is worse is it is practically impossible to work here legally, or illegally ~ This is very much a present concern of mine and would be difficult for you (and I) as well ~ It is essential to know some Italian ... I have been fortunate enough to meet a group of Americans here who have lived in Rome for a long time and who are cutting corners for me financially, etc. They have found me a small appartementino, in the central area (near the Via Veneto) complete with linen, dishes, heating, electricity, telephone, maid service, 2 terrazzas, with a complete view of all Rome, etc. for between 50,000 to 55,000 Lire (about 80.00 per month) and with no lease ~ This is a real bargain here! ... Although this group of people are somewhat older, and in the long run may not turn out to be my kind, whatever that is, I would be lost without them....

... This appartementino, I hope, is available this weekend and I expect to move in ~ I am waiting now for a telephone call for an appointment with the landlord, an American screen actor, Lex Barker, of 'Tarzan' fame[48] ~ I have not yet met him so I hope it turns out that I can have the place, which is normally kept for his guests ~ In any case, it will do for the present, and the view is fantastic ~

When you come to Rome, bring warm clothes ~ it is very damp, for all (practically) the buildings are made of marble being the cheapest commodity ~ the quality of woollen clothing here is not very good as well....

48 Lex Barker (Alexander Crichlow Barker Jr.) (1919–1973) was a well-known American film actor who played Tarzan in RKO movies between 1949 and 1953 but starred in many westerns as well. He moved to Europe in 1957, starring in some forty movies there, including three in Italy in 1959; this is probably the reason why he had an apartment in Rome.

October 1959   77

... our problems are unfortunately of [a] financial nature to a great extent and I am wondering how you propose to live for an extended period, here, or elsewhere in Europe ~

I am afraid of saying too much more until I receive your letter, because I seem to make a hassle of my letters when confused ~ It was marvellous to hear your voice Tuesday, and I do hope you have not lost too much weight ~ Have you been well, love?

Please write me very soon ~ I think of you so much ~

> Love, love and more
>
> Normie ~

HS to NB
Thursday [October 29]
Dearest Normie:

I feel a sadness I've rarely known before. I don't feel like eating, I can't sleep, in fact all the symptoms of those who require something like Carters Little Liver Pills. Perhaps I should try to write some 'happy' music like Dixie. Right now it's just the 'blues'. Ole Somers Blues. A pocket full of darkness. There's really too much for me to do. This is no time for one of my depressive periods.[49]

It was marvellous to hear your voice the other night, almost unreal. Letters were becoming so inadequate that I just had to speak to you directly and clear the air of so much misunderstanding. I love you so much.

Nov. 1st Sunday – Schöenberg's Chamber Symphony performed by the New York Philharmonic, Cavello or Decavello ~ the chap who taught at Tanglewood.[50] Such busy post Wagnerian music. I sometimes feel that that which is taken for profundity and feeling in music is really just so much pretension, noise and hot air. I suppose my mood is just contrary. There's a very nice schmaltzy second movement going on now.

49 See chap. 1, n. 25.
50 Somers was listening to a matinée performance of the New York Philharmonic under the direction of the Brazilian conductor Eleazar de Carvalho (1912–1996) who had trained in the US under Koussevitzky and taught many younger figures, such as Claudio Abbado, Charles Dutoit, Zubin Mehta, and Seiji Ozawa. The program also included Mozart, Strauss, and Villa-Lobos.

78   Between Composers

I finished one of those 24 hour sessions of copying from Saturday to Sunday, was completely senseless, had a sleep and am now enjoying these moments with you.

Today I had to deliver some music to Studio 4. It almost broke my heart to be in the same place where we first met. Everywhere I go your footsteps have been, everywhere I am reminded of you....

––––––––

... Monday [November 2nd] – I am enveloped in my love for you so that the sky, wind, the air is the sight and the touch of you. You'll be sorry that I love you so completely for I shall overwhelm you with the rush of my feelings into extravagant phrases which seek to touch and probe every part of your body and mind and heart, to arouse you with my caressing to the joy and pain of loving, to leave you exhausted with my intensity....

... Tuesday and your letter from Crispi – Oh Normie – tell me the truth, please, please!! – are you in love with some-one else now? are you going to or are you living with them? You must, you must. I'm desolate for I have finally given my heart to you completely, it is what I feared most to do because I always felt it would be cut to ribbons....

... There is no need to tell me I deserve what I get, I do, but it tears me apart I love you so completely my whole being is cracked. Just let me know and I shall cope with what I have to, but let me know the <u>truth</u>, please don't hedge for fear of my feelings. –straight out, Normie. I can hardly speak – Normie, Normie, a few days and I shall have more control, a few years and shall be old Harry again ... I love you with my whole being and have no interest in anyone else nor do I care for anyone else ... On the 15th I shall go down to Hartford Conneticut for the Canadian Music Festival there, more to simply get away and meet people in order to escape from my feelings than anything else.[51] They are doing my 2nd violin Sonata, works of John W. etc.

Please write as soon as possible of <u>exactly</u> what your situation is externally and internally. Don't worry. If this is it, then it will be it quickly and finally, no more trouble from me....

51 This mini festival of Canadian music was sponsored by the Institute of Contemporary Music at the Hartt College of Music in Hartford, Connecticut on 15 and 16 November. The Institute was chaired by the composer Isadore Freed (1900–1960).

October 1959   79

... Now I am yours, there is no other question to me, you have a kind of victory, my love for you is complete and that is where I stand –

Harry P.S. – Don't worry I am

not nor could I ever be really angry with you – only myself.

NB to HS

Roma ~

Oct. 30, 1959

Darling Harry,

Rapidly on the heels of one letter follows another ~ I received your letter this morning and felt the necessity to sit down and try to write more of what I feel ~

My love, I am sick for you ~ how much easier it is to be in a completely new land without endless reminders of the past every time you turn around ~ Undoubtedly I have achieved by this time a fair perspective, for even though there are extreme moments of loneliness and sadness, I am generally in a state of serenity, more and more every day ~ I have discovered that it _is_ possible to live with other people and that I actually _like_ people ~ This is not a desperate search for friends, either, but I suppose placing more value on friendships....

... I seem also to become less and less afraid of looking at the real values in life, at myself probably ~ I guess I realize that I have been running away for a while and if I have the soul of an artist at all (or of a true human being) this is a state which is impossible for long stretches ~ or should be impossible ~ I do not know entirely what I mean ~ I just have the sense of something ~ something important, I think ~

The other night I was invited out for dinner with a group of people ~ It was a wonderful meal, the first one I really enjoyed here ~ There were drinks and not too heavy (or even too interesting) conversation while outside raged the wind and a ferocious thunderstorm. (We have had a steady three days of storms) I got a little high ~ and felt very pleasant and removed from worries, etc., a state which I have felt desirable for some time ~ About 12:30 I left for home, and upon coming out of the building experienced the most fantastic sense of truth, or some word similar ~ The rain had stopped, there was wind and fallen leaves, and the air was perfumed with the scent of dead leaves and a rain that had passed ~ I thought, how can one ever run away when an atmosphere like this hits you in the face bringing you back to reality and truth ~ Oh darling, how sad I felt, but how happy on the other hand to know that these things touch me so deeply ~ I know you will understand what I am saying ~

Yes, I love you and want to be with you ~ If we meet one person in our life who understands us we are indeed fortunate ~ and if that person loves us then we must be blessed ~ I hope all the practical considerations can work themselves out for both of us ~

Now I must go and prepare to move to my new place (address on the envelope) ~ I _do_ [double underscore] wish to write you, contrary to your letter ~

Very much love
Normie ~

CHAPTER THREE

November 1959

HS to NB
Tuesday afternoon [3 November]
My dearest love –

This is my second letter to you to-day – a deluge, for you will receive the full downpour of Somers in love – in love with <u>you</u>.[1] The first letter, as you can gather is really a pouring out of my feeling. I'm in a fever over you but I think I am a little clearer now.

To love fully is not to question but to give, it just <u>is</u>. To be specific let me present my proposal - it is evident that I can't live without you, I need you, I love you. I want to live with you, to be together. Till you left all I could think of were my fears of what could go wrong, how I could be hurt, but they don't matter. When one loves fully one accepts all the chances as when one lives fully or writes or does anything fully. It's so ridiculous that I, who have taken chances in everything that is important to me should act with reservations about something which is as important to me as anything in my life....

... Should you at any time not feel love for me or love someone else then I shall never be bitter for I have finally given completely. To love is to give without question, to trust without doubt, to take what comes, to desire that the object of one's love be happy and alive to life....

... I'm enclosing Ken Winters's review of my 3rd String Quartet - <u>your quartet</u> which he wrote in the Music Journal.[2]

---

1 The first letter was the last part of the letter dated 29 October.
2 This was a review of Somers's String Quartet No. 3 (1959), dedicated to Beecroft, which had been premiered in August by the Hungarian Quartet at the Vancouver

82   Between Composers

I give you all my love, Normie, and loving you so I want you to live with the joy and happiness that I would give you and that I would have you have.

My self-righteousness is past. I hope you find peace in yourself and that your work goes well, though I have no doubt it will be difficult. Have courage, my dearest.

　　　　　　　　With all my heart –
　　　　　　　　Harry

NB to HS
Roma
Via Francesco Crispi 99
November 4th ~ 9:00 PM.
Darling Harry,

I had half expected a letter from you by this time but thought that I would try and write anyway....

... I have just returned from a recital given by Wilhelm Backhaus ~ four Beethoven sonatas ~ What a strange pianist ~ The first half of the program, an early sonata and the Appassionata, was incredible ~ he played as though he was completely bored with the works, audience, etc., tempi all wrong, timing, dynamics, and so on ~ It turned out that he was saving himself for the 2nd half ~ Op. 101, 111 (I hope these are correct) ~ both sonatas which he performed in a very personal way ~ I couldn't help thinking of our trips to Hamilton to Reg's concerts[3]....

... As you can see, I have moved into my new place ~ Everything didn't turn out to be as ideal as described in my earlier letter, but I am in a safe area of Rome, and have this fantastic view of Rome, so

---

International Music Festival. See *The Canadian Music Journal* IV, no. 1 (Autumn 1959), 26–7. Kenneth Winters (1929–2011) was a music critic, broadcaster, and editor (co-editor of the first edition of the *Encyclopedia of Music in Canada*). He had studied composition with Nadia Boulanger in Paris in 1959–60 but was chiefly known as a music critic. He wrote for several journals and newspapers, including the *Globe and Mail* (during the final years of his life). He also contributed reviews and served as writer and host for many CBC Radio programs over the years.

3 Reginald Godden (1905–1987) was an extraordinary pianist and teacher, specializing in the music of J.S. Bach in his later years. In the late 1940s and most of the 1950s, he lived in Hamilton, Ontario, where he served for a time as principal of the Hamilton Conservatory. Somers had studied piano with him formally for only one year (1942–43) but he became one of Somers's closest life-long friends and premiered a number of Somers's early works, notably *Testament of Youth* and the Piano Concerto No. 2.

November 1959

83

I am staying here for a while anyway ~ The place is rather charming with its antique furniture [~] I am writing to you from a desk that looks like 'Beethoven sat here', complete with a quill pen, with my back to Rome (the window) and surveying my domain ~ There is another old Venetian desk against the wall, a couple of comfortable armchairs, two little antique tables, a rather comfortable bed with bookshelves above, another bookshelf, and two electric heaters that don't work (my only source of heat, by the way) ~ To my left is the bathroom-kitchen, so small there is only room for a one-gas-burner....

... Shopping here is an experience too! The stores are open 9:00 to 1:00 and 4:00 to 8:00 PM. If you don't get up in the morning you can't do anything until 4:00! And when you do go shopping, it takes hours to find where to go for each little item ~ The Italian shopkeepers are very humorous and very helpful, but I don't trust their food entirely....

... I received a marvellous letter from your mother. Am delighted to hear she is writing, and hope some day to read her output[4]~

My Mother sent me a clipping of a League concert ~ Please let me know how it went and what was performed other than John's Wine of Peace[5] ~ By the way, I have not heard from either Weinzweig ~ I hope all is well with them ~ ·

4 Ruth Somers (1896–1964) was one of the most important and supportive figures in Somers's early years. She was an intelligent and perceptive person. As an active member of the Toronto Theosophical Society during the 1930s and 1940s, she wrote articles on theosophical matters and even gave several talks about theosophy on the radio. She seems to have written some fiction as well but virtually nothing of this part of her life seems to have been preserved.

5 This reference to a concert sponsored by the Canadian League of Composers is puzzling, since these ended in 1958 and the League does not appear to have sponsored a concert in 1959. There were, however, three broadcasts of Canadian orchestral works, as reported by John Beckwith in the *Toronto Daily Star*, in the fall of 1959. These included John Weinzweig's *Wine of Peace: Two Songs for Soprano and Orchestra* (1957), which the CBC Symphony Orchestra had already premiered in March 1958. (John Beckwith, "Audiences Hear More of Own Music," *Toronto Daily Star*, 31 October 1959). John Weinzweig (1913–2006), the eminent Toronto composer and teacher, had taught both Somers and Norma and remained a close life-long friend of both. His wife, Helen Weinzweig (1915–2010), was also a close friend of both in these years. She later became a highly respected writer, publishing two novels and a collection of short stories. Her novel *Basic Black with Pearls* won the Toronto Book Award in 1981.

84 Between Composers

Darling, could you arrange to have sent to me a subscription to Canadian Music Journal[6] ~ I can get news of the US. and can get Musical America here, but nothing on Canada, musically or otherwise ~ I would be glad to pay the charges for the subscription and air mail postage (otherwise it would never arrive)

Still no word from Petrassi ~ If I don't hear by the end of the week I shall again endeavour to write him....

... Darling, please write me soon ~ I am rather desperate to hear from you and want to know when you are planning to come over to this side of the ocean ~ or should I return?

So much I want to ask ~

Love

Normie ~

HS to NB

1 a.m. [4 November]

Darling Normie:

Tonight I had a long visit with John W. He sends his love and best wishes for your studies. Before too long he will probably write to you.

It is always good to see John. His views on music are so sound and his loyalty as a friend unchanging....

... I'll likely be going to Hartford Conneticut with John by the way....

... Night sounds, my heart beating in the solitude, no other sounds. At such times as this all the superficial smart phrases are flung back into one's face with the impact of garbage.

So ever back to my lonely tasks, in this case the last movement of my guitar sonata. Soon it will be done then to the Koussevitsky at last[7]

6 *The Canadian Music Journal* was published quarterly from 1956 until 1962 by the Canadian Music Council under the editorship of Geoffrey Payzant. Its articles dealt with a variety of historical and current issues about music. It also contained reviews of concert life, recordings, and books. The contributors included Marius Barbeau, John Beckwith, Chester Duncan, Glenn Gould, Helmut Kallmann, Udo Kasemets, Hugh Le Caine, Sir Ernest MacMillan, Kathleen Parlow, Godfrey Ridout, R. Murray Schafer, Arnold Walter, and Kenneth Winters.

7 This was a commission for an orchestral piece from the Serge Koussevitzky Music Foundation in the Library of Congress, a permanent endowment established by the original Koussevitzky Music Foundation in 1950. The original foundation was established by the Russian-born conductor of the Boston Symphony, Serge Koussevitzky, in 1942 to help promote contemporary music. It still commissions new works from composers and disseminates this music through performance and other means. Somers's commission resulted in the orchestral piece *Lyric*, which he did not complete until the spring of 1960.

November 1959　85

– possibly the Pittsburgh commission[8] – then the writing of music for an art film – studying Gregorian Chant[,] the music of Pierre Boulez and French as a preliminary to what I hope is a stay in France via the Canada Council.[9] I do have my work cut out for me, as Falstaff might say. So pull yourself together, Somers, and don't bother the fair lady with all your rumblings and surges.

———————

Wednesday a.m. –

A sleep and I feel myself regaining my strength and composure, an ideal state for writing. A wet day with the sizzle of tires and the closeness of a room.

Do remember to get the Stravinsky 'Poetics of Music' and 'Conversations' with Robert Craft.

Have a ball.

　　　　　All my love,
　　　　　Harry

P.S. My Passacaglia and Fugue has been done twice in Scotland and is to be done in Liverpool and London.[10] George Little's Paris performance was bad, he took the fugue half speed.[11] Vic did a great

8　This refers to a commission from the American Wind Symphony Orchestra, founded in 1957 by Robert Boudreau (b. 1927), a Juilliard-trained trumpet player and conductor. During the summer months, the Pittsburgh-based ensemble performed aboard a floating arts centre, named Point Counterpoint, a converted coal barge with a rudimentary stage that was towed from one venue to another along American inland and coastal waterways. Boudreau commissioned some 400 new works for the ensemble over the years. Somers did not write the piece for the ensemble, the Symphony for Woodwinds, Brass and Percussion, until 1961, during his stay in Paris (1960–61).

9　The Canada Council had been established in 1957, to, as its mandate from Parliament stated, "foster and promote the study and enjoyment of, and the production of works in, the arts," chiefly by providing grants and services to professional Canadian artists and arts organizations. Subsequently, Somers did receive a grant to spend a year in Paris in 1960–61.

10　The Passacaglia and Fugue (1954) was one of Somers's early mature works to become widely known through concert performances and, later, a Louisville Orchestra recording (1966). The piece demonstrates Somers's preoccupation during the 1950s with traditional contrapuntal techniques, such as fugue, combined with an individual and somewhat flexible use of serialism (applied only to pitches).

11　George Little (1920–1995) was a Montreal-based choir director, organist, and teacher. In 1951 he founded the Montreal Bach Choir, a group that premiered many

86   Between Composers

job from Winnipeg and the Harp Suite is to be done in Montreal in December, a performance I might drop down for[.][12]

NB to HS
Friday, November 6th
My darling Harry,

I have received two letters from you this morning and I have waited for them for so long ~ I am terribly upset and desperately lonely for you ~ I want to pick up the telephone and speak with you but I can't ~ it takes days here to place a long distance call ~ Will you call me again and let me pay for it ~ it is so much easier from your side of the ocean ~

You confess your love to me ~ I believe it ~ I don't want to believe it for it causes me too much pain ~ No, I am far from feeling love for another person ~ I love you very much, but have tried very hard to forget my feelings for you, for this is what I thought you wanted, for you and for me both....

... I have tried to exist by myself since I left America, and find it now harder than ever as I am finally in a place, totally alone, and supposed to be starting to work ~ I can't work, for I don't know how to really live with myself ~ I look for solace in my visits to the Savios, my shopping expeditions for a package of salt, watching the behaviours of the Italians, and for a while, a group of people that have parties, and hang out in Jerry's bar seem to help ~

Canadian works and performed a wide variety of music, ranging from the Renaissance to the twentieth century. This group received considerable national recognition and in 1958 did an extensive tour of four European countries, including a concert with the Orchestre Radio-Symphonique at the Théâtre des Champs-Elysées in Paris. This performance included Somers's Passacaglia and Fugue. It was recorded by Radio-France, and broadcast on the CBC in the fall of 1959; this must have been how Somers came to hear the Paris performance. The broadcast was reviewed in the *Toronto Daily Star* by John Beckwith, who wrote that "the performance [of the Passacaglia and Fugue] seemed more musical in many of its details than the recording made by the CBC own orchestra two years ago." See John Beckwith, "Audiences Hear More of Own Music," *Toronto Daily Star*, 31 October 1959. This review was republished in the *Canadian Music Journal*: John Beckwith, "Notes on Some New Music Heard on CBC Radio," *The Canadian Music Journal* IV, no. 2 (Winter 1960), 39.

12 "Vic" was the Canadian conductor Victor Feldbrill (1924–2020) who had been a close friend of Somers since the late 1940s and championed his music as well as the music of many other Canadian composers. At this time (1958–68), Feldbrill was conductor of the Winnipeg Symphony Orchestra. The Suite for Harp and Chamber Orchestra (1949) became one of the best known of Somers's early works and was even the subject of a short National Film Board film in 1953 entitled *Rehearsal*.

But I am sick to death of trying to find happiness in alcohol and things which flatter one's vanity like shopping ... I am frantically miserable in this charming little place, for above all, I must be true to myself if nothing else, and I can't live a life of nothingness ~

I am also worried sick about money, for this place is costing me plenty ~ $88.00 per month, plus telephone, food, and many things which I am required to buy in order to survive here ~ I doubt whether I have $1300.00 left and whether I can stay here for more than three months ~ my lessons, if that bloody Petrassi returns, will cost me plenty, probably $15–20. per hour ... So many things ~ I have to rent a piano which will cost $5–10 per month....

... It will be another six months to a year before any further distribution is made on the estate, so what do I do?

You say my letters are cool, but darling, what am I to do ~ I came here to try and work, and I haven't even started and my money is practically gone! I wanted you, and still do, here, and I don't know whether it would be advisable to spend all my money to have you come over, and worry after or what? What?...

... I so much want to wander around with you and see Rome and other areas of Italy ~ I want to sit and drink and talk or be silent with you ~ I want to sleep with you every night ~ How can we do that? Shall I send you a plane ticket? Please, please know that I care so much, I never look out at this view from my window that I don't think of you and how you would love it....

... Your letters make me so sad ~ Why, oh why did I come away without you ~

5:00 PM –

Darling, darling Harry Somers ~ why must we be apart ~ I am afraid now of falling away in pieces unless I can hear your voice and see you soon ~ Since I started this letter, I have had a small lunch and some Italian vino to help it down, and had a sleep full of unquiet dreams ~ Now two little Italian workmen have come in to fix the roof (which leaked) ~ and my letter and thoughts are being interrupted....

... Do you know that I love you, and that I am unable to love another, even if there were someone, which there is not! No, No, No ~ I am not living with someone else, or am I about to ~ even if it were available it is against my personal pride, dignity and everything else to live as a kept female ... I know that if I am not a composer,

I certainly have the soul of an artist, and that kind of life is against all truth to me …To live with you is not to live against truth ~ you know, darling Harry ~

I have read and re-read your letter, and re-read it again … Harry this is the first time in my life that I begin to feel as though I am loved by someone, by you ~ I am extraordinarily happy ~ and yet so sad to be a long way away ~ I am frightened of my own self as well … I believe sincerely and truthfully that I love you, maybe this is all I can hope to know.…

… We seem to have gone much deeper than many thousand others who exist together ~ I do not think it is too late and that we have lost each other ~ external problems worry me, however, such as money, your wife, etc ~ I wish that you could answer these for me ~

The more I write the calmer I seem to be becoming, but I so much want to hear your voice ~ Could you please telephone me again, darling, for to place a call to Canada is so difficult here a) because you need to have an 'overseas deposit' on your telephone and as it is not listed in my name, and b) it takes a century to call long distance in Europe with their antiquated system, and c) the language problem pertaining to (a) ~ My number here is 682.393 and there is a 6 hour difference (you are behind).…

… I have tried to tell you in other ways what it is like here, how I feel and worry and think ~ Part of me seems to have been missing, and still is, and now I am living alone I know that it is you ~ Oh God, how I have tried to condition myself to living a life of solitude ~ is it really a necessity to write music? No, no, it ain't!…

… Michael said in words and you said in music 'How can I hold within me all that is' ~ I hope I don't break.

So much love, my dearest one

Normie ~

PS. So delighted to hear again of the quartet ~ maybe someday I shall hear it ~
Are John and Helen travelling to Hartford as well ~?
Good luck with your performance ~

N.

November 1959 89

HS to NB
Friday, Nov. 6
Darling Normie:

I'm going through such a hell as I never dreamed of. If I tortured you for four years you may be assured I'm getting much more back. I wait only for your letters and am crushed when there is nothing, my only consolation being that there is another day and perhaps a word and again no and again another day of illness and fever and dying and the thought of your not caring.

It was Marion Grudeff who once told me that she hoped one day that I'd really fall in love with a woman who would leave and cut my throat.[13] She felt that I had never fallen in love and when I did I would get what's coming to me. She was so right. Sometimes for a whole afternoon I think I have control and then I suddenly retch up my feelings and thoughts.

I want only you, only to be with you, to love you, to live with you, to have children by you – everything. You think it impossible – we have exchanged roles....

... Please forgive me for all the hurt and cruelty I inflicted on you in the past. Now I know –
     All my love –
          Harry

HS to NB
Saturday Nov. 7
Dearest Normie:

Your letter of the pleasant dinner arrived. You cannot know the torment I'm in. I can't continue too long like this. You say so carefully "I hope all the practical considerations can work out for both of us ~" almost casually, then 'very much love' Normie Normie. I'm glad you have a perspective, I'm happy you're finding out, it's the purpose you went to Rome for....

13 Marian Grudeff (1927–2006) was a Canadian pianist, composer, and teacher who became known in the 1960s for her collaborations with Ray Jessel (1929–2015), most notably for the Broadway musical *Baker Street*, based on the Sherlock Holmes stories. During the 1950s, Grudeff was associated with the well-known Toronto revue *Spring Thaw*, eventually becoming its music director. From 1948 until 1952, she taught piano at the Royal Conservatory of Music in Toronto, and it is likely that she met Somers in the late 1940s through the Conservatory. In early 1954, on a European tour as a pianist, she performed his Sonata No. 2. One can only speculate as to the reason for her pointed remarks to Somers about his relationship with women.

90   Between Composers

... I want you to come back to me, I want us to live together and eventually be married. Will you come back to me now? Will you live with me now? Will you eventually marry me? I never dreamed how much I love you or how much I need you. Give me an answer. If I continue to live in this middle world I will go completely mad. I shall take whatever you write as your answer. For the sake of my composing, which is something I regard as something important outside of myself, a gift which I must preserve, I cannot destroy my sanity....

... You stated in one of your letters that an impersonal relationship with me was impossible – you spoke of passion and intensity.

Now you must answer me. By now you know your feelings and desires. It is all or nothing, I would surely die otherwise.

I love you to the depths of my whole being.

       Harry

HS to NB
Sunday Nov. 8
Beloved Normie:

I visited your mother this afternoon intending to stay for supper but I'm afraid I almost broke down completely and had to leave. We talked for a while for I asked her for her views on our relationship, about you, what she thought of my marrying you. She was very wise feeling fundamentally as I do, that you must have time to find out your own mind. She pointed out that after all a proposal from me required a complete re-appraisal by you....

... Who is Alex, Normie? From the sound of your mother (she read a portion of one of your recent letters), he is wealthy and it would seem tremendously attractive to you. Is this what you want?

A composer perhaps couldn't provide you with the things you want.

Do you love me Normie? Will you marry me? Echoes over and over. I'm in a death cell reliving my whole life. The expectations of people, the disappointment in people, the hurt, hurt to numbness....

... I cried for the first time since childhood and despised my weakness. I cried for my agony and the agony I've inflicted on others and for the suffering of the part of the world which feels and is sensitive.

The moons' gone down and the suns turned black.[14] (Lyrics from somewhere)

You are probably another person by now. Your mother said after all its' only been two months. Two months, when the last hour has been my whole lifetime! I should be an actor I'm so dramatic....

... All I need to know is that you love me as I love you, that we'll get married if you can find it in your heart to do so, that we'll take what comes together, rich or poor.

If this is not so for you, you must tell me as soon as you know.

My only solace now is listening to music. Music has been many things to me, I have given to it and now it is my refuge, I hope my works will mean as much to others....

... You see, because of my past behaviour, I have no recourse but to my own hurt. Norm has said to me "Well after all you deserve it you know," quite honestly and without malice. Gwen has said "You did treat her rather roughly, she will be very reluctant," for I asked her how she would react. My mother has said "If she really loves you, and I think she does, then everything will work out."

Helen McNamara just called.[15] It's 2:00a.m. She's tearful. Now I understand I'm going to drop over for awhile. She needs company dreadfully. "Ah yes. Norma loves you." she says.

---

4 a.m. Back from Helen's. Bumped into Norm on the way up so he came up. Almost like old times drinking rum. We almost called you reversing the charge just to have you join the party except we know what you're usually like in the morning. Rome time it would have been 7 or 8 a.m.

Better watch out. Norm, Helen and myself decided the only thing to win you back is the grand gesture. I fly in, knock on the door leaving the engines running, grab you saying 'You're my woman' and off in a blaze of protests....

... God, I wonder if I can sleep tonight. Anyway I must at least lie down and see if I can pretend, though one can't really deceive the night.

14 These are the first two lines of a short poem by the American poet and writer, Dorothy Parker (1893–1967), entitled "Two-Volume Novel:" "The sun's gone dim, and / The moon's turned black; / For I loved him, and / He didn't love back." It was published in her 1928 collection *Sunset Gun*.

15 See chap. 2, n. 23.

Monday noon and I feel somewhat calmer. It's as though I'm going through some nightmare. It is a true dying but is curious, I feel that I will emerge much stronger should I deserve it. In effect I've had to assess myself and to add it all up.

I am a composer. I live from the air not the earth. It is a little like having taken vows or sworn the doctors' oath. Stravinsky speaks of the sacred nature of the creative arts, their duty to present the shape of unity to the world, that in the desire to communicate and the desire to hear there is a profound purpose. Debussy speaks in one of his letters to Stravinsky 'of being servant to that art which we both reverence, and love.'[16]

I find that I am à dedicated person, that come what may I must survive. Composing is not just a game, it is my life to me and virtually a sacred duty. I am not a member of any religious group, but my art is my religion. (Which sounds a little pompous. Please excuse.)

If you couldn't live with a composer you must find this out too, I realize. It is a hard life for a woman to live and hard to live with a person totally emerged in it....

... Deep inside I know that if we have a real love it will survive and join. You have affected me as no one else in my life. I love you as I have loved no one else.

Strange that now perhaps more women are strongly attracted to me than at any time and that I couldn't care less and have nothing to do with them. I find that loving you as I do I have no feeling whatsoever for other women. Everything is held in my love for you....

... It is yours if you will have it.

I am more at peace now than for a long time –
You know you have all my love –
Harry

It is an incredibly beautiful November day. I had to go to the C.B.C. television building and actually went in without being sick to my stomach for memories, though my heart was certainly in my mouth.

---

16 The passage is actually as follows: "[T]he dedication on [the score of Stravinsky's *Petrushka*] is much too flattering about what I have done for the art of music, which we both serve with a similar disinterested zeal." François Lesure and Roger Nichols, editors, *Debussy Letters 1862–1918*, trans. Roger Nichols (Cambridge, Massachusetts: Harvard University Press, 1987), 258.

November 1959

93

NB to HS
Monday ~ 8:30 PM [9 November]
My darling Harry ~

At last things are looking up! I am bursting to tell you of the events of the last two days, so if I can contain my thoughts long enough to organize them on paper then you can share my excitement (if it is all that exciting) ~

Yesterday afternoon Pierre Monteux[17] was conducting the Santa Cecilia orchestra[18] ~ For me, Monteux is always worth seeing and as I hadn't yet heard the S.C. orch., I went ~ You were as usual much in my mind and especially as I heard the Bach Passacaglia, orchestrated by Respighi (naturally too heavy for my taste for it destroyed the eternal 'line') ~ reminded me very much of the P. + F. of that famous composer Somers ~ from Canada too![19]... and then Petrouchka, in full ~ I never cease to be fascinated by Stravinsky's marvellous sonoritys (ies) but it was an incredible performance ~ and orchestra ~ In the first place the orchestra never tuned at all ... In the first part particularly, the brass section completely fell apart (in Petrouchka, that is) and brass and ww. were missing and farting during the whole work ~ all over the place ~ Monteux, I am afraid is showing his age somewhat ... but what a concert ~ The Romans sit with rapt attention, and I am sure they aren't even aware of what a good orchestra or performance sounds like ~ God, I miss our marvellous conversations on music as well as everything else....

... However, for today which is undoubtedly more important ~ I met Petrassi, at last, for he has now returned from Japan no less ~ When I made the appointment on the telephone yesterday, I was

17 Pierre Monteux (1875–1964) became well known as a conductor in the years before the First World War when he conducted the world premieres of important ballets for Sergei Diaghilev's *Ballets Russes*, including Stravinsky's *Le Sacre du printemps* and *Petrushka*, and Ravel's *Daphnis et Chloé*. Among the orchestras he later conducted were the Boston Symphony Orchestra (1919–24), the Amsterdam Concertgebouw Orchestra (1924–34), L'Orchestre Symphonique de Paris (1929–38), and the San Francisco Symphony (1936–52).
18 The National Academy of St Cecilia (Accademia Nazionale di Santa Cecilia), founded in 1585, grew into an internationally recognized conservatory, with areas devoted to musical scholarship, education, composition, and performance. It has both its own choir and orchestra (the Orchestra dell'Accademia Nazionale di Santa Cecilia, which was founded in 1895). Between 1822 and 1870, the Academy expanded to include persons other than composers and performers, such as dancers, poets, music historians, musical instrument makers, and music publishers.
19 Another reference to Somers's Passacaglia and Fugue of 1954. See chap. 3, n. 10.

94

Between Composers

forced to confess my ignorance of his language for he couldn't understand why I couldn't speak as well as I write Italian ~ One's sins are always uncovered ~

He is a very energetic and preoccupied looking person, about 52, with a brush cut no less, and eyes that slightly protrude as though there could be some physical cause somewhere ~ A sensitive, intelligent face which looks as though it belongs to a banker instead of a composer ~ He has the most fantastic studio I have never seen ~ A fairly large room, with grand piano and three walls covered with books and scores and contemporary paintings, plus a spacious work desk ~ I looked at it with green eyes, believe me ~ I was interviewed for an hour roughly, during which time he pulled out my music and commented on several aspects, some of which I understood (actually most of which) ~ referring to my work as conservative but very musical ~ I showed him what had been completed of the Tanglewood piece (of Michael's) which he considered more interesting[20] ~ We chatted about many things general such as Tanglewood, and he questioned my previous training, whether I had studied counterpoint, harmony, etc. ~ The course at Santa Cecilia begins at the beginning of February and I seem to feel that is where he thinks I should aim ~ In the meantime, he has suggested that I complete Michael's work and at the same time begin a work for chamber orchestra (a suite perhaps) and at the end of December see what is the next move ... He asked me what kind of program I wanted to tackle, which was a bit of a surprise to me, so I simply said something very difficult, for I feel I need to be so preoccupied with work in order to discipline myself ~ Hence the chamber orchestra project!

All in all, I don't yet know very much about this man, but I have decided to give the whole thing a hell of a good hard try and see what happens ~ I started this afternoon by buying four scores ~ Schoenberg Kammersymphonie, Stravinsky Suite #1 for Chamber Orchestra, Hindemith Kammermusick #4, Webern Six Pieces for Orch. ~ all of which I intend to study in detail in the next short while ~ In addition I am renting a piano which I should have shortly ~ and have managed to gain access to the Santa Cecilia music library....

20 Beecroft recalls that Fram gave her some poetry entitled "Cantata," which he suggested could be for choir and solo voice. She worked on this project at Tanglewood in 1958 and again in Rome, but only managed to work on part of it, a short piece called Cantata for Mezzo Soprano and Five Instruments; even this was never completed. (Norma Beecroft, email message to the editor, 29 December 2020.) For Fram, see chap.1, n. 31.

November 1959 95

... I had my first real lesson today with Gazzelloni on the flute, and I played well ~ He is a very easy person, very warm and I guess he can get results from me ~ I also chatted with him about orchestras, concerts, here, etc. and I have been invited to attend a rehearsal on Saturday next of the Rome Radio orch., evidently very good. Naturally, I am anxious to meet the Roman musicians and it is impossible to hear a rehearsal without an invitation from a member as well ~ So I just asked! By the way, I am an unusual species here ~ they have no women studying wind instruments ~ isn't that strange ~ Gazzelloni is also a very busy man with concerts and recordings, etc. and plays and is interested in new music ~ so I can get a lot of information from him on what is happening ~ My lessons go, as I said, very well with him for I don't seem to have difficulty speaking Italian with him at all ~ But with Petrassi I will, so I will spend the next two weeks or so tutoring with a gal friend of Carla Savio as well ~

So my life starts to become occupied with important things again and I feel much happier, also because of your marvellous letter, so warm and so full of love ~

I am happy to hear that you are coming near the end of the guitar sonata ~ Are you pleased with your work? By the way Julian Bream[21] comes here in the early spring, so I shall endeavour to say hello, as I discovered in London he is also a friend of Thea's....[22]

... I think that I should have been a painter here ~ everything ~ the buildings, the earth, the people, the sun ~ has a burnt-sienna-bronzy-golden colour which is incredible ~ I have never seen such magnificent colour, and who ever said there weren't vivid sunsets in Europe obviously hadn't been to Italy ~ From my roof terrazza at 5:00 o'clock the sky is fantastic in colour and skyscapes ~ the dome of Saint Peters, the famous nine (?) hills of Rome, and roof tops and church campanellas are all viewed ~ You always wanted to live with a view ~ well, you had better join me for this place is available for only six months!

I love you muchly, and kiss you most tenderly goodnight my love ~ Buona fortuna and buon divertito in Hartford.

     As always, with much love for you alone

     Normie —

---

21 See chap. 3, n. 29.
22 Thea Musgrave. See chap. 1, n. 35.

96 Between Composers

NB to HS
November 10, 1959
My dearest Harry,

Today I received two letters from you the second of which I don't know whether to ignore or not, for I hope by now you have some idea of what is going on externally and internally with me ~ I want, however, to take your questions and individually answer each one as best I can ~

I do know the torment you are going through and that you can continue without question ~ Yes, I hope by this time I have some perspective ~ that is what I have wanted, especially after having four years wondering what I was and having very little perspective ~

If you are disappointed and hurt because of the tone of my letters I am sorry ~ I tell you usually what I mean one way or another ~ To someone in great heat everything else and everyone else seems cold or cool ~ Also I think that some of your thinking has rubbed off on me, as I expect some of mine has had its subconscious or conscious effect on you ~ be this only natural ~ But what you have helped to give me, and I hope the reverse is true, is a certain kind of strength and courage, and you may call it perspective, but whatever it is, is very good for me ~

I do realize the importance of what's happening, my love, very well ~ I know what you are going through, for that kind of torment existed very often for me with you in Toronto, and what made it additionally painful was that I was with you ~ and yet not with you....

... In any case, if my last letters haven't answered your questions, I will try again ~ but with questions of my own ~ The answer is yes, I want to live with you and eventually marry you and have your children ~ yes, yes YES ~ But what do you mean 'Will you come back to me now?' Do you want me to return to Canada now? What does 'now' mean?...

Wednesday ~
... Today a young American girl brought a young American composer here to visit me for an hour ~ This chap studied with Milhaud and another name in Philadelphia who I have never heard of ~ and has no respect for Copland or Foss whatsoever ~ says Copland should grow up musically ~ Why do all young composers have to be so opinionated? It is really very boring after a while ~ However, he seems rather bright (another chap who majored-in-musicology-turned-composer) and seemed to be very grateful to meet a junior colleague, and looked at my set-up here with very envious eyes ... I have invited him

November 1959   97

here to a little supper party on Friday night which I am giving for the Savios ~ Carla particularly, as she leaves Rome on Sunday for Paris and then to work in Brussels ~

I must say it was pleasant to have an argument with even an opinionated composer!

When they left, I trotted on down to a piano recital of contemporary music, played by David Tudor[23] ~ I admire him greatly for playing the 'music' of Stockhausen, Cage, and the gimmick-electronic boys with such conviction ~ Really, darling, I can't help wondering why these people who are so interested in sonority cannot see further than they do and use their bloody sonorities to create music and something that communicates something important ~ Some of the sounds on the piano interest me greatly, and if they were used musically, I think it would be ever so much more important ~ However ~ very stimulating ~ and I must say the audience were for the most part attentive and interested....

Thursday AM.

... Dearest Harry, I am sure you are losing your equilibrium after reading again another letter ~ You are crazy, my love, and I am crazy for you ~ But as you think I am avoiding your questions, I think also you are avoiding mine ~ Please, please, please, how can we be together soon? This is what I mean by practical considerations, my love ~

On the telephone you said you were going to try to come here as soon as possible, but since you have said nothing more in your letters ~ What is happening, darling? What do you want me to do? Trust the women to be always practical, but please don't resent me for it ~

Please write me always, and telephone.

Love and love and more
Normie

23 David Tudor (1926–1996) was one of the most prominent of the twentieth-century pianists who specialized in avant-garde repertoire. Although he gave first performances of works by composers such as Earle Brown, Sylvano Bussotti, Morton Feldman, Karlheinz Stockhausen, Christian Wolff, Stefan Wolpe, and La Monte Young, he was chiefly associated, in the 1950s and beyond, with John Cage, giving the premieres of works such as *Music of Changes*, *Concert for Piano and Orchestra*, and *4' 33"*. In 1958, Tudor selected the works to be performed for the 25th Anniversary Retrospective Concert of John Cage and performed in the premiere of the *Concert for Piano and Orchestra*, the closing work of that concert. After 1961, Tudor mainly concentrated on composing live electronic music.

98   Between Composers

HS to NB
Thursday night: [12 November]
Dearest Normie:

The overseas telephone is so damn frustrating! I have to shout in the receiver and your voice is quite often impossible to decipher, your sound being mangled by the infernal connections.

No, I am not sick, in the normal sense, but the churning up and facing of my whole life has caused a tension and upset equal to any illness. I felt sad and disturbed after talking to you because of the inadequacy of communications. My previous letter will explain, or answer, some of your questions.

There is a peculiar hopelessness about 'nothing concrete' but it's the way we must exist.

Tonight the snow is falling into the silent world. How beautifully melancholy it is. I feel 'down.' There are times it is difficult to accept – just accept....

... Friday morning. First winter sight of everything topped with white icing. First sound of snow shovel. The snow transforms and softens hard city outlines and the children laugh and shout....

... Right now I'm in the middle of a pile of copying for Wayne & Schuster show, trying to clear it up.[24] Bailey and myself will be driving down to Hartford either tonight or first thing tomorrow morning....[25]

---

24 "Wayne and Shuster" was a well-known comedy duo featuring Johnny Wayne (1918–1990) and Frank Shuster (1916–2002), both Toronto-born. They began doing radio programs in the 1940s and became part of *The Army Show* that entertained troops in Canada and in Europe during the Second World War. After the war, they continued on CBC Radio but in 1954 moved to CBC Television on a regular basis. In 1958, they began performing regularly on *The Ed Sullivan Show*, with great success. Their shows featured humorous sketches that were clever, with plenty of slapstick, often based on plays of Shakespeare.
25 Bailey Bird (1917–1992) was an administrator and publisher who had started out as a violinist before joining the publishing firm of Gordon V. Thompson Ltd in 1937. From 1953 until 1960, he was head of the publications division of BMI Canada and would have overseen the publication of a number of scores of Somers and his contemporaries. During this time, Bird co-founded Concert Associations of Canada, which presented Maureen Forrester, Glenn Gould, Lois Marshall, and others in recitals throughout southern Ontario during the 1950s.

November 1959

... I spoke to my wife and told her it is all over.[26] It is a hellish thing to have to hurt someone so deeply in order to live. It is tragic for her but perhaps it will be better in the long run. I just hate gaining happiness at the expense of someone else's hurt, it is dangerous, but she and I must free ourselves from the years of endless indecision and mutilation....

... I'm a person of many sides, as we all are, but one thing I know, I'm <u>not</u> a bachelor by temperament, I need a woman and <u>you</u> are the woman. Everything is in our favour for we share so many things and our curiosity runs in similar directions. During the past we have been moving closer and closer. I believe our love can grow and mature into a deep and profound relationship....

... John W. is going to Hartford by himself. John Beckwith's going with Pamela. Apparently it's been so long since they have had a holiday together they are making it one by staying in New York for a couple of days ahead of time. Murray Adaskin will be flying down. Couture and some others from Montreal will attend so that there should be a good representation.[27]

Bailey and Jean Beaudet are going down as observers.[28] We'll be driving back on Tuesday.

---

26 Somers had married Catherine Mackie (1927–1963) in 1949, shortly before leaving Toronto to spend a year in Paris. Three letters to her from Somers, written in 1953 and 1954, indicate that they had been separated since 1954 (see the introduction for more about this). At this time, she was working as a private secretary at American Biltrite Rubber Co. Ltd.

27 The Canadian delegation included some of the most prominent composers of the period: John Weinzweig (1913–2006), John Beckwith (1927–2022), Murray Adaskin (1906–2002), then head of the Department of Music at the University of Saskatchewan, and Jean-Papineau Couture (1916–2000), who was then president of the Canadian League of Composers. "Pamela" was Pamela Terry (1926–2006), a well-known theatre director in Toronto and John Beckwith's wife from 1950 until 1975. As well as raising a family during these years, the Beckwiths were both carrying on full-time careers. In addition to his composition career and teaching duties at the University of Toronto, Beckwith had recently begun writing music reviews for the *Toronto Daily Star.* It is little wonder that they had not had a holiday together for some time.

28 Jean-Marie Beaudet (1908–1971) was a conductor, pianist, educator, and administrator. His conducting career began during the 1936–37 season of the *La Société des concerts symphoniques de Montréal.* At the same time, he began a long association with the CBC as a program director and conductor. In these roles, he played an important role in the development of new Canadian music, from the 1940s on. At the time of the Hartford festival, he was the first executive director of the recently formed Canadian Music Centre. In 1964, he became the first music director of the National Arts Centre in Ottawa.

Between Composers

I'll be thinking of you all the time, my darling.

Please take care of yourself and don't worry about me. (As the song says.) You are the keeper of my love. Always be at peace and never, ever be afraid to be completely honest with me in the future as you've been in the past.

I love you so much –
      Harry

HS to NB
Thursday, November 12/59
Darling:

Above all, don't panic. By now you must think me possessed or mad, which might be quite true, but I want you to be calm, at least about the practical things.

As long as you have a return ticket or enough money for same, there is <u>no</u> worry....

... Do not spend money on a present for me, <u>please</u>, because your wishes and peace of mind are the only presents I want.

... Take careful stock of your money. Figure out a budget totalling expenses against your capital and determine just how much you can spend and how long it permits you to stay. Put everything down on paper and figure it out then <u>stick</u> with your budget spending no more than is permitted. You'd be surprised how things will stretch if you do not go outside essentials, I've had to find out this fall....

... Now, if you intend to do any work with Petrassi then you <u>must</u> regard yourself as a <u>student</u>, not a tourist or visiting fireman. You must live as a student, avoiding luxuries and only looking to needs.

My dearest, you have an iron will, organize yourself and put it to needs....

... The problem of money with us is difficult but I have shown you how you can resolve a good deal of this conflict by accepting our relative financial situations and living accordingly. Now that I know my love for you I have an inner calm that accepts the necessity of being apart. The more we know of ourselves at this point the better. For it was the very fact of being apart that made me open my eyes so that I could see what was in my heart....

... Now, musically – yes, Op. 111 is Beethoven's last sonata, the great work of which Thomas Mann speaks so beautifully in Dr. Faustus. (Your apartment with its Beethoven desk sounds really charming. I envy you!)

November 1959
101

Spent most of yesterday afternoon in conversation and listening to Julian Breem in his hotel room.[29] Showed him my new guitar sonata, which he likes and wants. Wonderful conversation covering many things of art and life. Good Lord he seems to know every composer in the world. Nono is a good friend of his.[30] Hilarious story about them being worlds apart in musical tastes.

His recital last night was fantastic!![31] He has gained unbelievably in a year and it was a pleasure to hear him....

... Must go to the dentist. Be at peace my beloved. Have no fear. Take time without pressure or worry to know yourself and to take advantage of the world you're in.

(Visit art galleries too!)

All my love, darling Normie —

Harry

---

29 Julian Bream (1933–2020) was one of the most celebrated and well-known classical guitarists and lutenists of the twentieth century. His career began in the early 1950s and his recitals included a wide range of music, including pieces by Bach arranged for guitar, popular Spanish pieces, transcriptions of seventeenth-century music, and twentieth-century music (much of which was written especially for him). In 1959, when Somers met him, he was on his first North American tour. A further connection with Canada occurred in 1965 on the occasion of Stravinsky's visit to Toronto to record the Symphony of Psalms, when Bream met Stravinsky in Massey Hall and played a pavane of Dowland's on the lute; this meeting is captured in the National Film Board film *Stravinsky* (1966).

30 Along with Bruno Maderna and Luciano Berio, Luigi Nono (1924–1990) was one of the major Italian avant-garde composers of the post-Second World War generation; much of his work had anti-fascist subject matter. *Il canto sospeso* (1955–56) for solo voices, chorus, and orchestra had brought Nono international recognition by 1959. This work commemorates the victims of fascism, incorporating farewell letters written by political prisoners before execution. Another then-recent piece for orchestra, *Diario polacco; Composizione no. 2* (1958–59), was based on a journey through the Nazi concentration camps in Poland.

31 This recital had taken place at Eaton Auditorium the previous evening; the critics pointed out that the auditorium was only about one-third occupied. The program featured both lute and guitar and included music by Luis Milan, Handel, Bach, Cimarosa, Ravel, and Villa-Lobos.

Between Composers

NB to HS
Sunday ~
November 15th, 1959
Darling,

The middle of the month again ~Another grey day here full of rain and wind ~ It rains all the time here it seems, and is damp ~ The other night before I telephoned you, we had such electric storms here as I have never seen before ~ From my sixth floor apartment the sight was incredible, great forks of lightning shooting across the sky and rain in torrents ~ An old professor, and lawyer, named Della Rocca, a friend of the Gazzellonis had taken me to see and hear L'Histoire du Soldat and Peter and the Wolf (Prokofieff) ~ nothing to be worried about, my love, only a lonely old man who is now a has-been, I think, in his profession ~ rather sad ~ But what a charming theatre and performance ~ The Teatro della Cometa is designed for intimate performances, chamber music, etc. ~ complete with two little balconies, chandeliers, and a charming arrangement of seats ~ The atmosphere of this little theatre I can only describe as très charmant ~ it seems more French than Italian![32]

In 'L'Histoire', which was performed in Italian, were some incredibly good performers ~ mime artists such as we don't have in Canada and possibly America too ~ Il Soldato was excellent ~ What a delightful miniature, this work ~ I thought that Norm Symonds would be interested in seeing it and examining the score, if he is still contemplating writing for the theatre ~ In any case, a delightful evening, followed by a walk in torrents of rain in which I ruined a pair of shoes completely, and got soaked to the skin, as my friend il professore was not very gallant!...

... I have just returned from another lesson with Gazzelloni during which time I played badly and enjoyed his views on modern music and activities in Europe ~ Evidently, the best summer music school here is in Germany, in Darmstadt (?), during the month of July[33] ~

32 The Teatro della Cometa was founded in 1958 by Countess Anna Laetitia Pecci, also known as Mimi Pecci-Blunt, a Roman art patron, who was acquainted with many of the leading literary and artistic figures in Europe in the years after the First World War. The theatre was part of the Pecci-Blunt family residence in Piazza d'Aracoeli and became an important venue for theatre, literary presentations, and concerts.
33 Darmstadt is a city in Germany located in the southern part of the Rhine-Main area. Beginning in 1946, it became the venue of a regular summer festival of contemporary classical music, internationally known as the "Ferienkurse für Internationale Neue

November 1959

103

There they teach and play only contemporary, in the real sense, works ~ music of Boulez, Berio, Messiaen, etc., ~ Sienna is passée, and not of too much interest to composers[34] ~

Gazzelloni's views on Petrassi and Dallapiccolo are very interesting ~ he praises Petrassi highly, for Petrassi is writing in tune with the times ~ Dallapiccolo has managed to stay behind, and has not incorporated any new techniques into his work, I am told ~ Naturally, this is contrary to what I have, or had, heard in America ~ But Petrassi has embarked evidently into 'new twelve-tone' or serial writing in the past few years, and has his ears open to new sounds etc. I pass along these views to you as I think they might interest you ~

Maestro Gazzelloni is touring in America next spring, Boston, Philadelphia, etc., probably playing music of Boulez and the younger generation on his famous Gold Flute, (a very beautiful instrument, by the way) [~]

Yesterday, I spent the afternoon examining scores and chatting with this young American composer who I mentioned in an earlier letter ~ a very pleasant afternoon ~ He looked at my music and put forth some interesting views, and I looked at his scores which I couldn't make too much sense out of without the aid of a piano, (and possibly with the aid of a piano)....

... I am getting some crazy ideas for a chamber orchestra project which I would like your opinion on if possible ~ I can't decide if I treat a work in almost a concerto grosso manner, i.e., featuring not necessarily soloists, but a string quartet and woodwind group, who state the ideas for the complete work, whether this idea would demand a kind of treatment too large or heavy for chamber

---

Musik Darmstadt" [Vacation Courses of International New Music in Darmstadt]. It featured lectures by composers, performers, and theorists about contemporary music as well as concerts of music by composers representing trends that originated in the serialism of the "second Viennese school," especially Webern and Schoenberg. In the early years, composers such as Karlheinz Stockhausen, Pierre Boulez, Luigi Nono, Bruno Maderna, Luciano Berio, Earle Brown, John Cage, Aldo Clementi, Franco Donatoni, Niccolò Castiglioni, Franco Evangelisti, Karel Goeyvaerts, Mauricio Kagel, and Gottfried Michael Koenig played important roles in the Darmstadt festival.

34 She may be referring to the Accademia Musicale Chigiana, a music institute in Siena, Italy. It was founded in 1932 as an international centre for advanced musical studies, including composition, and held concerts in the summer under the title of "Estate Musicale Chigiana."

104 Between Composers

orchestra consisting of one each of piccolo, flute, clt., Eng. hn., bassoon, bass clt, trpt., trb. (bass), harp ~ plus 2 horns, perc. and stgs ~ Perhaps I may decide before I receive your reply, but may I have your views?...

... I spoke of a doctor and his wife who Eric and I met in London in a pub, in an earlier letter ~ This doctor arrived in Rome Friday for combination business and pleasure ~ They invited me to spend Christmas at the Hague, which is very pleasant ~ I am afraid of that season very much, and if you are not able to come here, or Eric is not able to get away, I may accept their kind invitation ~ I really don't wish to move now for I am getting in a habit or schedule of work ~ but I don't know if I could be here alone at Xmas ~ which at this time appears to be the picture ~ God, so much bloody courage is needed when one is sentimental ~

I love you muchly ~ please write as always
Normie

NB to HS
Monday, November 16th, 1959
My dearest Harry,

Your very warm encouraging letter arrived this morning which made me very happy ~ reasons beyond explanation ~ All I can say [is] that it affects me very deeply, probably because of my own insecurity and loneliness....

... Today is a very sad day for me ~ while walking along the street I see couples, and a single thing like a hand on someone's arm makes me feel very tearful ... Oh darling, I do miss you so much ~ and do so need you ~ I try not to think of you, and home, and my friends and Canada too much, but once in a while just some simple gesture seems to break me up inside ~ 'Some subtle touch will break me ~ - etc'[35] you remember ~ I find myself quoting to myself these words and hearing the music so often in my mind and feelings ~ The 'Dark Songs' are so personal to me, my love ~ I can't tell you ~ but perhaps you know ~

This morning my new friend (and <u>please</u> don't be jealous) dropped in to pick up one of his scores ~ His name, by the way, is

35 This fragment is from the *Five Songs for Dark Voice*, beginning with the fifth song: "How can I hold within me all that is? /Some shape, some subtle touch will break me, / Some joy explode me in a rain of stars / To fall in ashes on this city."

November 1959

Peter Chrisòfides[36] ~ We inevitably got into more conversations on composition, and he has some very fine criticisms of my work and suggestions for further problems, compositionally, of mine ~ I am getting to appreciate these visits, for he is a rather intelligent boy and very 'simpatico' ~ We talked steadily for three hours during which time he mentioned a composer with Theodore Presser in Philadelphia by the name of George Rokberg (?) ~ Isn't he a friend of yours from Paris days? ~ I told Peter that you knew (I think) this man, and he was going to write George as well to find out ~ [37]

I have a feeling that this beautiful spot of mine will turn out to be the hangout for foreign musicians ~ It is central and comfortable ~ but I must watch here to avoid getting too involved in social life, for it seems to be very easy ~ But fellow composers and performers are necessary to talk to....

... So happy to hear that Bream likes your Sonata ~ Is it possible that you can send me a copy of your String Quartet as well? Bream comes here in January and I will try to meet him ~ Yes, concerts without you are also very difficult ~

I hope I have today found a piano which will arrive tomorrow ~ I have had so much trouble here finding a small instrument, it isn't even any longer humorous ~ I want to work and must, so if this floor holds the bloody instrument, and if I can get it up the stairs, va bene (OK) It has been very frustrating dealing with these Italian people who promise everything today! and nothing happens....

36 No information about Peter Chrisòfides could be found. Beecroft recalls meeting him when she went to check out the Academy of Santa Cecilia. She lost touch with him eventually. (Norma Beecroft, email 29 January 2021.)

37 This refers to George Rochberg (1918–2005), one of the major American composers of the twentieth century. He became interested in twelve-tone technique in the late 1940s and was one of its leading exponents in the US until the 1960s when, after the death of his son in 1964, he gradually abandoned this approach in favour of an eclectic style, often incorporating traditional tonal materials and stylistic references. He and Somers had met at a student composer symposium at the Eastman School in 1948 and corresponded by letter for about a year after that. There are five letters from Rochberg to Somers in the Somers fonds at Library and Archives Canada, dated from June 1948 until April 1949. None of Somers's letters to Rochberg seem to have survived. Rochberg also corresponded extensively with Canadian composer Istvan Anhalt over a period of years. This correspondence has been published as *Eagle Minds: Selected Correspondence of Istvan Anhalt and George Rochberg, 1961–2005*, ed. Alan Gillmor (Waterloo: Wilfrid Laurier University Press, 2007).

106 Between Composers

... I will take your good advice and try to work out a budget ~ it is rather difficult for me to live that way, but I would like to stay for a while ~ therefore a necessity ~

I must practice ye olde flauto now, so away with me ~

'Til later, my sweet!...

Tuesday AM ~ 10:00 AM

... I was sitting here in the window eating an orange this AM when out of the blue appeared some character on the roof ~ Who he is and what he is doing and how he got there is beyond my comprehension ~ but he has papers ~ either he is looking for an artist's view or he is a builder or architect ~ But one would expect some privacy on the sixth floor, you would think!

A day's work awaits me darling, so I will away again ~ So marvellous to love you and be loved by you ~ I miss you terribly ~

      Much much love

      Normie

HS to NB
Wed. Nov. 19/59[38]
Darling Norma:
Hartford was a good tonic for me. Extremely hospitable people with a terrific music school and a volatile president who infects all with his drive and enthusiasm. He says "These kids – I pound music in them 'till it comes out their ears – they play music morning, noon, night – they play every kind of music possible whether they like it or not – it doesn't matter a damn whether they 'like' it or not – they are here to become musicians and by God we'll make them musicians." And he certainly does. What an orchestra! A young girl did a beautiful job on John's flute divertimento! Can you imagine? All new and difficult stuff played to equal any professional group.

Before I forget, Tom Poucer (Tanglewood – he and Lombardo are buddies) wanted to make sure I sent his regards to you.[39] Had a

---

38 The date here is incorrect. Wednesday was 18 November, and the envelope is postmarked the 18th.

39 Tom "Poucer" was actually Thomas Putsché (1929–1983), an American composer who had had a piece performed at Tanglewood in the summer of 1958 on the same program as Beecroft's's Study for Woodwinds and Brass. His opera *Of the Cat and the Moon*, based on a play by W.B. Yeats, can be found on a CRI recording that includes

November 1959

chat with him during an evening when a few of the composers got together.

Ed Fuller, a young composer, played a tape of some 12 tone music of his for recorders.[40] It was excellent –

Had a chat with Francetti, an Italian composer who teaches there.[41] His father was an important musician in Italy. Francetti's comments on the direction of Italian music and on Petrassi were unusual and, needless to say, interesting. I won't reveal them as I want to hear what your reactions will be first.

In short there were a large number of composers, teachers, musicians – all sorts of stimulating conversations and exchange of ideas – excellent performances – a good deal of dull music from Canada – speeches – and of course when I'm on stage I can't resist hamming it up. (In front of a 'full house' audience – students, faculty, public – I was asked to comment on the 'respectability' of the composer. I replied by saying 'I really didn't know because I was drunk most of the time anyway.' The students loved it.)....[42]

R. Murray Schafer's *Requiems for the Party Girl.* "Lombardo" refers to American composer Robert Lombardo (b. 1932) who was a graduate of the Hartt College of Music and had studied with both Aaron Copland and Petrassi at Tanglewood in 1956. He was a prolific composer of opera, orchestra, chamber music, solo instrumental and choral music, and electronic music. He was at Tanglewood again in 1958 when Beecroft was there to hear the premiere of his Woodwind Quintet.

40 No information on Ed Fuller could be found.

41 Arnold Franchetti (1911–1993) [https://www.windrep.org/Arnold_Franchetti] was an Italian-born composer and the son of the well-known opera composer Alberto Franchetti. Before immigrating to the United States in 1947, he had had an interesting background, to say the least, studying with Richard Strauss in Munich before the war, and later working with the Italian resistance. He taught composition at the Hartt College of Music from 1948 until his retirement in 1979 and had an active career as a composer, writing orchestral, symphonic, and chamber music for solo instruments, receiving recognition and support from such organizations as the Guggenheim Foundation and the National Endowment for the Arts.

42 Yet, this differs considerably from the remarks made by Somers as reported in a *Globe and Mail* article about the gathering at Hartt College. According to this report, when asked to comment on "the respectability given composers by government grants," Somers replied that he was left "quite speechless" by such a question. He was quoted as saying "I'm not that respectable. This is the first time I've had a tie on in weeks, and I certainly do not look forward to being respectable." He is also reported to have said that the Canada Council was "very willing to take chances" on the work of young composers and that if a composer given a grant turns out "hack music then you know he is no good" but if he produces a masterpiece the grant has helped all art. Apparently all five Canadian composers present for the events at Hartt College – John Weinzweig,

... There is a tremendous amount of compositional activity and I feel their composers will one day, if not already, lead instead of follow. For the first time influences can come from American composers to younger composers. They have a tough struggle but will come out ahead. The level of technical competence and creative imagination is high. (Among the serious people.) As everywhere, Webern exerts a strong influence whereas ten years ago it was Bartok and Hindemith. We had some good exchanges about whether 12 tone is a 'leveler' or not. In the electronic field it is a fact that Americans were working at it before Europe but didn't receive the publicity.

My mind is on the track again as a result, — evaluating my work 'till now, accepting, rejecting etc. Most stimulating....

... It now looks like I'll be doing music for an 'art' film of Christopher Chapman.[43] What with my commissions I'm as busy as hell but I love it.

My chances for a fellowship are pretty good.

Normie, it's so marvellous to feel like I haven't felt in ten years! — to have no regrets, to not be weighed down by 'past" at every turn, to live and write with joy and strength again!! I've got the gloom off my back. Not that I can't be depressed anymore, (I'm slightly manic-depressive anyway) but when I take hold of the affirmative (You can sing it) I don't louse it up....

... As for me getting over to Rome it is obviously impossible 1) because of money 2) because of so much work to do. If I had had a thousand bucks you would have seen me weeks ago, that's what I meant.

I intend to get a divorce as soon as possible, this would take place regardless.

Jean-Papineau Couture, John Beckwith, Murray Adaskin, and Somers – spoke up in favour of government support of the arts. ("Composers Defend Ottawa Aid," *Globe and Mail*, 16 November 1959.)

43 Christopher Chapman (1927–2015), the Toronto-born filmmaker, had by this time already achieved major recognition for his first film, *The Seasons*, which won the Canadian Film of the Year award at the Canadian Film Awards in 1954. He is best remembered for his highly acclaimed and influential film about Ontario, *A Place to Stand* (1967), which used split-screen techniques. *Saguenay*, the film for which Somers was to compose the music, was commissioned by Alcan and depicted the use of the Saguenay River to generate electricity to manufacture aluminum.

November 1959

... Talked with Olnick about electronic music.[44] The laboratory should be ready in a year. You hit it on the head – it is only when these gadgets are put to a human artistic use that they become valid. Harvey concurs. In other words they still demand a composer and not an electrician. It's the same old problem.

Normie – listen carefully. If this fellowship comes through I could be over in Europe in June.[45] If you still felt you wanted a life with me and to marry me then we would come together....

... Now, if you should have to return before then (which I must confess selfishly I would love), then we would go over to France together. By that time I hope to have some extra money so there would be no worry. When a divorce could be made absolute then we could marry.

The divorce is an expense that would be difficult to meet now, but I'm investigating it.

So you work and study and don't be afraid of me in any way. Whatever truth you discover about yourself tell me, even if it should ever mean a change of heart of mind or heart. I cannot tell you enough that I love you completely, Normie, and doing so only want what is in your best interest, even if that would exclude me. My love for you does not demand qualification, it is all embracing.

Good night, dear heart ...

Harry

---

44 Harvey Olnick (1917–2003) completed an MA in musicology at Columbia in 1948 and began teaching this discipline at the University of Toronto in 1954, the first such appointment in Canada. Besides building up the music library at the university, Olnick was also instrumental in establishing the Electronic Music Studio (EMS) there, beginning officially in May 1959, only the second studio of its kind in North America. The impetus for this came from Arnold Walter, then director of the Faculty of Music. Hugh Le Caine of the National Research Council of Canada was responsible for developing the analogue equipment used in the early years, including an oscillator bank (an array of 108 oscillators that could be controlled by touch-sensitive keyboards), a multi-track recorder, and, most significantly, the "Sackbut," developed in the 1940s and now considered the first synthesizer.

45 "Fellowship" probably refers to the recently formed Canada Council's Senior Arts Fellowships, which were available to artists who wished to spend time out of the country for study and/or creative work.

NB to HS
November 18th, 1959
My love,

The time goes by, on and on ~ Your letter arrived this morning and you talked of the snow ~ Oh, how sad I feel ~ Here it is grey, grey overcast sky and I believe colder weather is moving in, as a cold spell has hit Europe ~ One of the little flower stands up the street was selling holly yesterday ~ what a sentimental creature I am, but I really am so afraid of that bloody season called Christmas ~ for the past years I have been almost paralysed emotionally....

... I miss you terribly, my sweet, and thank you for your frequent letters ~ I feel when I write that I am communicating with you somewhat, but there are times when I would die for your personal touch....

... Yesterday, for the first time, I recommenced work on Michael's songs ~ and then my piano arrived and I continued ~ Slowly I am getting into a schedule of work, but it requires great discipline, for especially in Rome, it is not easy to work hard ~ this is the whole atmosphere here which is marvellous for one's nervous system but you don't get much accomplished ~ Nevertheless, it felt rather good to work again and I was rather pleased with myself at the end of the day ~

Later ~ 2 AM.

My love ~ I said it was difficult to work here ~ It is! Let me explain how a day goes by, as I want to tell you of a strange but rather charming evening I have just returned from ~

I arose this AM about 9:30 ~ About 11:00 I started to practice the flute ~ at 12:00 I studied Italian for an hour ~ at 1:00 I had lunch ~ at 1:30 I worked at my songs for an hour ~ and at 2:30 I left for Italian lesson #2 which lasted an 1 1/2 hrs. I did then a bit of shopping and returned here about 5:45 ~ I was so depressed and tired I slept till 7:30 after which I made my dinner ~

My friend the Dr. from the Canadian Embassy called, and I asked him to ask some other friends of his who he was with at that time, to introduce me to some musician they (the other friends) had previously mentioned who could tell me about Santa Cecilia and the courses there.[46] Sounds all very complicated, but the last couple of

---

46 The doctor's name was Paul Chevalier, as noted in chapter 2.

days I have been a little troubled by Petrassi's vagueness (and really, not my lack of Italian) in stating the kind of program I would have, etc. etc. so I thought I would try to seek out some inner information about the set-up at the Academy ~ To shorten the story, I was told that I should go up to this house tonight and meet a man by the name of Rosenfeldt and some other people [47]~ who could help me probably ~

Now, normally, one just doesn't go trotting off to some house unannounced and uninvited, but here I do strange things ~ So I went! Well, I walked into this rather lovely apartment and I could hear a piano quartet playing Mozart behind a closed door, which I was immediately ushered through by the maid ~

During the course of the evening was played by this group of people the Trout Quintet, Schumann Quintet, etc., rather badly but with great enthusiasm ~ There were in total about a dozen people there, an American girl cellist and organist here in Rome studying old music, a New Zealand violist, a Czech violinist, and Italian cellist with a wig that just sits on the top of his head and a baby face, about 50 or 60, a young Italian composer whose manner and dreamy expression and whose music is right out of Debussy, an Armenian violinist, painter and religious student, plus 3 or 4 audience, plus Rosenfeldt at the piano ~ Quite a conglomeration of people, I would say ~

Rosenfeldt, I was told later, is a multi-millionaire who loves to make music (one of Franz Lehar's descendants) and collects amateur instrumentalists in his home once a week to play together (and students) Rather charming, don't you think? An ex-American living in Rome, a man in his 50's, rather energetic and extremely helpful to young students, even financially, I am told ~ His wife has the same attitude ~ Now don't you think that was a worthwhile introduction ~ I have been asked to join this group as their flautist, if you can imagine, and at the moment I think it might be rather good fun and experience to play in an ensemble ~ Again it was a pleasure to meet more students ~ so gradually one gets around ~

AM.

It was three when I stopped writing last night and I am so tired this AM. ~ However, cheerfully wakened up by another letter from you....

47 No information about Rosenfeldt could be found. Beecroft did not remember anything more about him than what she described in the letter.

... I must begin another day of trying to work and hope for success ~ At least the sun is shining today ~

I love you very much ~ and miss you terribly.

Love

Normie

HS to NB
Thursday, Nov. 20, 1959
Beloved Normie:

Today I saw the rough version of Christopher Chapman's film and am still elated. It is supposedly an industrial film for the great aluminium company of Canada but is really a beautiful film telling its story with the power and subtlety of Christopher's camera.

The opening presents the man-made result – six dams in Canada's Quebec north which furnish the power for the manufacture of aluminium. He opens with camera moving down a great slab of rock to the river to the base of the dam and up to survey an eerie scene of sunset then to loading of bauxite, or I should say unloading, from great boats – from this activity the picture moves upriver into fantastic country of great hills, rivers, lakes wild completely untamed into winter over a vast frozen lake into a forest.

Snow melts into the first drops of water – drops into pools, off rocks – lovely mists of spring – into rivers – lakes – rapids – torrents spilling through this breathtaking wilderness accumulating, raging – to be suddenly held by man's concrete fists to become damned up – camera captures a whirlpool.

Down, round, round into enormous generator wheels starting to move – accelerate – into pipes – into cables – into electric carried across the vast spaces by endless lengths of hydro-electric wires – the plan – box cars — elements transform themselves — solids to molten silver liquid — to solid forms – to aluminium – loaded onto freighters – camera returns upriver to this powerful brooding land – fini

Canada is the land not the cities – God how I love it, to see it, I want one day for us to travel this whole continent to absorb it. It is our country, our environment –

Forgive me, I'll sound like those documentary orators, but Normie, it is in my blood and I want some day that some of my music will speak for the strength, wildness, ruggedness, beauty of

November 1959　　　　　113

what I feel about this country outside the cities. Land of rocks lakes forest trees, sky.[48]

I love Europe, its cities, its being so civilized in its way of living. (Though not in killing.) I love good wine, conversation, the arts, the subtle beauty of its cities and countryside, but I love this uncivilized wilderness more.

Early next week I go to Ottawa to confer with Crawley films, who will handle it, and the company representatives. They wanted me after hearing some of my music.

Not until I saw Christopher's film did I agree to do it and now I'm excited by the prospect. It will mean high pressure because the deadline is early next year....

... Your letter of 15th – last Sunday –

'L'Histoire du Soldat' – both Norm and I saw the production of it a few years ago (before I knew you). A wonderful production with Marcel Marceau et company.[49] It would be difficult to surpass that presentation I would think but perhaps.

By the way, Lou Applebaum is trying to organize a congress of all the leading composers of the world at Stratford next summer.[50]

---

48 Somers is describing the landscape of northern Ontario, which he had experienced on many occasions since childhood. In 1948, in his most striking early composition, *North Country*, for string orchestra, commissioned for CBC Radio's "Wednesday Night," he tried to capture some of the qualities of this landscape in his music, resulting in a remarkably original work in the context of that period. He also attempted to depict certain qualities of the Canadian landscape in the earlier *Three Sketches for Orchestra* (1946). Certain aspects of the music of *North Country* are present in his works of the 1950s and beyond, forming an important part of his mature style.

49 Stravinsky's *L'Histoire du soldat* (1918) had been performed at the 1955 Stratford Festival, with the great French mime artist Marcel Marceau (1923–2007) playing the role of the devil and Canadian actor Douglas Campbell the soldier. It is likely that this is the production Somers had seen, since he had not yet begun his relationship with Beecroft.

50 Louis Applebaum (1918–2000) was one of the most important figures in the arts in Canada in the second half of the twentieth century. An accomplished film composer, he was the first music director of the Stratford Festival and in 1955 established the Stratford Music Festival. He continued to write music for theatrical productions until near the end of his life. His fanfares, written for the first year of the Festival (1953) have been played before every performance at Stratford's main stage since that first season. He was executive director of the Ontario Arts Council from 1971 to 1980 and in 1982

There would be talks, discussions, performances. Just how he intends to bring this off I don't know.

Gazzelini's views conflict with Francetti. Basically Francetti feels that Italian composers have, for the first time in their history, taken on, holus bolus, a technic and approach that is foreign and alien to their own historical evolution and natural temperament ...

... As you know, my views on adopting technics and approaches simply because they are the latest fashion, are strong. One must be conversant with all that's taking place in one's own time, with the adventures and experiments, but I wish to become a composer not a fad or fetish.

The individuality <u>must</u> come from within, it cannot really come from without. It takes years of work, of internal struggle, of searching. I am as excited as anyone by any new discovery or approach, but I don't automatically assume that it makes obsolete other ones, nor does it become any more valid simply because it's the latest.

I'm essentially a romantic in music – I wish to shape and put into an artistic form those things felt as a human being. Complexity is <u>only</u> complexity to me if it ain't got that intangible 'something to say.' A composition can never justify itself by an explanation of its parts. That is always <u>only</u> an explanation of its parts. That's all. The search for new or altered technics must come from an inner necessity to find the tools to speak for oneself, but it requires a hell of a lot of writing to reach that kind of maturity, and one must be aware of it.

I enjoy abstract shapes, design, proportions, fragmenting, organizing of pitch, duration and dynamic, in itself, for it is a <u>part</u> of the whole and must be disciplined in its organization (even disorganization) until finally one is free....

... If, for your projected 'concerto grosso' you use a large group of instruments as your 'soloists,' naturally, being almost as large as the 'orchestra,' it will only appear as another section <u>of</u> the orchestra. In effect you would have a little chamber orchestra and a slightly larger one. A concerto grosso concept for small chamber orchestra and large orchestra would be an interesting idea, but your original idea would be a sort of sectional orchestra writing. In the historical

---

he co-authored the Applebaum-Hébert Report with Jacques Hébert, the first review of Canadian cultural institutions and federal cultural policy since 1951. The International Conference of Composers did actually materialize at Stratford in the summer of 1960, thanks to Applebaum's organizational skill and far-ranging vision.

context the solo body, or group, set itself apart to display, state, answer, continue material and only occasionally join a tutti....

... Your mother will be disappointed not seeing you, but have no worry because all of us who love you want you only happy and well above all else.

The fever on my lips burns for your mouth –
　　　　All my love —
　　　　　　Harry
(I wonder if all my letters are reaching you?)

NB TO HS
November 22nd, 1959
My darling Harry,

I love you more than anything or anyone in the whole world ~ I miss you terribly ~ I wanted to write you to tell you this ~ this alone really ~ but I notice there would much paper empty if I didn't continue, so I will tell you the events of my life the past few days, if I am able to recall ~

You remember the Rosenfeldt 'soiree' that I mentioned and an Iraqi chap called Aram who I met there[51]~ Well this extremely talkative fellow is arranging to find out details about the Santa Cecilia course in composition from his solfeggio maestro for me....

... Although I am finding Michael's songs hard to get into again, I am hot on an idea for this chamber orchestra project (for Petrassi) ~ I do so want to talk to you about it but it is difficult to write ~ Suffice it to say that I am attempting a work with very strict organization ~ a one movement affair based solely on one idea ~ a five note series ~ I am evolving my harmony from so, and line, and transformations ~ I am attempting to work on a strict dynamic basis alla Boulez, etc, still employing my concerto grosso idea ~ All very exciting for me and very new ~ I am trying, ~~as usual~~, to try to work in a new technique, and with much discipline I hope to learn and understand

---

51 "Aram" was Aram Baboukian, a violin student from Iraq. Beecroft writes that "Aram became a valuable friend to me during my three years in Europe, and housed my brother Eric when he visited me in Rome. He was indeed an Iraqi, and had all the Eastern habits, including eating with one's fingers...[I] suspect he was not a very good violinist, but he was loyal as a friend, and obliging to everyone he met, inviting them to his flat in central Rome (near the Trevi Fountain) for food or drink or whatever. Toward the end of my stay, he married an Italian girl, and returned with her to Iraq." (Norma Beecroft, email to the editor, 31 January 2021).

much more which will facilitate what writing technique I already have ~ I know this will not convey too much meaning to you, but the whole idea is that I am excited ~ all stimulated by a walk in the Villa Borghese this afternoon to the Borghese Museum, and being constantly fascinated by these magnificent umbrella pine trees and golden colour of the late afternoon sun all the way, plus getting very angry at a series of articles on Canada in the Saturday Review saying that a) Canada is senza personality and without any distinctive culture, b) that Canada is intimidated by the U.S., c) that Canada has no angry young men, no jazz ~ etc. etc, the issue which included an 'article' on music by that has-been, Sir Ernest ~ etc.[52] Truly, I get so bloody angry once in a while, even though a little reason will tell me that maybe a portion of what these idiots write has a grain of truth in it ~ Oh well ~

I guess I am finding my personality darling ~ I get angry when I am, which upsets me very much ~ I speak my mind on just about any subject, ~ I am everyone's best friend, including the Italians who call me 'simpatica'... I am enjoying a very select group of people here (very few still) who enjoy me in turn and regard me as a good conversationalist and friend ~ Terribly good for one's ego....

Monday AM ~
... You mentioned America as a future leader in music ~ Well darling, from what I observe here, America is definitely now. In any

---

52 These articles appeared in the 24 October 1959 issue of the *Saturday Review*. Figures such as Frank Underhill, Granville Hicks, Robert Fulford, Herbert Whittaker, and that "has-been" (in Beecroft's words), Sir Ernest MacMillan, contributed articles dealing with general questions of Canadian identity, the role of the CBC in this respect, and in the various arts, literature, art, theatre, and music in particular. It was possibly comments such as the following, by Frank Underhill (whose essay was entitled "A Country in Search of an Image") that angered Beecroft: "Our young people, like those in the United States and Britain, seem to be chiefly security-conscious, non-political, other-directed, not much interested in literature or the arts. In these very days when rockets from the earth circle the moon they seem to be mainly intent on cultivating their local gardens. Canada hasn't even a minority of beatniks or angry young men. We are becoming more and more a homogenized, middle-class society." None of the articles claim that Canada has no jazz. Sir Ernest MacMillan's article is a wide-ranging account of the current state of musical activity in the country, including performance and education and creative achievements (a number of composers of John Weinzweig's generation are mentioned, including Somers's two recent ballets commissioned by the National Ballet).

November 1959 117

case, miles ahead of Italy in spite of the electronic school, but you recall the Atlantic monthly article on Italy[53] ~???

I said, and you have said, that I am growing up fast ~ well, it seems to be so ~ I really had no idea what I was capable of and I find my self-confidence being quickly restored ~ When you see me again, you will probably find a much stronger personality, much more secure in herself ~ How would you feel about such a change, my love? I remember Tanglewood so clearly ~

My God, you sound busy ~ forgive my ignorance but who is Christopher Chapman (?) ~ an artist? ~ The name Chapman rings a bell....

... Darling, a serious question! You realize probably now as I am beginning to realize that I <u>want</u> to write music ~ really ~ Although I am terribly excited about the idea of studying with you, do you feel we can exist together both writing music? Please tell me how you think on this subject, for although I realize ideally that it is a woman who should sacrifice her 'career'~ and that's me ~ at this moment, I can't contemplate the idea of giving up trying to write ~ every day the desire is stronger ~ the need is stronger ~ I am here in Rome to find out and I find that yes, this is what I want to do ~ How honestly do you feel, for I am worried a little ~

What a marvellous thought to have you here in June ~ Will you consider coming to this July music school in Germany with me[54] ~ (I mentioned it earlier) ~ for I should like to study with Gazzelloni there (contemporary techniques, for flute) as well as meet some of these world renowned composers ~ I believe that it is more of a meeting place for 'modern' composers and instrumentalists than a school ~ and I will try to find some more information on it from Gazzelloni ~

Darling, I too have written to the Canada Council for application forms which should arrive any day ~ should I ask assistance to help me last here till the end of June and to go to Darmstadt in July, or ask assistance to study in France next year ~? Please advise me on this, for you are involved very much....

... I wish you were here so much ~ I can't begin to tell you everything in one letter ~ My new project is very difficult, trying to write

---

53 She may be referring to an article that had appeared in *The Atlantic* nearly a year earlier: Massino Mila, "The Music Situation in Italy: The Break-Through into Contemporary Style," *The Atlantic* (December 1958). Massino Mila (1910–1988) was a prominent musicologist and critic.

54 A reference to Darmstadt. See n. 33.

a composition on five notes, but I will! I shall also have to learn the art of throwing away ~

All my love, dearest one

Normie ~

HS to NB

Saturday, Nov 22/59 [21 November]

My darling Normie:

I never thought a letter box could mean quite so much to me. Each day I very politely implore the box to give up a letter to me from you. Some days it is most disagreeable, refusing to co-operate and keeps its big empty mouth empty, or worse, teases me with bills and circulars. But today it was in a good mood and gave me your Monday-Tuesday letter. I said thank you and shut its mouth. It coughed and looked glum again but I was too happy to care.

Yes, dearest, I know how personal the dark Songs are to you. The words keep echoing in my mind. I remember our wonderful holiday at Snug Harbour where I finished and copied them out for performance.[55] How we hated and loved each other!!...

... Yes, George Rochberg is my friend, or was, (haven't seen him for a long time) but from a symposium of music schools held in Rochester in 1948 for the presentation of student composers' works, not Paris. His name keeps cropping up. Ed Diemente, a composer I met at Hartford, knows George well.[56] They presented a joint concert in New York, recently, of their works.

Evidently George's reputation as a composer is growing. He specializes in 12 tone technic and writes on the subject.[57] Ed told me

55 "Snug Harbour" may refer to the "Snug Harbour Resort" on Desert Lake, just north of Kingston, Ontario, but Norma Beecroft did not remember ever going there. She remembered that she and Somers didn't travel far from Toronto, since he was always working toward a deadline (and they were also short of money). The letter, however, indicates that he took work with him when on holiday. (Norma Beecroft, email to the editor, 9 August 2021.)

56 Edward Diemente (1923–2019) was a composer and organist who taught at the Hartt School for over forty years. He had been trained at the Eastman School as well. His output included orchestral, chamber, choral, and electronic works and was performed by groups such as The Hartford Symphony, the Boston Symphony Chamber Players, and the New York Brass Quintet.

57 Rochberg's main publication on the subject was *The Hexachord and its Relation to the Twelve-Tone Row* (Bryn Mawr: Presser, 1955).

November 1959

119

George has particular theories on the hexachord units within the full row, though I remember Ernst Krenek speaking of the same thing.[58] George also had a very good reputation as a teacher at Curtis. When I met him he was just beginning to get curious about Schoenberg. He worried that he was a late starter in composition, his service in the war taking a chunk out of his life – he was in his late twenties at that time. He was a guy I took to immediately sensing a great honesty and integrity in him.

My bloody guitar sonata is bugging me. I'm not satisfied with the 3rd movement so am writing another. The work is in my 'semi-diatonic-easy-to-listen-to-folk-like-at-times' idiom of the ballets. It's more difficult to produce than a 'set-technic' work. Of course there is the parallel struggle of trying to arrive at something 'guitaristic' without being 'cliché.'

Breem you would enjoy. Unpretentious thoroughly knowledgeable musician. Wonderful person, and, I believe, rapidly becoming a great artist, if not already one....

... I wish you would confine yourself to a workable medium so that you may solve straight composition problems. Small chamber works in which you set out to accomplish something pre-set and which would be more likely for you to hear....

... I quite often daydream of what you and I will do – taking walks, laughing, reading, studying, waking together.

I'm so happy to love you completely and to be loved by you! It's a gift I never thought I would have. Not until one gives can one love. My beloved Normie, to love without fear or suspicion, to trust, to

---

58 The Viennese-born composer Ernst Krenek (1900–1991), one of the major figures of European musical modernism, adopted Schoenberg's twelve-tone technique in the late 1920s. He moved to the United States in 1938 and taught at various American music institutions. In the summer of 1953, he taught a summer course at the Royal Conservatory of Music of Toronto. Among those who attended the course were Canadian composers Milton Barnes, Samuel Dolin, and Harry Freedman. It must have been on this visit that Somers heard Krenek speaking about twelve-tone procedures, such as the use of hexachords.

feel affirmation in love, to know warmth and beauty! I've been in such a torture chamber for so many years that I feel like a prisoner must feel when released from confinement....

———————

... Finished the new slow movement for guitar. Its derivation is the 'blues,' but very remotely. It is consistent with the style of this particular work, so much better. It's my hobby music, but nevertheless has my mark.

———————

Normie, it is only through seeming weakness we discover the measure of our strength. I want you to never doubt that you can depend on me. Actually what took place was one of the unique experiences of my life – a probing of myself of real repressions, which are difficult to examine, but the facing them freed me – elements that I had refused to recognize till now – the whole business of what it is about to love another and what it involves in the way of 'growing up' to defeat years of pain and misunderstanding – to let go of false pride and to see the essence of human relationship....

... I hold you to me. I see your face at the moment of pain and ecstasy and hear you exclaim, your body beating to a rhythm of total release. My heart, my beloved, my dearest one – I love you, I love you – take care of yourself for me who lives for you –

I kiss you, my darling –
Harry

HS to NB
Sunday morning. [22–23 November]
2 a.m. —
You wonder what I think of you! I think that when I saw you go on that boat I died.

Allright I'll tell you my reactions. Yes I died! You are the one woman in my life who has really loved me enough to leave me! You have given so much! I am sick, cynical, disbelieving! Normie I hate to the point of nausea. And it's too late. I know in my heart. But it's some satisfaction to you, surely.

Normie, I have no heart because it was destroyed!! Christ! Perhaps it was me that destroyed it! No matter (In the best manner of Victorian literature.) No matter no matter!! Leaves rotting!! Who cares. Vain vain egos displaying their intelligence. Oh baby! I could smash everything apart! Too late, too late, but I'll write about it! Something [*illegible*].

Ron Colliers wedding. Mr. and Mrs. Till and Marlene – and – and not <u>you</u> not <u>you</u>!! Not <u>you</u>!! Understand !! Will you!! Pierrot – Pierrotette

————

Sunday afternoon – I'm sitting here writing you to the tune of Gershwin's music on the radio. As you probably guessed my 2 am outburst was written whilst I was quite high.

Yes, the wedding – many people at the reception (Gershwin songs – embraceable you) many people asking after you.[59] O, I got so high! So lonely for you, such tension in me!! A number of pretty and absolutely dull young people! (now 'I Got Rhythm') What's the matter with young people? I believe I rather shouted this out more and more as the evening wore on. It was supposed to be a wedding not a funeral. (Of Thee I Sing.) – (Baby) Give me the great Slavic weddings!! It should be a joyous occasion! Oh well, I better not get off on that diatribe!

I [am] badly hung over. I do believe I drank more out of desperation than anything else. Marlene drove me out to the party in her new little Austin Healey Sprite,

(now – Summertime) She's a happy little person – loves her little car – loves Toronto – seems to love life in general[60] (There's a boat that's leavin now for New York). Ron Collier seemed happy. Had a brief chat with his new wife and I was pleasantly surprised to find her an intelligent girl who knows what she's doing and what she wants....

————

59 This section of the letter was written as a kind of counterpoint to the Gershwin songs he was hearing on the radio: "Embraceable you," "I Got Rhythm," "Of Thee I Sing," "Summertime," "There's a Boat Dat's Leavin' Soon for New York" (the latter from *Porgy and Bess*).

60 "Marlene" could not be identified.

... Well, it's Monday morning. A rather gloomy one indeed. Your Rome letter of the jazz concert and your reply to my outburst arrived.

Now I will try (sober) to tell you of my feelings, reactions, thoughts in relation to us. You are removed physically and I suspect by now emotionally, so it's safe.

First, I <u>can</u> read between the lines, my anger is more righteous than anything else. One way or another you've always spoken or communicated your feelings to me, something I've always admired about you no matter how I would be upset at the moment....

... Yes, committing myself is something I hesitate to do very easily for I am a committed person. When I commit myself it involves every part of me without reservations. This makes it so bloody difficult for me as I know that in so doing I make myself infinitely more vulnerable to profound hurt than most people ... Being such a person, knowing the measure of my ability to be hurt, I naturally shy away from involvement....

... Normie, it's a curious contradiction, but I felt that I knew my feelings towards you, but that you really didn't towards me. Of course this is why I regarded your trip as so important. By clarifying your feelings towards me you would clarify your feelings towards many things.

You have, in our time together, given me more real happiness than anyone I've ever known. It got so that I would rather have a 'battle' with you than a pleasant time with someone else. I'm afraid of happiness, as of many things. But I suppose, once again, that one of my greatest fears was that you really didn't know what you were, that you would get involved with me then quickly find out differently....

... I suddenly feel inwardly very tired. John Osborne is right – anger shows one cares.[61]

I've just about finished the guitar pieces which are to be called a Sonata because there are so many Suites in guitar literature. Then the Koussevitzky work and perhaps a commission from Pittsburgh

---

61 The play *Look Back in Anger* by John Osborne, first produced in London in 1956, introduced a type of realistic theatre in which anger and raw emotions are powerfully displayed, largely generated by class antagonisms between the main characters, Jimmy and Alison. The play was first performed in Canada at the Royal Alexandra Theatre in Toronto on 29 January 1958. The film version was released in Canada in November 1959. It is not known whether Somers had seen either version, but he seems to have interpreted the notion of "anger" in a very different manner than that implied by Osborne's play.

November 1959   123

for a wind ensemble. Yet right now I feel depressed. Cloudy sky. Russian thoughts. Emptiness.

Anyway, I hope Petrassi will prove interesting, he's bound to. Don't worry whether you are to be a composer or not, and <u>don't</u> worry how your decision, whatever, will appear in other people's eyes. One of the reasons you went to Rome was to give yourself a reasonable chance to find out. As far as I'm concerned there are no final answers anyway, there are only immediate needs. If this isn't the particular time of your life to compose, so be it. But whatever you do in earnest is never lost and always worthwhile....

... Indeed, what is freedom? But I think I understand Palinnurus.[62] 'To be free is to be lonely' should be qualified. No doubt it means to be free <u>from</u> – from those things which enslave most humans in bonds of materialism or common thinking etc. To think for oneself, to pursue that course which will isolate one from one's fellow men by virtue of it not being in agreement with them. Do you follow me? Then 'but the fear of bondage is the apprehension of a real danger' makes sense, for we simply choose our form of bondage anyway, which could be what freedom is.

Individuality is always lonely, be it an idea or a person, for the herd has to move as a crowd. It accepts those who think or act as they do, a 'regular guy' and they are trapped in their conformity to graze in valleys where all the things to fill their bellies are but never to view the world from those lonely heights whose compensation is in the sight ...Of course, Palinnurus's statement would apply to women if then it means what I imply. However women don't have to say it, men always have to grapple and fight in their chains.

Normie I'm sorry that the four years we were together might be regarded as a waste to you because it was leading nowhere, which can only mean marriage or something similar to you. It is not such a long time, as you will one day realize. I know your emotional needs,

---

62 Somers was not referring here to the mythological helmsman of Aeneas's ship but to the pseudonym used by Cyril Connolly for his book *The Unquiet Grave*, as pointed out in chap. 2, n. 42. Here Somers quotes two fragments from Connolly's text, both in the same sentence: "The fear of loneliness can be overcome, for it springs from weakness; human beings are intended to be free, and to be free is to be lonely, but the fear of bondage is the apprehension of a real danger, and so I find it all the more pathetic to watch young men and beautiful girls taking refuge in marriage from an imaginary danger." He has taken Connolly's remarks out of context and applied them to far wider concerns of loneliness and freedom. (Connolly, *The Unquiet Grave*, 11.)

124   Between Composers

darling, and believe me I am sympathetic. I know your frustrations, your anxieties....

... know that I love you with a passion and love so outside the bounds of reason and control that I have to exhibit all my reason and control in order to function. At times I have endeavoured to act reasonably – well, now I'm rather exhausted. I must go. Sorry to upset you so much. I hope your work will go well. Don't worry about not writing, for I can easily understand. All the best Normie dear.

Love – all my love –
Harry

HS to NB
Nov. 24/59 [23 November]
Monday
My dearest love:

I'm glad to hear of your pleasant musical evening with the amateurs. Yes, it would do you good to read music with such a group.

You would probably find Toronto a bore after all your activities and new people you're meeting in those exotic surroundings!

Petrassi might not turn out so well, it would seem. Don't worry, we both knew that he was only the excuse, not the reason for going to Rome. A pupil of Franchetti's had studied with Petrassi but left after a short while because he found that Petrassi would either just grunt when he looked at his work, or say that this was wrong or that was not, and that was that – and this chap spoke the language. This is what Franchetti told me.

So anyway, you're in Rome, there is art, culture and interesting people and these are your true education.

I sense that it is an education for you. Rosenfeldt sounds like a wonderful introduction to the 'haute monde.' I also sense that your sadness or happiness is dependent on whether you're mixing with people or not, dearest, so you are wise to cultivate a circle of people.

If that sad, strenuous, never-ending struggle, which is called composition, should prove secondary to you, or not what you thought you wanted, you would be wise to acknowledge it and get the most out of your stay through music generally and the life and beauty of Rome.

Already the city is in your heart and I guarantee that it is there for life....

November 1959

125

... When I studied in San Francisco in 1948, I had to make a choice between piano or composition.[63] It was an enormous decision for me at that time, but events made me realize there could only be composition. It was a different struggle than yours is, but I know enough about it to be able to sympathize with you.

There can never be a final answer for you. At any time in your life activity, interest can rise or fall in composition. Your study and application is never lost.

Remember that.

"Steal some money for New Years and visit you![64] I'm working on a bank holdup now. Oh would I love to! but I'm so flat, baby!...

... Normie, my dearest, you are my love. I die for want of you.

Live, my girl, enjoy, find out, study – be happy and be at peace with my love for you – my heart goes out to you –

Harry

HS to NB
Monday evening, Nov 24/59 [23 November]
My dearest Normie:

Gently raining, and inside my thoughts are of you, close and warm. Reed sounds – oboe, then cello, muted viola.

It's a night to sit around, listen to some Ellington, a bit of jazz, some chamber music, a few drinks, your head on my shoulder. Just easy and close.

'Sometimes I feel like a motherless child' — a whole people speak.[65]

---

63 Somers had gone to San Francisco in June 1948 to study piano again with E. Robert Schmitz (1889–1949), a French-born pianist who had developed his own special technique of piano performance, and championed twentieth-century music. At a piano competition there in August he tied for third place, a result he found bitterly disappointing. As a result of this, he resolved to devote himself entirely to composition. This was his decision; nobody told him he had to make such a decision. It was clearly not the same kind of decision as Norma deciding whether she wanted to continue to study composition.

64 From Beecroft's letter of 18 November.

65 "Sometimes I Feel Like a Motherless Child" is an African American spiritual that originated during the era of slavery. It expresses the hopelessness a child who has been forcefully separated from his or her parents might feel but also the consolation offered by prayer ("Den I git down on my knees and pray, pray!"). It was frequently performed during the civil rights movement in the United States. Somers may have heard one of the recordings of the song by Paul Robeson.

Did I tell you that awhile back I went to a party, thinking I could get out of the blues? All I could do was wait for you to come through the doorway. I felt sad and lonely. At a point in the evening a Scotswoman sang the Skye Boat Song and some other Irish and Scotch songs unaccompanied.[66] When one is lonely they mean a great deal, but never so much as now.

Right now I'm copying out the guitar sonata on transparents.[67] Tomorrow I'm driving up to Ottawa with Christopher Chapman for the film discussions. It should be pleasant to drive into the countryside.

―――――

Whew! Just finished copying my stuff, and that after a day of regular copying.

A variety of music over the radio while I work – now 'West Side Story' – rather superficial but likely effective theatre. Previously music from 'Jazz Export U.S.A' a rather good jazz score – Purcell's 'Fairy Queen' music, some contemporary Hungarian composer much influenced by Bartok with touches of Stravinsky and un morceau of Schoenberg, he's head of some conservatory in Switzerland, etc.,[68] with a talk on the 'American novel' in between.

By the way, Harvey Hart's production of The Crucible was a striking success in every way. It was present on T.V. about a month ago.[69] I must write him. University Alumnae presents 'Endgame'

66 "The Skye Boat Song" is a late-nineteenth-century Scottish song relating the escape of Bonnie Prince Charlie to the Isle of Skye after his defeat at the Battle of Culloden in 1746. The air had been collected by Anne Campbell MacLeod in the 1870s.

67 In those years, composers generally copied their scores by hand on transparent "onion-skin" paper in black India ink. These "transparencies" were then subjected to the "Ozalid process," in which positive images were printed on chemically treated paper through exposure to ultraviolet light. This technology was widely used at the time for making technical drawings and architectural plans. Multiple copies of composers' scores could then be reproduced from a set of transparencies.

68 This composer may have been Sándor Veress (1907–1992) who studied with both Zoltán Kodály and Béla Bartók. He left Hungary in 1949 and spent the remainder of his life in Switzerland, teaching at the Conservatory of Music in Bern.

69 This CBC Television broadcast of Arthur Miller's play The Crucible was a specially condensed version (seventy-seven minutes) prepared by Mavor Moore. It was broadcast on 27 October and starred some of the leading actors in Canada, including Douglas Campbell, Douglas Raine, and John Drainie. The production was directed by Harvey

November 1959

of Beckett's next month with Uriel Luft, (remember 'best actor' of D.D.F) in the leading role.[70] Must go.

Saw a performance of O'Neil's 'Ice Man Cometh' with a striking performance by the lead actor – an all-Canadian company.[71]

Theatre and painting seem very active now. Many small acting ventures and great deal of gallery activity. Had an interesting chat with Graham Coughtry some time ago.[72] He had some curious remarks to make concerning Jack Nichols work and what he feels to be a lack of development.[73] I just ask and listen. Graham is constantly evolving. He devotes himself entirely to painting now having quit C.B.C.

The Bach Choir under George Little is doing Chorale & Fugue in Montreal this Friday.[74] Sometime this season, probably Spring, the Montreal String Quartet will give a performance of the 3rd quartet

---

Hart (1928–1989), a prominent Canadian television director and a theatre and film producer.

70 This production of *Endgame*, directed by the *Globe and Mail*'s drama critic Herbert Whittaker, was put on by the University Alumnae Dramatic Club at the Coach House Theatre on Bedford Road for ten days in the first part of December. The part of Hamm was played by the German-born actor Uriel Luft (1933–2017) who had immigrated to Canada in 1957. He settled in Montreal, and began working for *Les Grands Ballets Canadiens*, later marrying the founder of the company, Ludmilla Chiriaeff. He had been named best actor in the 1959 Dominion Drama Festival (DDF).

71 Eugene O'Neill's *The Iceman Cometh*, directed by Basyar Hunter, was presented in mid-November by the Arts Theatre Club at the Toronto Central Library's theatre. The part of Hickey was played by George Sperdakos (1931–2000) – presumably this was the actor to whom Somers was referring. In his review of the production, Nathan Cohen, the *Toronto Daily Star*'s drama critic, wrote that what interest the production had was "due almost entirely to George Sperdakos." (*Toronto Daily Star*, 14 November 1959).

72 Graham Coughtry (1931–1999) had spent time in France and Spain in the mid-1950s and was highly influenced by the art of Pierre Bonnard and Alberto Giacometti. His mature work was almost exclusively concerned with the abstracted human figure. Until 1959 he worked as a graphic designer for CBC Television in Toronto. He was probably encouraged to work freelance when his canvas "Night Interior" was accepted for the Second Biennial of Canadian Art in 1957. Later, Coughtry became a well-known member of the "Isaacs Group" of artists, a group of Toronto post-war artists who exhibited with the dealer Av Isaacs.

73 See chap. 2, n. 27.

74 See chap. 3, n. 11. Although Somers refers to this choral work as Chorale and Fugue, its correct title is *Where Do We Stand, Oh Lord?* The piece was commissioned and first performed by the Hamilton Collegium Musicum in 1955 under the direction of Udo Kasemets. It was not possible to find the date of the Montreal performance referred to in this letter.

128   Between Composers

in Montreal.[75] What with the Harp Suite[76] being done there next month I'm being heard in that city!...

... This coming Saturday evening the Guitar Society is presenting Alirio Diaz, whom Eli says is a terrific guitarist.[77] I shall go and see....

... Tuesday noon –
The day is colder and more sombre. Leave shortly.

My Normie, we take ourselves wherever we go, but I also take you wherever I go. I have always felt much and said little, a serious mistake sometimes. Please take care, I love you so terribly much, my dearest. Words always seem so completely inadequate to express or convey deep feelings – I hold a timeless, endless loneliness, longing and love for you –
         Harry

NB to HS
November 24th, 1959,
Darling Harry ~

I am writing the craziest piece of music you have ever heard ~ I dare say that all my ideas are in the first three pages and I shall probably have to start all over again ~ It is a shapeless piece at the

---

75 There were three quartets in Montreal called "The Montreal String Quartet" during the twentieth century. The last one was active between 1955 and 1962. Its members were Hyman Bress and Mildred Goodman, violins; Otto Joachim, viola; and Walter Joachim, cello. During the 1959–60 season, the quartet presented two series of six concerts in the Ermitage, sponsored by the Canada Council. These concerts included quartets by Claremont Pépin, Otto Joachim, Jean Papineau-Couture, and John Weinzweig but, evidently, not Somers's Third Quartet.

76 See chap. 3, n. 12. The date of this performance (if there was one) could not be found.

77 Eli Kassner was correct. The Venezuelan guitarist and composer Alirio Díaz (1923–2016) is considered one of the most prominent composer-guitarists South America has produced and one of the most important classical guitarists of the twentieth century. In the early 1950s, he studied with Andrés Segovia at the Accademia Musicale Chigiana in Siena and later developed a major concert and recording career. He also collected Venezuelan folk songs and arranged much of this repertoire for guitar.

November 1959   129

moment ~ a free (not by design) study in sonority and although I am having a ball ~ it probably is worthless ~[78]

I find myself in a very peculiar position now ~ not sure what it all means but will find out! For so long I have rejected new ideas for fear of falling into a trap ~ writing only for newness' sake ~ John and I never embarked on any Schoenberg or Webern either ~ Now I find I am not happy and cannot write out of past knowledge, (hence the difficulty with Michael's songs) that is out of past knowledge alone, am terribly curious about Boulez, Berio, etc., and am frustrated by lack of knowledge re developing my own radical ideas at the moment ~ I guess I will have to embark on serious score study which I hope can be supervised by Petrassi, and go right into the beginnings of twelve-tone ~ I don't know what has come over me, but I know I haven't lost my perspective on musical truths and validity, so I guess everything is OK ~ Quite an interesting feeling though ~ another stage in the development of NB.

25th – AM

This morning I called Petrassi, who was very friendly over the telephone, and I will see him tomorrow afternoon at 3:30 so I guess all will be straightened out ~ I am going to have to tell him what I have just written and see what he suggests ~

This afternoon I have another flute lesson and Italian lesson, and I am so bone-weary at the moment I don't know whether I'll be able to stand for an hour ~ The weather here is grey again....

... Last night my friend Peter brought some scores over and a book on a particular twelve-tone technique which he thought would help me ~ Three piano works and the 'row' book by George Rochberg who I asked you about[79] – Peter studied with him in Philadelphia, as well as Persichetti, Milhaud and Sessions ~ Rochberg evidently has some stature in the US as a composer and is a new editor of Theodore Presser in Phil. ~ I am dying to know if this is the same person you knew ~ a man in his 40's somewhere??

---

78 This was probably the strictly organized piece for chamber orchestra she describes in the 22 November letter: "a one movement affair based solely on one idea ~ a five note series ~ I am evolving my harmony from so, and line, and transformations ~ I am attempting to work on a strict dynamic basis alla Boulez, etc, still employing my concerto grosso idea."

79 George Rochberg, *The Hexachord and Its Relation to the 12-Tone Row* (Bryn Mawr: Theodore Presser, 1955).

I met another American composer the other night, Sam Gale, a 23 yr. old studying with Petrassi and one of his protégés, Porena (?).[80] He was not able to give me much information on the Maestro for he only had a 1/2 hr. interview ~ It is indeed pleasant to sit and chat with composers, even young ones! These people are quite knowledgeable about the American scene musically which really makes me feel as though I have been somewhat isolated ~

Darling, re Darmstadt and Boulez: this summer school in Germany is the only place where Boulez teaches I am told ~ Although he lives in Paris, he evidently does not teach ~ Darmstadt is evidently a school for very advanced composers, etc., working in the pointalist style probably, which makes me question whether I could qualify or not[81] ~ To be accepted there one is required to submit scores, and if your work is slightly on the conservative style, they are anxious to convert you ~ It sounds like an interesting place, but unless you have some knowledge of how these boys like Boulez work, it will be over your head completely ~ Evidently classes take the form of lectures ~ This is one person's opinion ~ I will question Petrassi about it tomorrow ~ But it might interest you greatly....

... Darling, I try not to be jealous very much, but you mention taking 'people' over to Norms, escorting Marlene to and from a party[82] ~ Would you tell me if you are escorting anyone around for I am terrified of hearing it from anyone else as has happened before ~ I trust you, and trust that you love me very much, but also know

---

80 No information about Sam Gale could be found. Boris Porena (1927–2022) was a multifaceted Italian composer, writer, and teacher, a student of Petrassi, who wrote about Petrassi's music but also had an active career as a composer himself. He was interested in the political and sociological aspects of music, resulting in a long hiatus in his career as a composer, from 1968 until 1988, during which he published, among other things, *Musica-società: Inquisizioni musicali II* (Einaudi, 1975).

81 The usual term for what Beecroft describes as "pointalist' is "pointillist." It refers to a then-new texture in modern music called "pointillism," whereby notes were presented as somewhat isolated, non-linear occurrences, "points" of sound, usually several at a time, not as a continuous process as in a traditional melody. Anton Webern was considered to be the originator of this approach, and this was a typical feature of certain "serialist" composers of the post-war period. An example would be Karlheinz Stockhausen's *Kontra-Punkte* [Counter-points] for ten performers (1952–53).

82 This paragraph indicates that Beecroft was uneasy, at best, about whether Somers had remained faithful to her since she left Toronto. Her phrase "as has happened before" suggests that in the course of their relationship she had heard reports from people about his relationships with other women. This lack of trust seems to have operated on both sides in their relationship, as will be seen in later letters.

November 1959   131

that women are attracted to you, and vice versa sometimes, but you must love me enough and trust that I am capable of understanding your need for feminine companionship to tell me if you have women friends ~ I mention my friends here to you for I know that you are able to understand and I do not want you to be jealous of anyone, for I love <u>you</u> only....

... I must go and practice more now ~ I will write you of my interview with Petrassi ~

Love – so much love, my sweet blond one
Normie

PS. Why do you ask if I receive all your letters? I think I do darling ~ N.

HS to NB
Ottawa –
Nov. 25/59
(Wed. night.)
My Dearest Love:

Know this – that all beauty is bittersweet without you. I cannot enjoy fully what I see without you to share it. In fact it is a kind of pain, not pleasure for me.

I am writing to you in front of a warm fire – but let me describe this.

The Crawleys, of Crawley Films, have been kind enough to put me up in their wonderful home set in the most extraordinary location – the Gatineau Hills north of Ottawa.[83] How can I describe it but to say it is my ideal! (And I think yours.)

This is an enormous room with a fireplace at one end. (Opposite which I write.) On all sides are long windows, which, in daylight, view the magnificent panorama of hills, woods, sky – not unlike the Berkshires, but more rugged.

They are only 25 minutes from Ottawa, yet quite isolated. The wind howls and thunders, the snow carpets the earth, the fire crackles yet there are no noises of cars or people, no lights, no sign of the world, yet only of the world.

83 Crawley Films was founded by Frank Radford Crawley, known as "Budge" Crawley (1911–1987) and his wife, Judith Crawley (1914–1986), in Ottawa in 1939, and grew to be one of the major independent film production companies in Canada. Among its early successes was *The Loon's Necklace*, a short film inspired by British Columbian folklore, which won first prize at the Venice Film Festival in 1949.

But the world makes sense to us humans finally in terms of people, and these people are wonderful. The Crawleys, man and wife, are dedicated to film making, they both are devoted to the medium.

In this particular film I am given 'carte blanche,' in fact the 'farther out' I go the better.

I have spent 10 hours of work at the studio – inquiring, getting information – specific and general – everything – viewing films – in order to understand more the medium. Everyone is co-operative and enthusiastic.

This film means a great deal. –

It is to be widely shown through Europe and South America.

My responsibility is great – this film will be shown with a German film which used music concrète – synthetic music – which, I understand was exciting.[84]

I must create from the 'natural', which is the story of the film.

Canada is certainly on the threshold of wondrous things in the arts, services, industry. We've had talks and seen examples of this. There is an awareness, growing, of those elements which are unique.

My beloved Normie – it is to arrive at general truths through one's particular environment. It is fake otherwise, even if for a moment successful.

Italians must do it through Italy, Canadians through Canada, etc....

... We must know and create our own identity, I don't give a damn how timid and self conscious the rest are....

... Here there is an environment, a temperament (So terrified of being identified for fear of being called 'provincial') of even evolution!

I feel it and know it!! It does not negate another culture, but it affirms my own!

---

84 "Musique concrète" was one of the two main approaches to electronic music in these early years of the medium. This approach began in France in the early 1940s with Pierre Schaeffer, Jacques Copeau, and others in the *Studio d'Essai de la Radiodiffusion nationale*. They used various kinds of recorded sounds to produce sound-based compositions using radiophonic techniques as well as those derived from cinema. By 1951, the *Groupe de Recherches de Musique Concrète, Club d 'essai de la Radiodiffusion-télévision Française* had been established by Pierre Henry and others, with an electronic music studio that attracted major figures such as Olivier Messiaen, Pierre Boulez, Jean Barraqué, Karlheinz Stockhausen, Edgard Varèse, and Iannis Xenakis. In 1958 a new group was formed, called Groupe de Recherches Musicales (GRM). The other approach, centred in Cologne, used electronically generated sounds that could be modified by filtering, reverberation, changes in speed, and other procedures.

November 1959 133

Jazz, Indian, Eskimo – are our folk music – Europe is our inheritance – it is colourful and multilingual. Unlike U.S.A. we have not felt cut off from Europe. We know the continuity yet are the new world. Normie dear, it is a unique position, and we have something unique to say if only we are <u>not</u> intimidated by what we think we should say.

Thursday – late afternoon. (Nov. 26 or 25?)

Excuse the writing but it's difficult on a train (As what isn't!) I'm seated in parlour car luxury, surrounded by the eminent and successful. C'est très drole, n'est ce pas?...

... Budge and Judy Crawley are such genuine straight people it's a pleasure for me to be associated with them. Christopher Chapman is the essence of an artist – lean, absent minded, quite vague yet absolutely one pointed and unrelenting in his search for artistic perfection – in short he has artistic integrity.

I will have to return to Ottawa a number of times. They made an offer of $1000.00 for the music for this 10 minute film, but I haven't accepted yet. From their standpoint it's a good fee, but I must consider. The project is so unique that I hate to quibble, but the work involved creatively is enormous – naturally a movie composer could knock it off in no time, but I would write it as a through composed piece – which is another story.

It would be much simpler if some electric pen could be wired to my head to write as the thoughts occur. How lazy can I get? Answer – very....

... Kingston – 15 years ago a weekend pass – 36 hours was a bonanza from above – to be able to 'sleep in' one morning –how I prized it – Kingston to Toronto – how much has happened in between?[85]

---

85 "Fifteen years ago" – around the beginning of March 1945 – Somers was posted at Barriefield Camp near Kingston as part of his military training. During this period, he travelled more often to Ottawa than to Toronto on weekend passes to visit John Weinzweig, who was stationed there, as well as a young woman named Dorothy. By the spring of 1945, as his correspondence with his mother shows, he had become depressed and disillusioned with military training.

One day last week I went into a University restaurant filled with young students – alive – righteous, gay, superficially serious – A weird feeling came over me – that the last 20 years were a dream that occurred last night and that then was now – this is 1939 – the war has just started – that I had a dream that would soon be forgotten – that I had all these things to live through that I was just starting –

How could I tell them of my dream? What is to happen? Finnegans' Wake.

One day it will be a second before my life has ended – before the dream is over. Will I suddenly wake up? It will have been a tick of time then over. In the face of it reality seems a silly word. We are so vain in the face of time, but time wears a cynical smile we don't understand....

... Here I sit, suspended in time between the before and the after. Join the three points simultaneously and it is a 4th dimension.

You may look at me as an empty cube projected into space – not a handsome nor a fed one, but one quite full of booze – a great improvement on Canadian Railways....

... I sit here and the steward keeps pouring me drinks – he is, perhaps, Old Nick in disguise pouring poison into my diseased soul in order that he may eventually cut it out at the end of this journey. Or is it ever to be ended? I might never get off the train – forever – you will never read my words – the Flying Dutchman....

... Another swig. I'm pouring myself from Ottawa to Toronto. I'm a stream, baby....

... Norm just had an operation to remove the pins from his leg.[86] He's excited about the opera and from what he says has some exciting ideas. We both have to meet about the same deadline.

Darkness, night flies by. Soon I will be in Toronto. How strange....

---

86 Beecroft recalls that before she left for Europe, she and Somers and Norm Symonds were visiting the jazz columnist Helen McNamara. Apparently, while Somers and Symonds were energetically trying out some judo manoeuvres, Symonds was thrown in such a way that his leg (or ankle) was broken; this probably explains why he had pins in his leg.

November 1959

12:30 a.m.

... On the radio some delightful scherzo music by Prokofiev, preceded and followed by some rather tawdry stuff by the same gentleman – all Romeo and Juliet music.

The Russians so often sound like they live in a bloody circus – jugglers, high wire acts, clowns 'And now ladies and gentlemen –' noise. biff bang – oom-pah oom-pah oom pah – change the goddamn key – then the false relations – oom pah oom pah – do dodeedo – trumpets, now fast – always oom pah oom pah – slow oompahs – fast oom pahs – medium oom pahs – forever oom-pahs!!

Thank God he's finally out of the Ringling Brothers business and into the lush stuff - peculiar Wagnerish feel....

... Friday noon: Snow and the annual grey cup fever, for the game is to-morrow, an excuse for a great mass orgy.[87] Thousands of years to develop the individual and the cover is so thin. I have seen a happy singing mass of people turn in an instant into a destructive mob, hurtling crashing out of control. I hope I never see it again.

Meanwhile it's colourful and festive. The air is clean and cool and people are in the mood to celebrate.

To-night I go to Eli's – a dinner for the visiting celebrity, Alirio Diaz.

I study, write, work, my mind hums along through high voltage wires, high tension wires –

> You are always in my thoughts and heart –
> Much love –
> Harry

NB to HS
November 26th, 1959
My dearest Harry,

... This morning I woke up with one of those terrible heavy heads, first cousin to a headache ~ It is heavy and grey weather here in Rome and so much rain! It has just started to come down again in

---

87 The 47th 1959 Grey Cup game took place on 28 November at Toronto's CNE Stadium. The Hamilton Tiger-Cats were defeated by the Winnipeg Blue Bombers 21–7. https://web.archive.org/web/20130819211410/http://cfl.ca/page/his_greycup_recap1959.

great large drops and although the sky-scapes are fascinating it is so depressing sometimes.

I find it hard to imagine that 2 1/2 months have passed by ~ Now more than ever, it seems like yesterday when I saw you for the last time from the deck of the Liberté – such a sad occasion it was, bringing great tears to my eyes every time I think of that parting ~ But you are very close to me even though we are far away from each other, and it sometimes is very hard to bear....

... All I am trying to say I guess is that I am desperately lonely for you, that I need you very much, love you very much ~ and am finding life and work 'trying' these days – and Rome ~ I am a little homesick too ~ Courage, old dear, they always say!

Please come to me soon, my darling ~ it's hell without you ~ and forgive my self-indulgence a little ~

> Love as always
> Normie

HS to NB
Nov. 29 /59 [27 November]
Beloved Normie:

Your happy and energetic attitudes and projects sound wonderful.

How would I feel about finding a stronger personality, more secure? About such a change?...

... To be strong and secure in yourself would delight me now. As I said before, a relationship to last must be built on strength, not weakness. One person can suffocate another through insecurity, they can kill all affection. As a matter of fact the strength you're discovering in yourself is <u>essential</u> for a successful relationship....

... "Can we exist together both writing music?" – "ideally that it is a woman who should sacrifice her career" – "can't give up the idea of writing – stronger need" – "you have found out 'yes' in Rome.

Yes, these are serious questions. In the past you were sometimes jealous or else were competing with me. You want your place in the sun as Norma Beecroft, composer or artist. You want a career. You want recognition as an individual.

These things I must carefully consider, they can be destructive seeds in a marriage.

I believe we could exist quite well together writing music. We would simply be two different composers when working. It would likely mean a separate studio for one or the other to work in. But

November 1959

that's the only complication. Normie, I've always respected you as an individual and respected and encouraged, I hope, your desire to compose....

... <u>Understand</u> that you may rest assured that I have always have, and always will respect your needs. Outside of that you would take care of a reasonable amount of a woman's duties and I would take care of a man's duties....

... It's too bad John W. didn't give you a basis of serial technic, but he must have had his reasons, John always does. I started right out with John in 1942 doing 12 tone and serial technic – I've been going backwards ever since! (Like 'Through the Looking Glass.') If one is going to work outside of harmonic or diatonic, or even tonal centre logic, then serial technics are the only answer. There are, I understand, some excellent books on the subject....

... A five-note series. Yes. You sound very stimulated by the idea and I can get a vicarious excitement from your excitement.

But in any style of composition certain basic problems remain constant – how to maintain unity of technique, or consistency of technique, yet avoid monotony of texture.

Serial technic is in essence a constant form of variation....

... Your Canada Council application – I would advise you to apply to go where you feel in accordance with your study needs and plans, for your application must have logical presentation and conviction. I want you to have every opportunity to study, to develop to discover both the inner and the outer world. I will simply continue with my plans....

... Had a magnificent meal at the Kassner's last night. How Naomi can cook! Then a fine evening of talk and music with me ending up, as usual, on the floor.

The Spanish composer from Madrid who came over to study with John, was there. We all had to talk half French half English and those what could, Spanish. Diaz is Venezuelan and an exceptional guitarist. Tonight the recital and after the Youngs for a party....[88]

... All my love, my beloved Normie, may it give you warmth and joy and happiness.

Always, always, your Harry

P.S. I'm very happy for the way things are going for you, dear.

---

88 The "Youngs" were Ken and Marguerite Young; Ken was the secretary of the Guitar Society of Toronto. See chap. 2, n. 26 for information on the Youngs.

NB to HS
Roma ~
Friday – 7:00 pm [27 November]
Darling Harry,

I have just returned from a two-hour session with Petrassi ~ and I feel quite exhausted ~ I built myself up to quite a state of worry and I guess this is the relaxation following ~

However, I had telephoned him to tell him I was having problems and could I talk with him again ~ My reactions are quite different from this meeting ~ for I found him quite helpful, open and friendly ~ He inquired after the state of my Italian, my flute, my living situation here, etc., and I answered in turn ~ Then out comes the work ~

This morning I worked like hell and finished the re-writing of the first section of the songs ~ As this was not the major problem we spent no time on that, but he looked at my sketches for the chamber orchestra piece and gave me his criticism to date. He told me that to try to write a work on five tones immediately limits me, and with the specific five tones I had chosen ~ a series C, D-flat (9th), G, F#, Eb ~ there was interval duplication in inversion ~ I presume he meant the -9th -+7th sounds ~ in mirror inversion ~ A more skilled person than I would be courageous taking that particular series! So after much chat, it was decided that I commence a strict 12-tone piece for pianoforte as an exercise ~ This, I suppose, I had almost anticipated and felt a little relieved ~ He did not seem to remember that he had given me this chamber orch. project, so I did not mention it ~ My God, what concentration is required to understand being taught in Italian ~ It's exhausting ~

After this I questioned him about the course at Santa Cecilia for I told him I felt a bit insecure not knowing my future program ~ It's like this: it's his 'baby'; there are no subjects other than composition and this class is limited to 10 (mostly foreigners) and it costs nothing ~ It is for advanced students of composizione ~ I asked him about my possibilities of being accepted ~ there is evidently a board of examiners who examine your work ~ deadline for entries ~ the end of December ~ He encouraged me to finish writing the songs for submission ~ said my chances are good ~ At the end of the course one received some kind of diploma or something or other ~ So I have decided to try it out which will mean hard work between now and another month ~

I questioned him ~ 'what do I do if not accepted ~ can I study privately with him, or with whom?' ~ He says that he does not teach

November 1959   139

privately but I would be looked after by a young 'professore, molto brava' ~ as with the Fullbright students here, and probably receive his criticism once a month or so ~ So – OK!

There are no listening facilities connected with the schools of music here, so Petrassi has kindly lent me a couple of albums of Schoenberg, Webern, Boulez, Nono – music (records) ~ We chatted more ~ I asked about his work and was given a book in English to read about him ~ (it always works with composers) ~ a 'present,' he said ~

We talked about the state of music today ~ and he seems to be just as horrified by what he calls 'musica brutta' ~ a bad, ugly music ~ as I have been, but acknowledges the talents of certain composers like Boulez, Castiglioni, Berio – etc – I found him generally very pleasant ~

So now I write a twelve-tone piano piece and call him in about a week ~ This is much better for me ~ I really need someone to bat me over the head once in a while – or need to have the sense to abandon, temporarily at least, what is beyond my means ~ Perhaps this is acquired with age ~ but I do find my ideas so damn interesting that I am reluctant to give them up ~ We will learn ~

All in all, even though I know my reactions to people make me go up and down like a thermometer, I feel relatively pleased with this meeting and more secure about the future ~ I also after thinking a bit feel that maybe class work wouldn't do me any harm for disciplinary purposes ~ I would like to eventually be able to write with a little more technical facility than I possess at this time ~

Perhaps what your friend Franchetti says about Italian composers may be true in part ~ however, there is always something to be learned, and I think I can learn something from Petrassi even though the twelve-tone technique (or its offsprings) may be basically foreign to him ~ It is foreign to me for that matter, but I should certainly be fluent in that language before I can begin to understand the musical language of people like Boulez, whose scores I do not know even how to read ~! Getting into this course will also force me to work hard and provide the opportunity to meet other younger people which I have a tendency to reject ~ but here in Rome, it is important to know my contemporaries.

... So pleased to hear George Rochberg was (is) your friend ~ I have just finished reading his book on twelve-tone ~ hexachord principles ~ slightly pedantic, but covers and proves his hypotheses ~ Peter told me today that he will be coming to Europe in July for

140   Between Composers

they are doing 6 performances (in different centres) of his, I believe, Sixth Symphony[89] ~ He will be here for a month – so perhaps you can meet....

... In spite of the fact that I somehow feel that Europe is not too sincere in attitude musically and Rome not too active in contemporary music, I find it very stimulating to live in this environment, and somehow feel perhaps a little bitter that Canada seems to be so backward in its interest in contemporary music ~ I am passionately attached to the country and physical beauty and space, but find the people, in retrospect and not for certain in the long run, so content to sit and wait for leadership from elsewhere, which makes me angry ~ Am I crazy, or is this just a natural reaction ~ Canada produces seemingly passive people to me ~

I would be most curious to know what Coughtry said about Jack Nichols ~ I have had some thoughts on him and his work in the last couple of weeks ~ It occurs to me that Jack lives in a world of illusion ~ although an excellent artist ~ but doesn't seem to create anything out of <u>his</u> <u>own</u> background or environment, but simply rebels against it in every sense ~ His art on Spain, etc. - Is this unfair judgement ~? what do you think? The Saturday Review I told you about and the article on painting does not mention his name as a representative of Canada at all ~ which started me thinking ~ Coughtry's name <u>is</u> mentioned ~

Darling, I must go and work or practice ~ As always I wish you were here ~ There is nothing so lonely as not to be able to share something exciting with the one you love so much ~

Take care, my love and don't forget to eat once in a while ~ I am getting fat, I believe!

I love you, I love you
Normie

PS. You would be staggered to see all my gray hairs now I am keeping my hair long for you darling N.

HS to NB
Sunday, November 29
My dearest love:

89 This would likely have been the Symphony No. 2 (1955–56). Rochberg's Symphony No. 6 was not written until the 1980s.

November 1959   141

It's like an evening after a battle. Very quiet with a few bodies strewn about, left-overs from the game.[90] (Winnipeg won, by the way. I know this staggering bit of information will likely alter the course of your entire life.)

Elirio Diaz proved to be an excellent guitarist.[91] He married an Italian girl and makes Rome his home. Small world, huh! A very pleasant man.

At the party I succeeded in getting quite stoned but nevertheless had an interesting discussion with Ken, Margueritte, Norm and Gwen towards the close....

... Also a good talk with an engineer about aesthetics, the physics of sounds in relation to human response etc. A subject in which, a while back, Ted Shadbolt revealed himself to be very intelligent.[92]

... It's so quiet here. At least it's right for study and composing, but it's not so good when my heart is suddenly gripped with a fearful longing and loneliness for you.

I wrote my wife asking her for a divorce.[93] Now I will have to wait and see. I shall speak to her next week. It is in her interest as well as mine, so I don't foresee any difficulty outside the financial one. She is not a vengeful or a spiteful person, so this should lessen a naturally nasty situation. (Of course one cannot always be absolutely sure.) I want to get it over with as quickly as possible. Almost ten years of torture is just too much for anyone's emotional stability.[94] It must be finished quickly....

90 See n. 87.

91 The correct first name of the guitarist was Alirio. See chap. 3, n. 77.

92 See chap. 2, n. 37.

93 He had begun a long letter to Cathy the day before (27 November) and completed it the following day. He tried to convince her that it was best for both of them to finally end their marriage and put an end to the emotional distress they were both suffering. He admitted in the letter that he had treated her badly – an interesting parallel to the present correspondence with Norma.

94 "Ten years of torture" seems a curious way to describe his marriage to his first wife Cathy, since they were married in the fall of 1949 and there is little indication that things were going badly until 1953 or 1954, when they separated. During his years with Beecroft (1955–59), his correspondence with her does not mention Cathy, so one wonders exactly how "tortured" he was. It may be that he felt considerable guilt about the way he had treated Cathy during their few years together and was interpreting this as "torture."

Between Composers

... Jimmy Guiffrey and his guitarist are in town, so Norm invited me over later to chat with them.[95] When I'm at Norm's I do silly sentimental things like have him play records we used to hear together, you and I, and pretend you're there.

Wonderful evening ... Guiffrey played his latest records, (He met Berio in Italy and was impressed.) (Guiffrey's group enjoyed Italy as much as anywhere in Europe.) Norm played some of his music, and I played the Passacaglia & Fugue and the 2nd Piano Concerto. Guiffrey and Jimmy Hall (his guitarist) were so impressed they were almost speechless. A tremendously gratifying reaction for the composer, as you can understand. It is nice to get this from one's fellow musicians. Norm got more out of the 2nd piano concerto than he ever had before. Naturally I was happy about the response....

Monday a.m.

... Your interesting letter concerning Boulez, Darmstadt and your new interest in 12 tone. Sounds good, Normie dear. After all, 12 tone has been evolving for 50 years and is now an accepted part of compositional technic that anyone seriously concerned with the art should familiarize themselves with.

Jean Beaudet knows Boulez and seems to feel it would be possible to do something with him in Paris. Naturally I would investigate further. (This depends on the old Canada Council, of course.)

As to it being over my head, I'm willing to take that chance.

---

95 James Peter Giuffre (1921–2008) was an American jazz clarinetist, saxophonist, composer, and arranger. Starting out as an arranger for Woody Herman's big band, he became an important figure in West Coast Jazz in the early 1950s, and later in the 1950s formed several trios. In 1959, the trio, featuring Giuffre, guitarist Jim Hall, and bassist Buddy Clark, played a concert in Rome; that is how he came to meet Luciano Berio (as mentioned in Somers's letter). James Hall (1930–2013) was a jazz guitarist, composer, and arranger who had a distinguished career as performer and composer from the late 1950s on. From 1957 to 1960, he worked with Giuffre, notably as a member of the Jimmy Giuffre Three.

November 1959

Dearest Normie, as to escorting other women, let me give you the exact picture for like me, you have absolutely no reason for doubt, fear or jealousy. Trust me and love me as I trust and love you.

Because people can be malicious I will tell you of every woman I know. My life is an open book to you. I have nothing to hide. I want you to speak to me of every doubt you possess. Don't ever be afraid to. I love only you.

The French girl's name is Joan Ferry, married to a Tony Ferry and has a baby boy.[96] She is, as is her husband, very interested in theatre. They spent 3 1/2 years in London, England mixed up in avant-garde theatre. She's an actress and writer – he a writer. Sometimes the both of them come out with me, on occasion just Joan does.

Marlene I only saw once, when I mentioned her to you. You know her – pleasant, happy person.

Now, let me see – Malka Jessner (Mrs.) old fellow student at the 'Con'.[97] Singer, works as a film editor for the music, her husband being one of the best cameramen in the N.F.B. They live in Montreal. She comes to Toronto to visit the Birds, old friends. Had lunch with her at the 5th Ave. one day.

A very strange case – Francie Jones (the 'Black Witch').[98] I was dumbfounded one day when she told me she loved me! I said that I love only one person, Norma Beecroft, she has all my love, there could never be another, and I am true to her. That finished that. I said I would welcome her as a friend but under no other circumstances. The girl finally went back to Ken Jones after attempting suicide twice.

---

96 Joan Ferry (née Maroney) (b. 1932), an actress and writer, was born in Ottawa and studied at the Central School of Speech and Drama in London and in Paris with the Barrault-Renaud Theatre Company. She was the co-founder and editor of *Encore Magazine*, a theatre magazine in London, but she is best known as the co-founder of Toronto Workshop Productions, which nurtured actors, playwrights, and would-be directors. Her husband, Anthony Ferry (1930–1970) was a writer. See Ferry, "Experiences of a Pioneer in Canadian Experimental Theatre," *Theatre Research in Canada / Recherches théâtrales Au Canada* 8, no. 1 (1987): 59–67, https://journals.lib.unb.ca/index.php/TRIC/article/view/7378.

97 No further information about Malka Jessner could be found.

98 Francine Jones (? – 1980) and her husband, Ken, were friends of Somers. A handwritten eulogy by Somers, dated 7 June 1980, is among his papers at LAC; this was probably delivered at her funeral. She is listed in the Toronto Directory of 1960 as an actress, living at 596 Church Street in Toronto, very close to where Somers lived at the time. His eulogy indicates that her life was chaotic and that she was emotionally unstable, with numerous suicide attempts and many lovers.

144 Between Composers

Robie Ivy, script assistant to Andrew Allen.[99] A fine person. Only a speaking acquaintance, but some idiot could misconstrue it no doubt.

Helen you know all about.

Donica D'Hondt – a former Miss Canada, actress, dancer, studying music with Sam Dolin[100] – English – a fine person, intelligent and simply pleasant company.[101] The English have a nice reserve and the women can enjoy men simply for company, which is the only thing I wish, the only thing they wish.

Who else? Once I bumped into Grace just before Ron Colliers wedding. Had a beer with her. You know, Normie, things like that.

I do not go out very much, but on occasion Joan Ferry might invite me to some play rehearsal, or Helen will want to talk, or I think Donica might enjoy meeting some musicians etc. I regard these people as women friends and if certain people see me out with them and choose to make scandal out of it, then of course they will....

...We need each other so desperately, my Normie. I just can't see how I could get over for Christmas. If the divorce were to come through it would cost a minimum of $300.00 (Which I don't have.) If the film comes through I would have a frantic deadline – it's terrible! As it is I'm doing a great pile of work....

...Yes, you must feel completely free to discuss anything thing with me and to convey any feelings whatsoever to me. It is all the way now and you must never be afraid to be completely frank with me, as you love me and I you. I cannot stress this enough.

99 Andrew Allan (1907–1974) was the national head of CBC Radio Drama from 1943 to 1955. Beginning with the Stage '44 series on Sunday nights, he created a kind of national theatre on radio, encouraging Canadian playwrights and performers to achieve a consistently high level of production. Among the writers and actors in the Stage series were Lister Sinclair, Mavor Moore, W.O. Mitchell, Jane Mallett, John Drainie, and Barry Morse. The Stage series lasted until 1956. No information about Robie Ivy could be found.

100 The Montreal-born composer Samuel Dolin (1917–2002) had been teaching composition, theory, and piano at the Royal Conservatory since the late 1940s. Along with Somers and John Weinzweig, he was one of the founders in 1951 of the Canadian League of Composers.

101 Danica d'Hondt (b.1939) is an English-Canadian actress, writer, and businesswoman. She won the Miss Canada pageant in 1958 and went on to compete for the Miss America competition in 1959 while still a student at the University of British Columbia. In the fall of 1959, she was in Toronto working as a television panellist and actress but in 1960 began a Hollywood career that lasted for some thirty years. She starred in "B" movies, played supporting roles in major Hollywood movies, and guest-starred on TV shows of the time, such as The Man from U.N.C.L.E. (1964).

November 1959   145

Sweetheart, you are my woman.
I give you <u>all</u> my love – be at peace –
Harry

NB to HS
November 30th, 1959
Dear Harry,

Another low day in the life of NB ~ For the past two days it has
been pouring rain and just now it has cleared a little ~ My God it's
depressing ~ especially when your work is not going well, no one
calls on the telephone, there is no radio, no sound but rain ~ only
you talking to yourself ~ The days pass by here very slowly sometimes and I feel really quite desperate for need of you ~

This morning I decided to get up at 7:00 so I could start to work
early ~ I got up, got organized, was just getting into a tone row when
a knock on the door comes, and two Italians start carrying bags of
cement through my apartment to the roof naturally leaving half the
cement and muddy footprints all over my floors and rug which took
all Saturday to wax and clean ~ You can't win ~ they came in and
out of here for an hour ~ putting me in a very foul mood of course ~

There are just some days when I don't have a musical idea in my
head and today is one of them ~ then I start to worry and then everything is miserable ~ What do you do then!?...

... Darling, can't you arrange to come here before June ~ If I sent
you a one-way air ticket, don't you think you could make it – or we
could make it somehow financially ~ Other people seem to manage
somehow ~ I feel often as though I am in absolute agony here and
don't know how I can summon up the energy to do anything but
sleep, hoping that when I wake up I won't have to face just myself
and my misery, but that you will appear from somewhere as though
you have never been away....

December 3rd
Darling,

... I am sorry not to have finished this letter but have been suffering the most incredible kind of depression I have ever experienced
~ For days there has been no sun ~ for days it has rained ~ all my
fellow students are depressed and having much trouble working,
and I have been so desperate with worry that I have been sort of paralyzed here ~ I can't tell you how terrible it is to be completely senza

friends that are dependable and of long standing when you feel like this ~ Yesterday I broke down in tears (first time for months) and wailed from my lonely room for about 1/2 an hour....

... Please write me love ~ It's hell without you I really don't know sometimes how long I will last ~

It now looks as though I am going to have to buy a new flute if I am going to make any progress on the instrument at all, for I am afraid I, and Gazzelloni thinks, that I have a hopeless instrument which will do nothing but tire ~ Oh money, money, where are thou!

So much love dearest one
Normie

CHAPTER FOUR

December 1959

HS to NB
Tuesday, Dec. 1/59
My beloved Normie:
Snow gently falling. The very pores of my skin sensing your touch. My innermost feelings reaching out to you ... my dear sweet love whom I love more than anyone else in the world, who creates the greatest sadness and the greatest joy in my life, who gives reason to my heartbeat.

———————

2 p.m.
So there I was, comin' out of the Chinese Laundry when who should I bump into but Marlene. Naturally we popped by the local for a pint.
She sends her regards....
... Got to talking of art, Graham Coughtry, (Exhibition of Canadian painters at the Art Gallery.[1] Must go.) She met Graham

1 This exhibition ran from 13 November 1959 until 4 January 1960 at the Art Gallery of Toronto (as it was known until 1966) and featured work by members of the Canadian Group of Painters. This was the successor to the Group of Seven and had been formed in 1933, with a membership of twenty-eight artists. In her review of the exhibition, Pearl McCarthy mentioned Coughtry's *Emerging Figure*: "In addition to noting the increase in romantic subjects, visitors will find this interesting – check on how many of the paintings deal with the idea of how some visual image emerges and isolates itself. Graham Coughtry's Emerging Figure is only one of these." "Group of Painters Exhibition Controversial," *Globe and Mail*, 21 November 1959.

148   Between Composers

twice – at a party and at your place. Graham struck her as pompous, opinionated, and that people cow-towed to him, (A strange picture from my viewpoint.) so she had offered her own views, apparently some verbal pins in his balloon – and ever since he has been rather cool towards her. I told her that to any artist if you praise him you become in his eyes a penetrating, discrimination judge of art with profound insight and sensitivity. If you criticize him you are an insensitive clot without an ounce of perception, no judgement, a product of bourgeois ignorance and vulgarity.

She's going to hear Yves Montand to-night. He's at the Royal Alex for four nights. A fabulous entertainer-singer in the French-manner. His wife is <u>Simone Signoret</u> of 'Room at the Top.' Remember. I must hear him. Hmm.

Jimmy Guiffrey,[2] of all people, is in the group accompanying Montand....

... Disturbing dream last night. You were having a violent argument with your father over me. He was disgusted – "how could you marry a man who didn't play the Rachmaninoff 2nd piano concerto!?" You were in tears. I was hunting through enormous piles of music for the damn thing but couldn't find it. Charles and Caroline were huddled in the distance. I was frustrated and furious. You were dreadfully upset at your father and tried to reach out to me. Crazy, eh?

Must go to my French....

———

... Wed. noon. Sunny day. Feels like a good day to work. Bonjour, Norma, comment ca va aujourd'hui? Ca marche bien, j'espere. One feels like a bloody idiot re-learning a language. It's like – 'La plume de ma tante' all over again.

Your letter of Friday arrived....

... I must correct one error – for I have, since you left, discovered Canada under the surface is in quite an exciting ferment – composers, poets, painters, writers, theatre etc. The whole thing will explode to the surface one day not so far away....

... If the council came through, I'm not absolutely certain I could make Europe in June. (Though I would certainly try.) If my work burden is too heavy I might have to delay 'till the fall. However that decision is far away and I have much to do before then.

2 See chap. 3, n. 95.

December 1959   149

By the way, big to-do in newspapers about the new electronic laboratory being set up – Olnick, Walter.[3] Beat the drums. Be-dum dum dum....

... I've exciting ideas in my head re. Koussevitsky work.[4] My concern in composition is to constantly evolve – use my experience always as a base from which I move – continually evolving, transforming, adding. As you know, I feel Ives has raised certainly stimulating and interesting musical questions I find nowhere else – multi level writing on plains of sound. The pointillist techniques are too penny pinching for my temperament at the moment. An English critic called Webern a parsimonious composer. Perhaps a facetious comment but nonetheless pertinent. Spatial relationships etc. hewn down to their essentials and exposed as a composition make one acutely aware of these essentials. It becomes an abstract pleasure such as the observation of balance, proportion, symmetry – or – asymmetry in a mathematical equation made visual.

It is curious the evolution of a technique which had its roots in the 'expressionists' of pre first war Germany – Austria. Roots farther back in Mahler and Wagner – products of a 'romantic' movement. It proves how versatile and creative and right the formulation was that it should prove so fertile to many different minds.

Now it runs the risk of dogma, formulation to the point of crystallization, becoming a religion. (It has.) Certain idiosyncrasies keep reappearing. The do' and don'ts force the composers to stand on their heads balancing a screwdriver on one foot and a metronome on the other. But the history of music has been the making and breaking of rules. There is an article on 'the semi-tone in 12 tone music' in one of the music journals[5] – the tyranny of the semi-tone, which allows only a limited number of possibilities. (Semi-tone and its inversion to a maj. 7th or minor 9th.) – (and I would add 'tritone' which hexachord technic seeks to break but which forces it into the semi-tone.)

3 The *Globe and Mail* ran a story about the new Electronic Music Studio at the University of Toronto, the first such studio in Canada, on 26 November 1959, featuring comments about the new facilities by Arnold Walter, then director of the Faculty of Music, and some information about the instruments designed by Hugh Le Caine. "Music Machine Plays Drisody, New Style Electric Tune," *Globe and Mail*, 26 November 1959.

4 See chap. 3, n. 7.

5 This was likely Henry Leland Clarke's article, "The Abuse of the Semitone in Twelve-Tone Music," *The Musical Quarterly* 45 (July 1959), 295–301.

150   Between Composers

Sorry, got carried away!...

... Good luck – as always I am extremely interested and curious about your progress and understand you are writing vividly of your life –

        All my love – I love you into infinity –
        Harry

HS to NB
Thursday evening,
Dec. 3 / 59
Dearest Normie:

I feel strange, lonely, sad – unreal. As though something is taking place but I don't know what it is. 'The night grows colder....

... It's December. How many more Decembers? Into the distance, lives and time numbers. Dice keep rolling, cards are cut, the jokers wild. It's all written, play your hand. Circus music with the sad clown face and laughter. A big tear, how funny, corrodes ravines, and in it are reflected all the lights. Walk the tightrope to the oohs and aahs. And always the shadows. Shadows on shadows dancing, the objects never seen.[6] We are all alone in the service of the night. Put the shovel in and dig up sand.

        But at my back I always hear
        Time's winged chariot hurrying near,
        And yonder, all before us, lie
        Deserts of vast eternity.[7]

But I must remember to "Never deny, when you return to darkness, that you have seen the light."[8]

---

6 The notion of the "shadow," as image or symbol, and the connection between shadow and dance, seem to have been in Somers's mind from an early age. An early poem of his entitled "Fantasy," written in 1944, demonstrates this: "Last night I dreamed / Of people who were dancing, / Dancing in a world of fantasy. / Shadows among shadows, / With motion never ceasing, / Momentum ever increasing."
7 These lines are from "To His Coy Mistress," a poem written by Andrew Marvell (1621–1678). It is one of the best known "carpe diem" poems in English.
8 This is part of an aphorism written by the Victorian poet Coventry Patmore (1823–1896), from his book The Rod, the Root, and the Flower (London: George Bell, 1895), 16: "'To him that waits all things reveal themselves,' provided that he has the courage not to deny, in the darkness, what he has seen in the light." I am indebted to Dr Elaine Bander for finding the source of this statement.

December 1959 151

It would seem that this is my winter. Buried under mounds of snow is emerging life. Yeh dad, yo-yo, yah yah.

Back to work, Somers....

———————

... Quite often lately, I have thought of Jane, to what profound depths she must have searched, fallen, probed, before arriving at her decision.[9] That in a sense she is seeking the true world of reality. Though part of her action might have been psychologically motivated, (Family history, taking on burden of guilt, etc.) the consequences within herself will far exceed the motivation....

———————

... I'm concerned about the aesthetics of music to-day. Perhaps it has never been any different. The real composer is rare in any age.

If art removes itself from a human purpose and intent, if content is a despised thing and construction the primary thing, then art becomes a mechano set, a petty vehicle of intellectual vanity.[10]

Technic is a prerequisite of any accomplishment, research and invention essential elements of a vital art, but unless they are servant to human ends – communication, enlightenment, the struggle and search for truth in terms of values, of a purpose higher than both the bowels and brains, of nobility of spirit etc. – all words and attitudes quite often vilified and despised in this century which is terrified of honest emotion and intent – if it is not concerned with these things then it is indeed just so much farting Anny Laurie through a key hole.[11]

9 Beecroft's older sister Jane had recently taken her first vows as a nun at Loretto Abbey in Toronto. She left the convent in December 1962, not long after her sister had returned from Italy.

10 "Meccano" was the name of a set of metal construction materials for young people, first introduced in 1898 in England. Various models (vehicles, bridges, etc.) could be constructed by assembling different metal shapes, along with wheels, gears, and other pieces, secured by small nuts and bolts.

11 This expression was taken from Joyce Cary's novel *The Horse's Mouth*: "Why, your ladyship, a lot of my recent stuff is not much better, technically, than any young lady can do after six lessons at a good school. Heavy-handed, stupid looking daubery. Only difference is that it's about something – it's an experience, and all this amateur stuff is like farting Annie Laurie through a keyhole. It may be clever but is it worth

I'm concerned because cleverness for its own sake is an ever-present temptation, and I'm quite aware of the 'all heart' school which is often an excuse for shoddy material ill-conceived and poured out in endless clichés.

But statements I read of many avant-garde composers bother me because they indicate such a great deal of intellectual vanity, and absolutely no humility in the true sense.

Perhaps the age will become, if it has not already, an age of total science in which the human being is only one of many factors....

———

... 3 a.m. Can't sleep. Ideas for the film score won't let me rest. That and the Koussevitsky work.

The whole concept for the film score is evolving. An incredibly difficult problem – writing a score which when heard by itself makes sense as a composition, yet with the film supports it both in general and at certain specific points. Since Chris's film is composed and has a rhythm the problem is not insurmountable. It's not unlike a ballet score but has to do more. Most of the film will be without dialogue – just the pictures and music. Where dialogue will appear (If any. Not sure yet.) I would use the technic of cantata – that is the voice would be regarded as part of my concept and I would write 'around it' rather than having the music 'pulled' down when the voice is heard.

Music, then, will be evident as such rather than subconsciously suggestive. It will be companion to the film in order that both may contribute to the total effect.

The specific elements – thematic, harmonic, rhythmic – are shaping. The harmonic concept is interesting. The 'subject' demands the vertical weight. Whether my harmony is to be arrived at by verticalization of the horizontal material (which I previously have done in any 'serial technic' work) or whether I will devise the vertical logic first and have the horizontal evolve from this, I don't know yet. Some interesting things in extending intervals for harmonic purposes but related to serial principles have come up. By alteration and inversion I've found some quasi tone clusters which have a hell of an impact. At the moment just fooling around but will see. The ups

———

the trouble." Joyce Cary, *The Horse's Mouth* (Harmondsworth, Middlesex: Penguin, 1948), 186.

December 1959 · 153

and downs of composing. Probably wake up to-morrow and think it stinks.

The 'sense' of the Koussevitsky work is hovering about – use of silence in the dramatic and as a component of continuing line. (Rather than a distance between two dissociated points) Use of plains – how to achieve them. Tone clusters as harmonic units varying slightly in width, height. Dynamic relationships. Rhythm as a vast sense of phrase arch (As in Gregorian) etc. etc. all churning about. Don't want to talk too much about, I'm superstitious – talk an idea out and it can bleed and die (Joyce Cary – 'Talk of an idea you nail it down, When you nail it down it bleeds and dies')[12]

However talking in the general sense can serve to clarify one's approach, even if it appears confusing to anyone else.

Fire engines wailing in the distance, in the night. Tragedy somewhere....

... Good night sweet love....

––––––––––

... Afternoon – My love for you is pain, joy and sadness to me. It's a popular song, a symphony, a flute, a lonesome harmonica in the night....

... Hell Somers, you should write soap operas!! Think Lever Brothers would buy it? A thing like this could go on for years – 'Harry and Norma' – or 'Just Harry and Norma' or 'Harry and Just Norma' – when will they be together again?[13] What will happen to Norma (or Just Norma) in Rome? Will Just Harry (or Just Plain Crazy Harry) finish the score in time? Will Norma (or Just Norma) become a career composer touring Europe forever eating spaghetti and meat balls? What will happen to her figure? Will she become a meat sauce or a bottle of wine? How much can Just Plain Crazy Harry drink before the bar closes?

12 This is another quotation from *The Horse's Mouth*: "Dangerous to talk too much about your work. It fixes it. It nails it down. And then it bleeds. It begins to die." Cary, *Horse's Mouth*, 215.

13 The "Just" in "Just Harry and Norma" or "Harry and Just Norma" may be a reference to the "Just Mary" programs for children, which were aired on CBC Radio, starting in 1939, written and presented by Mary Grannan (1900–1975).

Between Composers

We could make a fortune, baby! And no work, just be our own little selves! Oscar Levant would be jealous, Life would write it up![14] – fame, fortune, success – we could pin them to the wall for all to behold – and we owe all our success to soap and an ocean!...

... You know, seriously, that I am more deeply in love with you than anyone in my life –You are the first woman I've really loved and am in love with – it's hell and heaven.

All my love – Harry

NB to HS
December 6th, 1959
Darling ~
The beginning of another week! I hope this one will be brighter ~ I can't begin to describe how grisly this past one was for me ~ It is truly a hard battle here ~

I have never been so depressed in my life for such a long period and I ended up on Wednesday by crying my eyes out practically ... Friday night I had not one hour of sleep ~ and at four AM, got fed up and started to study Italian which I did for two and a half hours ~ then got up and piddled around ~ I had an Italian lesson for 2 hours at 10:00 (she came here) in bed, and in the afternoon this little American singer, Marguerite, came over ~ Saturday night, I had asked Gazzelloni for a 'invito' (a ticket) to the RAI Orchestra concert, so I was obliged to go....

... It is very strange, my love, but nothing seemed to be able to lift me out of this depression ~ I was busy this week, in the evening ~ having dinner with a group of ex-Canadians on Wednesday ~ going to see a remarkable Italian film 'La Grande Guerra'[15] with the old university professor on Thursday, going to an orchestral rehearsal

---

14 Oscar Levant (1906–1972) was a multifaceted American composer, pianist, actor, author, arranger, radio game show panelist, television talk show host, and comedian. In California, in the late 1920s and 1930s, he wrote music for films and popular songs, even studying composition with Arnold Schoenberg. He was so well-known and successful that Somers jokes that his proposed soap opera will be even more successful than something of Levant's.

15 *La grande guerra* [The Great War] is a 1959 Italian war film directed by Mario Monicelli starring Alberto Sordi and Vittorio Gassman. It depicts the story of two First World War soldiers and friends who meet in a military district during the call to arms and are eventually shot by the Austrians as spies. The film was nominated for an Academy Award as Best Foreign Film in 1960.

on Friday night and meeting two Italian composers, Ghedini[16] (principal of Milan Conservatory) and another, Pellini (?), who teaches here in Rome ~ and going to the sea for dinner with the group ~ and the concert Saturday night ~ I have felt somewhat better today … I am worried for I haven't been able to think of a damn musical idea for the last few days, and am somewhat paralyzed by the thought of writing an 'exercise' for Petrassi using all twelve-tones, strict technique….

… I don't know whether I told you I now have to buy a new bloody flute if I want to continue to study and make any progress ~ Gazzelloni has repeatedly told me that playing this instrument will only tire me for I have to work too hard to get any sound, the low register is impossible, it is too heavy, etc. etc. I am convinced, for I have been practicing scales daily, etc. for 2 hrs each day, and now I feel that this instrument is giving me an inferiority complex!…

… More news about Darmstadt ~ a 13-day course only – July 7 to July 20th ~ Gazz. is going to find out or get information to me on how to enter the school ~ this man is a valuable person to know ~ I am kept informed each lesson of 'what's going on' in contemporary music here and elsewhere in Europe ~ I found out the other day that Shostakovitch has written an excellent flute concerto for him, as well as Boulez (and probably others have dedicated or written flute scores to/for him)….[17]

… This feeling I have now is an exaggerated feeling as I have experienced in Canada ~ just bloody loneliness and lack of strength or something to fight it all the time ~ I hope I don't have to say that I miss you for that should be understood – but I do not feel I would be happy or that I am ready to return home yet ~ How peculiar to want something and to know in the same breath that the time is not right to return to it ~ I wish I could answer what holds me here ~ perhaps just to discover me I guess ~

This letter must sound very low in spirits, so perhaps I should try to finish it in the morning and hope for a brighter day ~

Goodnight my darling ~

---

16 Giorgio Federico Ghedini (1892–1965) was an Italian composer, conductor, and teacher who taught at the Milan Conservatory from 1951 until 1962. Among his pupils were Claudio Abbado, Luciano Berio, Guido Cantelli, and Niccolò Castiglioni.
17 She was mistaken. Neither Shostakovich nor Boulez wrote a flute concerto.

Monday –
Good morn, my love ~

Received your letter ... a letter from Mother ~ Oh my darling, how sad the family situation is ~ Charles is suffering badly and Carolyn is in a daze....[18]

... So Mother feels her responsibility there and is not coming here ~ I do wish you could help her if at all possible ~ for even though she is strong ~ it must be very difficult ~

I love you darling ~ and need you so much ~

Take much care and don't get too thin.

Love Normie

HS to NB

Sunday, Dec. 6 / 59

My darling Norma – si valés, valéo.[19]

I'm listening to excerpts from one of my favourite operas – Don Giovanni. I've always loved it. I remember many years ago Michael Fram and myself celebrating New Years by listening to the Don.

I'm using an interesting new book for my Latin Studies. The exercises are derived from Latin literature giving the whole approach the sense of a 'live' language, as well as giving an introduction to Roman experience and thought.

Apprendre une langue, c'est vivre de nouveau.

At the end they have Loci Antiqui – excerpts from Catullus, Cicero, Pompey, Horace etc. enough to whet one's appetite....[20]

... My mind is getting so active I find it difficult to sleep at night, so I study 'till 4 or 5 a.m. Outside all the strange night sounds – wild parties down the street spilling onto the street – fights – endless

---

18 The family situation alluded to here and elsewhere in these letters has to do with the aftermath of Beecroft's parents' separation and divorce in 1947. Her father Julian retained custody of the five children in Whitby, while their mother, Eleanor, moved to Toronto and pursued an acting career. During the next decade, the children gradually left their father's house and moved to Toronto to be with her mother. Carolyn and Charles, the youngest, still needed her; she chose not to go to Europe to visit her daughter in Rome but to stay home with them. Norma had moved to Toronto in 1950 at the age of 16.

19 Latin for "If you are well, I am well." The words should not have accents.

20 "Loci Antiqui" are passages chosen from ancient authors that have been adapted to meet the linguistic level of beginning students of Latin.

December 1959   157

arguments of drunk gamblers waiting three hours for a bus from 3
'till 6 a.m.!!! "You're full of shit." echoing about. Then the night
stillness – my solitary street and the city will awaken before long....

––––––––

... 3 a.m. Monday
Had a pleasant evening at Joan and Tony Ferry's. Norm and Gwen
came down and Powys Thomas dropped in all bearded[21] – he's playing Macbeth at the Crest.[22] Fine discussions – situation in Canada,
attitudes, artist in society etc. and Beckett 'Endgame,' a form of
nihilism which infuriates Tony....
    ... The Ferrys believe in 'group theatre' but are having a tough
battle here getting good actors interested. They have a little basement theatre at King and Dufferin and trying to make it work is
exhausting. Of course their hero is Brecht, the kind of 'holy' name
of modern theatre....[23]

––––––––

21 Powys Thomas (1926–1977), a distinguished Canadian actor and teacher, was born
in Wales. He graduated from the Old Vic Theatre School and acted with the Royal
Shakespeare Company (1952–54) before coming to Canada in 1956. Besides working
with the CBC, and acting at the Stratford Festival for twelve years, he co-founded the
National Theatre School of Canada in 1960 and was artistic director of the English
section until 1965.
22 The Crest Theatre, located on Mount Pleasant Road in Toronto, was founded by
Donald and Murray Davis and their sister Barbara Chilcott in 1954. Over the course
of twelve seasons, the theatre put on some 140 productions, giving actors and directors
an opportunity early in their careers to get experience with classical and contemporary
theatre, as well as presenting contemporary plays by such figures as Robertson Davies,
John Gray, Mary Jukes, Marcel Dubé, Ted Allen, and Bernard Slade.
23 The group that became Toronto Workshop Productions had obtained free use
of a basement underneath a printing shop in the heart of Toronto's industrial zone
at 47 Fraser Avenue, several blocks west of Spadina Avenue's garment district. In
December 1959 (at the time of this letter) they were playing Chekhov's *The Boor* and
Lorca's *Don Perlimplin*. Powys Thomas had been one of the actors involved in the early
stages of the group but when he was appointed director of the National Theatre School
in June 1959 he could no longer participate. See Ferry, "Experiences of a Pioneer in
Canadian Experimental Theatre," *Theatre Research in Canada / Recherches théâtrales
Au Canada* 8, no.1 (1987): 59–67. Retrieved from https://journals.lib.unb.ca/index.php/
TRIC/article/view/7378.

158   Between Composers

... Monday afternoon –

A furious blizzardy day. My God, I heard on a news report last night that ships were floundering in 80 foot waves in the Atlantic!! I'll fly, thanks. (Oh that I could!!)

I have to be in Ottawa to-morrow morning to complete film arrangements. Weather's so bad I might have to take the train or borrow my mother's car and drive up.

Sent off the Guitar sonata to Segovia. Interesting to see if there's any reaction. I regard the work as presenting absolutely no problems idiomatically, in fact quite obvious, but Eli has a great difficult[y] in comprehending it musically!! However he is working hard at it. Times I feel quite insane.

Eli has 80 pupils! Can you imagine the work involved!

Leon Major has publicly claimed (via newspaper) that he is quitting theatre in Toronto.[24] "Actors are phony – no support" etc. etc. Trouble is he threw all his resources – financial and otherwise – into one production which didn't pay off, a very unwise move.[25]

Tony's attitude is right – adjust your theatre to circumstances, keep your pretentions modest, form a group who share labor etc, work within practical needs with the view to establishing a group theatre over a period of years[,] building your reputation gradually much as London's east end. Unfortunately I have a feeling Tony's group is heavily larded with amateurs, devoted to theatre, but amateurs nonetheless. I shall see.

The situation for actors generally is very bad this season....

... Happiness and well-being to you my beloved. I want life to be only good for you. All success in your studies, dearest –

>   All my love – ever –
>   Harry

24 Leon Major (b. 1933) is a Toronto-born opera and theatre director. He was the founding and first artistic director of the Neptune Theatre in Halifax, Nova Scotia, and served for ten years as artistic and general director of Toronto Arts Productions. In 1967, he directed the first performance of Somers's opera *Louis Riel*. In an article in the *Toronto Daily Star*, appearing a few days before this letter, Major was quoted as saying he intended to leave Toronto theatre because it was characterized by "hypocrisy, phoniness and inertia" and by actors who didn't really care about their work, only about how much money they could make. He felt that a "worthwhile Canadian theatre can be carved from the rocks and people of Northern Ontario." ("Toronto Actors Too Phony," *Toronto Daily Star*, 5 December 1959.)

25 The production that failed was the first play by the British playwright Bernard Kops (b. 1926), *The Hamlet of Stepney Green*.

December 1959   159

HS to NB
Tuesday night, Dec 7 [8]
En route – Toronto. Ottawa

My beloved Normie: –

Ah – this time I have a roomette!! Coming up in the world!! There is one thing missing – <u>you</u>!!!!

Dear soul, can you know how much you mean to me!!?? I'm stark raving mad about you! You are the centre of gravity about which I revolve!

Here I am in this crazy world bouncing around like some pea in a pod without the one person who gives me sense out of all this madness....

... Please understand what a <u>dreadful</u> part past experience has played in my life – it produced eternal suspicion, doubt, denial, hurt, unwillingness to take a chance, etc.

For you I throw all this garbage out! For you I finally take a chance because you are worth my life to me and I trust you with it!! I love you with every part of me – there is nothing left out – my need for you – my giving to you – my wanting to share with you – you are <u>the woman I love</u> with <u>everything I've got</u>, there is <u>no</u> other question to me....

———————

... Tuesday night – Dec. 8

Now I return to Toronto in another roomette thinking of you going off to Tanglewood....

... Well, I've finally accepted to do the film. An easy-going day. Met the public relations man from "Alco' who is responsible for the whole business.[26] Interesting and amusing man in his forties. At a certain point he got my back up and I was ready to throw it all up, but I kept relative control. He's really all right but I was tired having slept for only an hour all told, and was in a fighting mood.

26 The Northern Aluminium Company Limited was founded in 1902, in Shawinigan, Quebec, and officially registered under the trade name Alcan in 1945. Somers's use of the name "Alco" probably derives from the company name "Aluminum Company of America" or "Alcoa." It was not known as "Alcan" until 1966.

I asked Budge Crawley for $2000.00 feeling it to be worth it. He's an honest guy – he said $1000.00 and if the film really came off he would see that I got the remainder saying the whole film was a risk. He's one man I trust so I said what he feels to be right is fine with me, so I would go along with it because I believe in the film. No bluster – just preserving our viewpoints.

So at a minimum I get $1000.00 – maximum $2000.00 – we'll see. I hate bickering over dough so now I immerse myself totally in the work.

After all my talk about Webern et company, I think I will open with the titles with Webernish ideas. (An abstraction of drops of water) hitting the viewer a fearful wack later when I cohere it into solid Somers. It's a tough project, because as usual I set myself tough goals. I'm stimulated by it and hope to come up with something striking and worthwhile.

The Gatineau Hills are so beautiful – snow covered under a dramatic winter cloudscape. Had lunch at the Crawleys where we completed our discussions....

... Present also was the Crawleys' French governess from Paris, a sad woman whose husband was killed in Indonesia (Indo China).

The Crawleys have five children from 19 to 9, 6 horses, a couple of goats, a duck which think[s] it's human, a pet raccoon. It's a delightfully mad household and as I said before I think they are quite wonderful people whom I would trust completely.

A fantastic variety of colourful birds make use [of] free sunflower seeds kept in a box outside their window.

With a $500.00 advance I'm free to devote my energy to the work....

... Before boarding the train I had a few drinks by myself by way of a solitary launching, at the Chateau Laurier. Just sat in the middle of the crowd thinking of you and enjoying the warmth from my thoughts of you. Businessmen, call girls, wives etc. provided a babble background to my thoughts....

Home (Dec 9. Wed.)

... Your depressed letter arrived, love. The mail seems a bit slow. I guess Christmas is buggering it up....

December 1959 161

... Everything will be fine for us one day, sweetheart, we'll be together and start to really live our lives with joy! (No doubt a few fights. After all it wouldn't be right without them. We make up so well!)

As to coming over before June – it's a tough question for me, to say the least. When I see you so 'down' and I'm so 'down' without you I just want to fly right over or have you return to me immediately. A place just becomes so much scenery without the one you love.

It's just that I have 1) Finish the film score. Probably by the 1st of February. It has to be. 2) I should wait 'till I hear re: Canada Council. But this should be made known by mid or late February or 1st of March. 3) If I got an award it would be extremely wise to complete the Koussevitzky commission before embarking on the fellowship. It could be sticky otherwise and the Koussevitzky money would be insurance money for us. 4) If the fellowship didn't happen I would see that we were together as soon as possible. 5) A divorce – I spoke to Kay and though it actually stunned her and broke her heart when the reality of divorce was in front of her, she said she would consent to my wishes. There was no bitterness. When I get ahead financially I can start proceedings. After years of tears, hurt, loneliness I hope there can be come happiness for both her and myself. You can well understand the tragedy for a woman, my love....

... I'm sorry to hear of the Whitby trouble. God! I hoped you could be free of those family entanglements which have bogged you for years....

... Please take care, and feel the heat from my love – always –
Harry

HS to NB
Thursday, Dec. 10, 1959
My beloved Normie:

Last night I was talking at some length with your mother. She will likely give you all the details, so I won't go into it.

Suffice to say that I'm extremely sorry for all concerned that she won't be going to Europe for Christmas. It's a miserable let down.

In view of what the situation was, and still could be in relation to Whitby, it was the only thing she could do. Your mother has taken on a stature in my eyes that I didn't realize she possessed. She has put the needs of Carolyn and Charles ahead of her own without question. ....

162   Between Composers

... I would <u>strongly</u> advise, almost insist, that you and Eric get together for Christmas. Get him to Rome, if you can, or else go to England. You must make arrangements immediately.

Your family is a close unit, you are very close to each other – so be sure to see Eric one way or another at Christmas, eh darling? It will help both of you at this difficult and sentimental time of year....

... My only love, my Normie, take care not to get too down – I'm with you.

Try to study, to work as best you can. When you are depressed as you can be, don't be afraid to put down your thoughts and feelings on paper to me. I've found it helps sometimes to write about it.

Composition is tough. We work with so many intangibles. At least with an instrument one knows what one has to do and there is a sense of accomplishment in doing it, there is something to measure it by.

I've often found that if I'm not 'inspired' to work, that to just sit down and work on problems, with no thought of their being music, is a good way. Sometimes good ideas emerge, one never knows, and the unemotional approach allows you to clarify certain aspects which otherwise would escape you.

Try not to dwell on the family situation – it will be fine. Your mother is strong and the children can always be assured of a home....

... [I] embrace you with all my love and wish you to be free to search, study, discover yourself to learn from your surroundings without pressure or intimidation from the le nouveau monde –

   Valē –
   Harry

HS to NB
Thursday afternoon, Dec. 10 / 59
My dearest Normie:

I was quietly minding me own business, walking along the street to post my last letter to you. A honk, a shout and there's Harvey Hart.[27] A coincidence because a couple of days ago I had written him a letter of congratulations on the success of the 'Crucible', something I had intended to do for over a month.

We had coffee together over at the C.B.C....

... We had a discussion on Arthur Miller, American drama,

27 See chap. 3, n. 69.

government, world situation etc. He also spoke of his background research for the Crucible at Salem. Harvey's always a most interesting guy to talk to. February he's doing Ibsen's An Enemy of the People.

One evening I shall drop up and visit at Betty Ann Drive next week.[28]

I'm now the proud possessor of a stopwatch, the kind you used to have at the C.B.C. I was always a little jealous of it and found you most glamorous – clicking, stopping, jotting down, clicking again, you sexy bitch!

The watch will be an income tax deduction, it's essential to this movie. Every bar has to have the seconds numbered. The conductor uses the watch held in left hand checking it against bar timings. When you think that the film moves at 24 frames per second you realize how important exact timing is....

Friday noon:

... Meant to send you an article Harvey Hart wrote on a group who are dancing nightly at the 'First Floor Club' – the 'beat' club, but forgot and threw out the paper, damn it! Apparently they are doing dances of India, as Harvey said, "Part amateurish, part pretentious, but one part excellent." He felt the effort to be honest and sincere and felt that from such activity real dancing will emerge along this line. Part of his article was written in a very amusing manner without being cruel.[29] A lot of activity seems to be coming from small groups about town....

... Correction!! – the new snack bar across the corner is called 'Adam's Snack Bar.' Adam's. Isn't that significant! The beginning, garden of Eden, Eve and all that! It has poetry – Adam back to feed the world as penance. God's short order cook! What marvels are witnessed here on Church St. Isn't that extraordinary?! Adam's Snack Bar on Church St. An evangelist could make a song out of it! "I'm in the mood for pie, – simply because God made it, – I'm going

---

28 Somers's parents, Ruth and Russell Somers, had moved to North York in the late 1950s.

29 In this article, Hart actually said that the dancers and the dancing were "uneven, a mixture of commercialism, amateurism, theatricality and authenticity" and were "spotty in execution." See "In Off-Beatnik Club," Toronto Daily Star, 9 December 1959.

164   Between Composers

down to Adam's, – Snack Bar on Chu-hurch Street." (Copyright Hellish Harry Somers, Pub. member of H.O.R.S.E.S.H.I.T. MMMMMMMXIV.)

I know my material is dreadful. But some things are so bad they are good....

... Take care my only love, my dearest love –
     Love, love, love – a thousand times love!!
       Harry

NB to HS
December 11th – 10:00 PM
My darling Harry,

Another Friday night rolls by without you ~ for some reason Friday nights have always been the nights to go out, to me, the small-town girl ~ Rome is humid and heavy, bad for colds and headaches (I have the latter) ~

I have had today another flute lesson on my lousy flute ~ a strange lesson ~ Gazzelloni has a frightening cold, so the lesson was interspersed with shots of straight whiskey (I took it to be sociable) but by the time I got through playing all the major scales, the chromatic scale three octaves, and numerous other exercises, and the 'difficult stuff' arrived ~ Marcello Sonatas[30] – 2 of them, the mind was a little fuzzy ... halfway through the allegro movement, the power went off, and I continued to play in the dark, and then by candlelight ~ The lesson concluded with another shot of whiskey ~ Nice people, these Italians, but now of course, I am only capable of sleeping....

... I am truly frustrated with this time element ... I have to do all my washing in the bathtub, shop every day for I have no refrigerator, keep the damn place clean ~ and try to study in addition ~ Italian, the flute, and composition ... What suffers most is my composition, for I am not on a rigid schedule as with flute and Italian, and have much trouble exerting discipline over my lethargic mind and body ~ Some day perhaps I'll have a maid, a husband, and time ~?

---

30 Benedetto Marcello (1686–1739) was a prolific Italian composer (and a writer, advocate, magistrate, and teacher). Beecroft was likely working on one of his twelve Sonatas for Flute and Basso Continuo op. 2, published in Venice in 1712.

December 1959　　　165

I am pondering however on the principles of 12-tone writing ~ and have commenced to write a piece for piano ~ It is much more complex than I had ever dreamed to write a <u>piece</u> of <u>music</u> using such a strict technique, which, on the other hand, is not strict enough (there aren't enough rules or something) ~ To observe my tendencies now is interesting ~ I certainly am breaking away from 'yesterday' ~ not sure where it is heading exactly ~ ma non importa adesso! (It doesn't matter now) ~

Sometimes, my dear, I feel as though I am losing my marbles ~ It is incomprehensible to me, why we are not together now, and why we didn't come together when I was in Canada ~ I ask myself 'does this mean it was not meant to be?' ~ 'does this mean that perhaps I, and you have another purpose conceivably higher in this life?' ~ What does it mean? Or do I have no purpose at all? Ezra Pound wrote a poem, 'Portrait d'une femme' ~ which makes me ponder myself, and you[31] ~

I have passed Round #1 Depression, but something else seems to be niggling away at my ~ my what? It is a kind of half-bitterness, near acceptance, desperation, emptiness ~ You wish my happiness, darling ~ but do I know really what will create that for me?... Dearest Harry, I am afraid, <u>so</u> afraid, that I don't <u>believe</u> any more, and yet I have to, or I couldn't live now I am struggling with myself to believe that happiness could ever be found together ~ Please forgive me for writing these things, darling ~ naturally, all answers are found in time ~ I know this ~ I read, and re-read your letters, and at first felt such relief to know that you found your answers, and found you care and love me ~ Now begins the struggle with myself to try to recreate the dream and bring it to a reality ~ to believe again in that dream....

... Please send me your quartet, darling, and I would love to see the guitar Sonata ~ I too will be anxious to hear Segovia's comments

---

31 This poem was first published in 1912 in *Ripostes*, a collection of twenty-five poems by Ezra Pound. The collection is considered an early example of Imagism, a poetry movement concerned with directness of presentation, economy of language, and the use of non-traditional verse forms such as free verse. The speaker in the poem tries to define the woman's identity through the objects she's given and what she gives back, much as the sea gives up certain objects and absorbs others. A central concern of the poem is woman's role as muse in artistic creation; perhaps Beecroft was considering her own role in that respect in relation to Somers's creative work.

on the work ~ I suspect his old head might not appreciate 'new' music ~ is that true? I am very pleased that your work goes well and that you are so busy ~ life in Toronto sounds very active, and you seem to have made a number of new friendships which sound stimulating. I was rather overwhelmed by your list of women! Please give my love to the Kassners, and the Youngs, and Norm and Gwen ~

I love you my sweet and
ache for your love
Normie

HS to NB
Saturday, Dec. 12 / 59
Dearest love:

You say – 'but I do not feel I would be happy or that I am ready to return home yet' ...

... The important part of your statement is that you do not feel ready to come home yet. You <u>do</u> have a great deal to solve and find out. I understand this.

Happiness is something else. If one seeks it it is like the rabbit trying to catch the carrot projected beyond his nose by a stick tied to his head.

Naturally it hurts me, but I accept it, Normie dear. I hope you realize what you've said – in essence that happiness is <u>not</u> a thing called Harry....

... At a party for Duke Ellington last night, Norm got to talking of the whole problem, his doubts, his fears of taking a chance with a woman when he knows too much about women.

I said that now, even knowing what human nature is ... there is <u>no</u> question in my mind – there is one woman, Norma, I love her completely, I take my chances, I have thrown the dice.

He said 'Well why isn't she with you.'?

I said that I had dragged you through the coals for four years. That my one great gift I can give her is to be free to make up her own mind and to find herself....

... I am with you and understand. It is an important struggle as any in your life, but you will emerge from the sickness with maturity.

Ever – all my love – all my being –
Your Harry

December 1959　　　　　　167

HS to NB

Saturday night – Dec. 12 / 59

My only love:

The 'chorale' part of the Berg violin concerto.[32] A re-broadcast of the Philharmonic broadcast I spoke of.

A wet snow night. In my room in my solitude and loneliness – words which are my constant companions.

And the hand that wrote the music is dead, is dust. 1935....[33]

... Now the Brahms double concerto – music from another era. Rose and Stern.[34] There are times the mellow warmth of Brahms' music is good.

My thoughts circle, hover, take flight into darkness.

———

4:30 a.m.

Jeremy and Mary Wilkin have just left.[35] They dropped in at 2 a.m. Interesting, amusing, witty conversation. Jeremy brought a bottle of wine....

———

32 The last part of the Berg Violin Concerto features the quotation of a Bach chorale ("Es ist genug") by the soloist and orchestra. The first four notes of the chorale melody, a whole-tone scale segment, also form the last four pitches of the twelve-tone row upon which the concerto is based. This was Berg's last completed work (in 1935).
33 Berg died at the age of only fifty on 24 December 1935 of sepsis caused by an infected insect bite.
34 Cellist Leonard Rose (1918–1984) and violinist Isaac Stern (1920–2001) were two of the great performers of the twentieth century. The performance Somers heard on this occasion was probably a 1956 Philips recording of the Brahms Double Concerto with the New York Philharmonic conducted by Bruno Walter, taken from a performance in 1954.
35 Jeremy Wilkin (1930–2017) was an English-born actor who had emigrated to Canada after completing studies at the Royal Academy of Dramatic Art in London. In Toronto he appeared on the theatrical stage and in television productions for the CBC, appearing with figures such as Patrick Macnee, future *Star Trek* star James Doohan, and Lloyd Bochner. With Bochner, he appeared on the Broadway stage in New York in 1958 in a production of Shakespeare's *Two Gentlemen of Verona* at the Phoenix Theatre. In the early 1960s, he and his wife, singer Mary Catherine Newland and family, returned to England.

[Monday] 5 p.m.

... Just returned from the Chapman house, beautiful spot overlooking Rosedale ravine, a house in the English manner – wood, stairways, leaded windows – Tudor in style. It was there many years ago I studied piano with Schmitz.[36]

Chris showed me the German film on aluminum which is to be companion to his. The tape–electronic music suited the purposes perfectly, ideal for such a film. At times it sounded like a keyboard organ of some description.

Also saw the Lorent classic, music of Virgil Thompson, 'The River'.[37] Many excellent things about the music but still had me doubts.

Last week I went to a party for the models, dancers, some musicians and executives of G.M. as a guest of Norm and Gwen. (Gwen's dancing in the G.M. show at the 'Ex'.)[38] A ridiculous gathering for us to be at. But Norm had an opportunity to say what we both had wanted to say since reading an episode in Fitzgerald.

36 For information on E. Robert Schmitz, see chap. 3, n. 63. Schmitz had been visiting Toronto since 1934 and by the mid-1940s was coming to the city some three times a year, attracting the interest of several dozen musicians among Toronto's pianists and piano teachers. Among these were Reginald Godden and Weldon Kilburn. Somers studied with both of them and went to the United States twice after the war to study with Schmitz himself, in 1946 and 1948. The Chapman house, located at 93 Roxborough Road, had been designed and built in 1927 by Chapman's father, the prominent architect, Alfred Hirschfelder Chapman (1878–1949). Alfred Chapman's wife, Doris Dennison, had trained in England as a concert pianist. This is likely the reason why Schmitz gave classes at the Chapmans' house when he visited Toronto.

37 *The River* is a short documentary film produced in 1938 to raise awareness of the New Deal. It shows how farming and timber practices had caused topsoil to be swept down the Mississippi River and into the Gulf of Mexico, leading to catastrophic floods and problems for farmers. Written and directed by documentary filmmaker Pare Lorentz (1905–1992), the film won the "best documentary" category at the 1938 Venice International Film Festival. The score for the film was written by the American composer Virgil Thomson.

38 The G.M. show at the CNE's Automotive Building was sponsored by General Motors and was part of the "GM Motorama" exhibition for 1960. It ran for about ten days in early December and featured thirty-two dancers, as well as the American duo of Gordon and Sheila MacRae. The director was the Toronto musician/arranger Howard Cable, for whom Somers copied music to help support himself.

December 1959   169

A gorgeous dumb blond asked Norm in a coy sweet voice "And what do you do."

"I fuck!" Norm replies and the girl jumped through the roof telling everyone there was a dirty old man who said something to her she wouldn't dare repeat. It was really very funny from our viewpoint.

I never thought the day would arrive when I could find an externally beautiful woman a bore, but it has. Both Norm and myself couldn't get out soon enough....

... 9 p.m. Mother just phoned to inform me that an old friend of mine had just died at 5 p.m. He was a bank manager, age 49, Ron Bernand.[39] In the '40's we used to play a great deal of table tennis, talk. He was fond of my music. I'm a bit shocked for I have had a presentment of death lately but passed it off as Somers being dramatic. There are times my intuitive streaks frighten me.

I haven't seen Ron for a number of years. Somehow one gets in the habit of thinking life will just go on until one is jolted by the death of someone one knows. He had finished his days work, left the bank and dropped dead on the street.

All around is death but we are never really aware until it comes close to us.

He was married (her second) to the mother of a boyhood chum of mine who was killed in the war. Finis.

I am saddened so will write no further.
Take care, my dearest love, you are the world to me.
I love you with my whole being –

Harry

---

39 Ron Bernand had worked at the Imperial Bank at Wilson and Keele in Toronto. He was married to Audrey Morine, the mother of a boyhood friend of Somers.

170   Between Composers

NB to HS
December 14th, 1959
My darling Harry,

I receive your letters with much excitement, always ~ This morning I had two at once, one letter from my dear Mother, and a
Christmas greeting from your Mother ~ How marvellous to have so
much mail....

... One of the things which would provide great delight and fascination for you here are the swallows ~ I have never seen anything
quite so interesting, and I am told one finds these bird formations
in many Renaissance paintings ~ Thousands of these birds fly over
Rome and near church domes, seemingly always at 4 or 5 in the
afternoon, and form different shapes, constantly moving like wisps
of smoke ~ It is really incredible and I can't take my eyes off this
abstraction, especially when the background is a sunset ~ (there are
few these days) but the cloud-scapes are fantastic ~

I must tell you of my evening here last night ~ I had promised
some of my 'stranieri' friends a shiskabob, made by Aram[40] ~ the
gent from Baghdad ~ Well, what a fiasco it turned out to be ~ I
shall describe in detail, if you can put up with it ~ First of all, I had
borrowed this outdoor bar-b-que, and the meat was going to be
cooked on the terrace ~ naturally it rained all day ~ I had invited 4
people here ~ Aram, who arrived at 5:30 and together commenced
to prepare the meat Iraqi style and vegetables, Marguerita Lamb, a
young American singer-student, Beatrice Delilah, a Bostonian gal,
who brought 3 uninvited guests, all Italian males, and Roberto Savio
(Carla's brother) ~ At 8:00, all but Roberto were here ... Aram commenced to light up the Barbque ~ (the rain had stopped but the
terrace was wet) ~ After 3 hours, the stubborn Easterner finally gave
in to my pleas to give it up ~ the fire wouldn't burn, there was char-
coal and paper all over my wet terrace, in the kitchen, bathroom,
floors, everywhere ~ it was a mess, and my guests were getting very
impatient ~ Aram still wouldn't give up the idea that he <u>had</u> to cook
the bloody meal ~ and got in my way in the kitchen which is only big
enough for one ~ knocked over a pot of cooked potatoes ~ next the
shiskabob hit the floor ~ and I almost threw him out....

40 No doubt she means "shish kebab," skewered and grilled cubes of meat. In 1959,
this must have been a far more exotic dish than it is now. Aram was the violinist friend
she had mentioned in earlier letters. See chap. 3, n. 51.

December 1959

... Tomorrow I again see Petrassi ~ I have written one piano piece ~ 12 tone ~ very short and causing me much concern ~ We'll see what he says, although I am always terrified to see him ~ But I find this damn technique very difficult to handle, and I really need guidance, plus a weekly push ~ So far he is <u>teaching</u> me, and without asking for money. I don't know whether I am one of the preferred few or not, for I know the Fullbright composer doesn't receive this attention and I am told he doesn't teach privately (others have said he only takes those whose work he likes!) I am afraid to tell him that I can't complete Michael's work by the end of December ~ it is too gross a task ~ too long and requires too much thought and technique which I as yet don't have (ie. the facility to work quickly)

Poor old Gazzelloni still has a terrible cold and he has to play on TV tomorrow evening ~ I am going to the concert and then after will look at these new flutes from America ... I can't figure out whether to buy a new one or not....

... I have decided to write to the Canada Council, as an emergency application, in January when I know whether I will get into the course at Santa Cecilia or no, and ask them for assistance to complete this year of study and also Darmstadt ... In February I will submit an application for the next year if I deem it possible to stay in Europe....

... Please forgive my depressed, worried letters ~ the moods pass ~ more than moods, I believe ~ and somehow I find the will to continue ... We really must learn to live with our loneliness, I suppose, for a while anyway ~

I am sending a wee parcel to you ~ please forgive the size ~ I hope you receive it ~

So much love
Normie

HS TO NB
Tues. Dec. 15/59
My beloved:

Your mother just called to tell me you called on Monday morning while her toast burned on and on. She said you sounded happy and well, which is good to hear....

... From my own well of loneliness has emerged certain musical ideas that I might one day develop. I've just jotted them down.

Between Composers

I feel to sublimate human experience into an artistic shape is one of man's noblest acts. Creating of shape out of chaos. One can do this out of one's life or out of the specific materials of art. (I'll always be a romantic.)....

––––––––––

... Saw an amusing film of Peter Sellers – 'The Mouse that Roared,'[41] a very charming French companion short film – 'The Golden Fish'[42] about a small boy, a gold fish, a canary and an alley cat, and a news reel of Eisenhower in Rome. – I just caught a glimpse of your apartment as you opened the window.

The hour is quiet and conducive to work....

––––––––––

... More sad news. Paul Scherman's wife died in Paris. They have been separated for a couple of years. She was a very sweet woman, daughter of Creed, the furrier. She was only in her thirties.[43]

––––––––––

It's difficult for me to raise my spirits at all this time. I'll be known as funky Somers, except I manage to put on a pretty good face most of the time. Sometimes cynicism is a defence against my sadness and loneliness.

41 *The Mouse That Roared* (1959) was a British film, based on the 1955 novel of the same name by Leonard Wibberley. It starred Peter Sellers (playing three roles), and co-starred Jean Seberg. The film satirizes the relationship between a tiny fictitious European country and the United States, chiefly involving a lethal new bomb and various deals to determine who should have possession of it.

42 *The Golden Fish (Histoire d'un poisson rouge)* was a French short film directed by Edmond Séchan and released in 1959. It won an Oscar in 1960 for best short subject. The film has a musical score but no dialogue and features a boy, a gold fish, and a black cat.

43 Paul Scherman's wife, Donna, was the daughter of Jack and Dorothy Creed, who owned Creeds, the exclusive furrier in downtown Toronto. She and Paul Scherman had two children, Theo and Tony, and the family moved to Paris in 1955. In 1958 the parents separated and in December of the following year, Donna, a rather "troubled soul" (as her son Tony described her years later) sent the children to their father in London and committed suicide. In fact, they had only been separated for about a year. See *Toronto Life* 41, no. 3 (March 2007), 66–72.

December 1959173

I hope that Eric will help you have a happy Xmas, my love.

My emptiness without you, my longing and need for you, my love for you are limitless.

Harry

NB to HS
Tuesday [15 December] ~ 11:00 PM
Dearest Harry,

I have just returned from a concert to receive your letter, which I know is meant as encouragement but which seems to upset me ~ I said I was not ready to return home yet ~ The 'why not' is a grand question ~ I am sorry if this hurts you but I think you must have written your letter without thinking about that question ~ I have tried to explain to you many times as much as I know each day ~ and nothing is very clear to me right now except this knowledge that I can't return ~ I feel freedom to breathe here, freedom from family, freedom from gossip, freedom to move alone when I wish ~ otherwise freedom to live independently ~ This is the first time in my life I have felt freedom (I am not saying it doesn't have its enormous disadvantages) but at this time I don't want to feel as though anyone is chaining me to anything ~ I alone chain myself, I know, and that is enough to cope with ~

You say, in other words, 'happiness is not Harry' ~ What is happiness anyway? Although I bask in the love and warmth of your letters, I still am afraid of you ~ The hurt has gone very deep with me my darling, and I fear that I have been moving into a kind of bitter, emotional condition, one of non-belief, which you are just moving out of ~ Such is the life cycle of human beings ~ All I know now, is that I can depend only on one thing ~ myself ~ and I intend to do my damndest to write music which cannot change ~ that the expression of myself is positive and will last, and is only dependent on me, and I on it ~ This should make sense to you ~ No, I am far from being happy away from you, for I need you very much in many ways ~ No one can fill that need, but you – but I am afraid that I cannot find 'happiness' with anyone and have felt this way for a long time ~ My darling, what can you expect me to think when I have had a lifetime of being loved and pushed away at the same time....

AM

I stopped writing last night for I found myself starting to sink into that god-damned depressed, hopeless state which I must try to avoid....

174 Between Composers

... Today is Wednesday, my love, two weeks before the end of 1959 roughly ~ I told Petrassi yesterday that it was impossible to finish Michael's work before the end of December ~ that I could not work that quickly ~ He was very sympathetic with my problems related to twelve-tone writing, explaining to me that it is another form of thought and one cannot use old forms and parallelisms etc. ~ that one must be free of the past thinking ~ He has given me another project ~ a piece for piano, using all four forms of the row, not repeating a note or rhythmic idea ~ I am enjoying my work with him very much ~ I believe he is another self-made man, and seemingly very intelligent ~ I spent 1 1/2 hrs with him ~ I told him that I wish very much to enter his course (I need the discipline) and he again repeated that I stood a very good chance ~ I must submit works by the end of December, so I am cancelling flute and Italian lessons until January to prepare my scores ~ I think he likes my work, calls it musical and 'simpatico' ~ he must, for I continue to work with him without paying which is astounding to my fellow student composers (mind you, I think that all Italians like pretty women around, even if just to look at ~ but I am also sure that I wouldn't be receiving his attention if my work didn't have some merit!)....

... There is no snow here, of course, so this season is a little easier on me, sentimentally ~ I loathe shopping in the stores and seeing all the Christmas decorations, but try to keep my perspective ~ Eric will arrive next Tuesday and he and I, and the young composer Peter and Margaret Lamb (the two Americans) will attempt to cook a Christmas dinner here ~ I have asked to use the Barker's oven ~ so I guess we will make out OK....

... Please enjoy yourself as much as possible at Christmas, my love. I will be thinking of all those wonderful people I have known in Toronto, and wish for everyone's happiness ~

I sent yesterday a parcel by registered air mail ~ If you do not receive it, please let me know ~

So much love to you, it hurts

Love, love, love

Normie ~

HS to NB
Thursday / Dec. 17 /59
Dearest Normie:

I woke this morning with a lightness I haven't felt for many months. The day is beautiful, the weather like early spring. (To-morrow might be a blizzard.)

December 1959

Yes, the feeling that it is god-damn good to be alive – that there is much to do and feel and study and write – that there is the gift of life and what's the point of being in a bloody funk – there is too much to do!

So, for the time being, the fog has lifted.

All sorts of ideas. I'm gleaning much wheat for bread. I'm always concerned with a music which can set up relationships so that I can create contrast to the listener's ear. We know now that it is simple enough to create 'decentralized' music which avoids the establishing of permanent or even temporary tonal centres of relationship. (Though if there is any duration of a note there is always a centre, no matter how slight.) Music concerned only with abstract balance and relationship – very often 'paper' works – hell, I better shut up or I'll be talking it instead of writing it! There's already too much talk in relation to composition. It will get so that the composers will give talks and prepare notes which are longer than the composition! Was there ever a previous age of composers who sought to justify their music by explaining its parts, by using words? In opera there have been manifestos but never the taking apart of the watch in public. If a composition must be explained verbally rather than aurally then what is it? Me thinks it's bull shit, in effect, it _is_ bull shit.

Well, back to my own particular brand of same.

---

5 p.m.

Was browsing about at Gerrard & Bay when I gets a knock on the window and there's Helen W. beckoning from inside the Artisan shop.[44]

---

44 At the time, this small area of Toronto was comparable to New York's Greenwich Village, with such establishments as the Bohemian Embassy, the original framing shop of Avrom Isaacs, and shops such as The Artisans and The Fiddlers Three. "Helen W." is Helen Weinzweig (see chap. 3, n. 5). It is not clear whether he means that Helen Weinzweig admires the fact that Beecroft went away to do what she wanted to do or merely that she is doing what she wants, i.e., creative work and study. In fact, Helen Weinzweig had plenty of self-will; by 1959, she was writing fiction and her first short story was published in 1967, followed by two novels. The woman who "worked" in the shop was Mildred Gelfand Ryerson (1913–2003), a dear friend of Helen Weinzweig. She was a social activist and pioneer in occupational therapy who had trained in that field at

176 Between Composers

So I look around for cards and chat with Helen and another woman who works there.

This woman was in China about a year ago with her husband who was doing film work there. They found it fascinating. So much that they allowed their 16 year old daughter to stay in Peking to study Chinese for which she seemed to possess a special aptitude....

... The woman brought back some Chinese music which I want to hear. Knowing the infinite subtlety of Oriental art which makes the French even appear vulgar, I would suspect that the music contains a similar subtlety.

Helen expressed admiration for your will and determination. I suppose you are doing something she has always wanted to do, but one doesn't have to go away to do it so that it comes right back to whether she could anyway. But she admits she doesn't have your self-will....

... My god-damn fever's back. I get so sick of sickness! All summer that unnameable hay fever and now this! Don't worry, I'm only blowing off steam....

... Just to say I've got a brilliant idea for the Koussevitzky work. It always happens that when I should be working on one work I get ideas about the other. I can use this by bouncing between both works.

Before I go up to your mother's to-night I'm going to see what's cooking with the Ferrys' little theatre group. George Luscombe directing.[45]

---

the University of Toronto and had spent some time in the United States. Her shop, The Artisans, on Gerrard Street, was an outgrowth of her work using crafts to help rehabilitate psychiatric patients. In 1944, she had married Stanley Bréhaut Egerton Ryerson (1911–1998), an historian, educator, and political activist. I am indebted to Paul and Daniel Weinzweig for identifying the woman in the shop.

45 George Luscombe (1926–1999), one of the most important figures in Canadian theatre during the 1960s and '70s, was an exact contemporary of Somers. He had spent five years working in Joan Littlewood's Theatre Workshop in the 1950s, then returned to Toronto. In 1958, he founded Workshop Theatre, which later became Toronto Workshop Productions. Luscombe served as director of this company from 1963 until 1986. From Littlewood's Theatre Workshop, Luscombe brought the concept of group theatre, in which an ensemble of actors, directors, designers, carpenters and others work together to create theatre that was often politically or socially engaged, as opposed to

December 1959

Now back to work.

6:30 p.m. Grant Strate just called to say 'Ballad' was an unqualified success in Montreal this year.[46] Last year they had doubts – 'derivative' etc. – but this year they seemed to grasp its originality. 'Fisherman' is being done three times and Ballad four at the Royal Alex this year – (that is in February) I guess I'll have to have a look. Grant said Ballad has tightened up considerably.

He's looking for a 28 min. score for an abstract ballet. I said I didn't have one. (I can just hear a ballet orchestra trying to play my symphony!) It would be fun to write a long score for ballet which had no programmatic implications....

---

2 a.m. Back.

The theatre was much better than I had expected. The Chekov 'The Boor' was set in the Old South for some crazy reason.[47] They attempted to change the accents but neglected to change the Russian names 'At you service, m-a-am' Says Grigory S. Smirnov. 'Thet thar hoss cost me 1000 rubles, ma-a-am.'

'Don Perlimplin' was another matter.[48] This extremely poignant story of a middle-aged man and his young bride by Lorca was well

---

the lighter fare that had previously dominated Canadian theatre. One of the best-known productions of those years was a theatrical version of Barry Broadfoot's Ten Lost Years, a book about the Depression years in Canada. See Anthony Ferry, "Ten Good People and an Idea," Toronto Daily Star, 5 December 1959.

46 Grant Strate (1927–2015) was a Canadian dancer, choreographer, and academic. He was an original member of the National Ballet of Canada, from 1951 until 1970. By 1959, Somers had written two scores for the National Ballet, The Fisherman and his Soul and Ballad. In 1964, he wrote the score for a third ballet entitled The House of Atreus.

47 The Boor (sometimes translated as "The Bear") is a one-act comedy by Anton Chekhov, first produced in 1888. It centres around a confrontation between the widow Elena Ivanovna Popova and the landowner Grigory Stepanovitch Smirnov, who is owed money by the widow's late husband. The two prepare to fight a duel but before this can take place they realize they are falling in love with each other.

48 The Love of Don Perlimplín and Belisa in the Garden is a play by Federico García Lorca, written in 1928 and first performed in 1933. The play tells the story of an elderly bachelor, Don Perlimplín, who marries a much younger woman named Belisa. She only realizes that she loves her husband after he appears in the garden disguised as a mysterious man in a red cape, mortally wounded after a duel with a rival for her love.

178   Between Composers

done. A young pupil of Eli's played solo guitar which lent a nice atmosphere to it all, though she was a trifle nervous.

Afterwards went back by way of a beautifully lit Exhibition grounds to 112 Admiral Rd, where, to the drinking of slow gin your mother and Linda decorated the tree while I fiddled on the piano and the boarder watched, though he did take a crack at some left hand.[49]

Good night dearest, you are always in my heart and thoughts.

Friday A.M. – Ahha! Fought fever. Won same!
　　　All my love dearest, peace be with you –
　　　　Ever yours –
　　　　　Harry

HS to NB
Sat. a.m.
Dec. 19 / 59
Dearest:

Your voice came over the phone clearly this morning. It's likely the best hour to call.

Not having heard from you in over a week (Your last letter being dated Dec. 6.) I was very worried about you. It was great to hear your voice but I wasn't re-assured ... Is there any trouble?...

... Let me know what it's all about, will you love? I can't help but feel there is something wrong.

That your studies with Petrassi are going well was a happy note....

... If your depression eventually prohibits any kind of study or work it would be difficult for me to see just what the value of Rome would be. But of course that would be up to you to decide.

I'm very worried about you – that you sometimes are trying to prove something to your father's idea of the infallibility of self will – that there is only will or failure. You could have a break-down because of that damn foolishness. You feel that this is to prove something, always proving something! Look what your father has

----

49 Linda Jones had emigrated from the UK to Toronto in the 1950s to work in CBC Television and became a good friend of NB and her mother – "a sort of fixture in the household, especially at holiday dinners and such." (email from NB, 25 December 2020.

December 1959   179

proved! It's the product of North American Horatio Alger immature adolescent philosophy which has led to a bunch of people in middle age with stomach ulcers and broken lives!...[50]

... I do not deny work and application. I do not deny purpose and intention, but they must be for the right reasons. You must study and compose because you love music, because you wish to work with sound, because you wish to acquire craft which will equip you to understand and communicate much more.

As to becoming a composer – do you think for one moment Rome or anywhere else will <u>prove</u> this?! (That goddamn word!) It's not like becoming a bank clerk or graduating from College and going into business. If you left to-morrow because you just couldn't work there it wouldn't <u>prove</u> a thing, any more than staying would.

Relax inside and work hard with only the view to learning. Let the love of music and learning itself be reason. Do not regard the matter of staying or leaving as success or failure. You are always trying too hard and expending your energy too quickly. Composition is a long-distance run – it requires persistence over a long period of time....

... Do not worry about your mother, she is a very strong woman inside. I am here whenever she might need me, as I am to Carolyn, Charles or anyone else who needs me, so you have <u>no</u> worry....

... Be confident in my love for you. Give me all your thoughts and feelings. Give me your fever and your sickness. Take heart.

Ever – all my love –
Harry

NB to HS
Sunday, December 20th, 1959 – 6:30 PM
Dearest Harry,

How marvellous to hear your voice yesterday morning but please forgive me for perhaps sounding a bit in a daze ~ Your calls, or calls from home, seem to take me by surprise ~ and half worry ~ and I end up by having not much to say ~ You and I seem to alternate with our periods of depression ~ I am so sorry that you are now

---

50 Horatio Alger (1832–1899) was an American writer of fiction about impoverished adolescents who succeed in overcoming their poverty through virtuous behaviour of one kind or another, rather than hard work and determination, thus attaining middle-class security and prosperity. Therefore, the moral character of the protagonist plays an important role in improving their circumstances.

feeling low in spirits, and truly think it is a great pity that you cannot come over to this new environment ~ Most of the time it is very stimulating ~ like starting a new life in a way ~ You said learning a new language is a new life in essence, which is true, but what better situation than also living in a new environment!

Christmas festivities here seem very plentiful ... Last night I was invited by a friend of the Gazzellonis and some Fullbright artists to go to the American Embassy Christmas ball ~ Even with a Christmas tree, turkey and decorations one certainly didn't have the feeling of Christmas at all....

... I am slowly beginning to meet the intelligentsia and artists here, mostly through the Gazzellonis ~ which delights me very much ~ This chap who invited me, Peter Chinni by name is an American painter-sculptor of Italian extraction[51] ~ a rather quiet, sad creature, with a kind of mystic quality ~extremely intelligent and interesting in conversation, with his head screwed on the right way artistically speaking ~ The Gazzellonis had invited me to a Christmas party at Peter's Thursday night, where I met some of Italy's foremost painters (two women, no less) and even though the conversation was in Italian, one could certainly understand the quality of these people ~ I am delighted of course to finally meet some artists, real artists ~ but it does take time ~ You must understand that there is nothing personal in these relationships, darling ~

Some observations on Italy and Italians: I remember you once remarking on how rude the Italian Americans are to American women ~ the stares etc ~ Well you would be shocked the way they behave here ~ I find it very humorous, but most of the American male students that I have chatted with are rather annoyed by the behaviour of the Italian male to women ~ It is nothing to make a 90° turn to stare at a female, complete with comments about her appearance, etc (you can imagine) ~ Here in Italy, the double standard is <u>very</u> prevalent, mostly because of the powerful influence of the church, the fact that Italian girls are not allowed to go out alone with a boy before the boy is presented to the parents, and most of the marriages are pre-arranged ~ This breeds hypocrisy of the worst kind, of course, because

51 Peter Chinni (1928–2019) was born in Mount Kisco, New York to immigrants from Calabria and studied at the Art Students League in New York City. Beginning his career as a painter, he developed an interest in sculpture in the 1950s while in Rome. By 1959, he had his first one-man show of sculpture in New York and, subsequently, a distinguished international career.

December 1959

the marriage is <u>only</u> family life, divorce is illegal, and both Italian men and women are constantly on the make....

... Naturally, my personal reactions to this attention and flattery were at first ~ I was revolted ~ It is amusing to me now, but only as long as they don't go too far in their conversations (I have a butcher down the street who gets carried away by his attraction to me, and needs his face slapped)....

... My command of the language improves with each day and it will be great fun to have Eric here, who doesn't know a word of Italian, to practice my speaking and translating for him ~ He arrives Tuesday night (for a week) and there will be much for him to do ... I am endeavouring to cook a Christmas dinner for Eric, Marguerita and Peter (my American young friends) so we will see how it works out ~ It is a pity he doesn't speak Italian for there are some people who he might find interesting ~

I am a little worried about finding the hours to write and copy when he is here ~ I must have my work prepared for submission to the Academy before New Years ~

I have been invited to go to Torino after New Years to meet some artists and Rudolf Serkin ~ As I have also a standing invitation to go to visit Claudio and his family in Milan,[52] I may take the opportunity to make the whole trip, for once February arrives, I will not be able to see any of Italy until the end of June if I go in this course of Petrassi's....

... Darling, at this moment, I am not depressed as you probably can tell ~ I am truly too busy to have that time ruined by such feelings ~ However, I think I am catching another cold ~ May I wish you again a Merry Christmas, and will await the sound of your voice Christmas morning ~

All my love
Norma

---

52 This refers to the eminent Italian conductor Claudio Abbado (1933–2014), whom she had met at Tanglewood in 1958. That summer, at Tanglewood, he won the Serge Koussevitzky Competition for conductors, which helped launch his career.

182 Between Composers

HS to NB
Monday, 6 p.m.
Dec. 21 / 59
This is the second letter, my dearest....

... I have had time to re-read your letters with greater care and I am profoundly moved by your honesty, your search, your doubts.

I will phone you later to-night to tell you that I am going to come over and visit you in February upon completion of the film. I must. If it hadn't been for my enormous responsibility to this work (It means a great deal to many people and much hinges on it) I would have been over next week.

I must show you that what I feel for you is true love, we must talk together openly and for hours, we must walk and be silent together....

... I will also work on the Koussevitsky work over there.

Before coming I will study enough Italian to at least ask for a glass of wine.

I hope that I can stay for about a month, depending on money.

Forgive my explosions in letters. I do know your problems and doubts but I occasionally go off the deep like the 'a thing called Harry' bit because I'm in love with you and because I'm so bloody dramatic for an Anglo-Saxon. I sometimes feel as mad as Hector Berlioz....[53]

... I hope the flowers arrived, each one is painted in my heart's blood.
I love you, my dearest Normie –
Harry

HS to NB
Monday, Dec. 21 / 59
The day of 3 letters
Dearest Normie:
God, sweetheart, how can I convince you I love you?!

Surely that I want to marry you, that I'm getting a divorce, that I ask you to live with me means something about loving you!!

53 The French composer Hector Berlioz (1803–1869) was not actually "mad," but in his youth he saw the Anglo-Irish actress Harriet Smithson perform Shakespeare in Paris and fell passionately in love with her, pursuing her with an intensity that Hugh Macdonald has described as "emotional derangement." (Grove Dictionary Online, https://doi-org.proxy3.library.mcgill.ca/10.1093/gmo/9781561592630.article.51424). Eventually, after seven years, Berlioz succeeded in marrying Harriet, but the marriage was not a happy one. Perhaps this is what Somers was thinking of when he described Berlioz as "mad." Perhaps he suspected that his pursuit of Norma Beecroft was similar.

December 1959   183

I write you happy gay letters saying I'm fine not because I feel that way but because I think they will help you. The truth is that these past months I've been wretched. I can't eat, sleep, friends worry about me because I'm full of such tension and wasting. I force myself to work but there is no joy without you.

If I destroyed myself would that prove I love you? Because that's what I'm doing.

Don't do what I did or you will wake up too late one day!! I'm hopelessly in love with you – you're the only woman I've ever loved – surely, my recent actions prove it?!!!...

... Normie, come back to me. I will get an apartment. We will live, love, take our chances. This is _real_, don't make the mistake of your life....

... I'm still a young man but I'm too old to say 'I love you' lightly. I was always honest with you, _refusing_ to tell you what I didn't believe to be true, _remember that_. Even though it would have been to my benefit, I never did. You hated me for it, but _when I say now_ that I _love you_, I want to marry you, you _must know I mean it!_ I cannot play children's games nor write what I don't believe, I really never have.

Please consider what I have said with great care.

I love you beyond measure –
Harry

HS to NB
Dec. 22 / 59
Tuesday
Deare Love:

Inflamed by passions' intensitie my quill took feverish flight to paper stopping not to consider nor to stay the heat which burns my soul consuming all control.

Now that reason has, for the moment, returned to me mad mind which, under love's duress, doth oft take flight into realms of wildest fancy, I may peruse the last three letters that thee didst sendest me endeavoring, e'en tho my eyes do still reflect the dancing light of my heart's conflagration, to answer to the inner doubts which beset thy sweete person.

– of Dec. 11 –

In a country where it is possible to only do a little, then only do a little – that is, composition and Italian.

12 tone, shmelltone, you are learning a great deal about music –
never worry where it leads – remember Symonds & Somers – 'just
write!!'...

... I pushed you away so far because you were suffocating both
yourself and me thereby not solving the essential problem within
yourself but substituting me for an answer. You are an answer to
me as I hope I am to you. But at that time you had an inner need
which was not related to me, a need to understand yourself as you
are doing now, a need to become an individual, to answer to the
infernal domination of your father – I was an escape in part. For
my part I had to have time to answer my own questions for my life
and my attitudes were basically cynical and bitter. I needed moments
of solitude and you were crowding me for answers so I shoved you
away at a time I hated to face answers.

Your departure has given me the chance to answer all my questions – or at least the ones which were destroying our chance to live
and love without fear. I shoved you away so that we could come
together as two people who really love each other in such a way that
they can make a life together and not a shambles together....

... I will bring over my 3rd quartette and guitar sonata in February
when I fly. It will be almost as fast, likely....

... Take care about Petrassi. Study and accept the bounty but hold
reservations. Be flattered but hold reservations. Be flattered but not
overwhelmed by his attention. Keep in mind that one never gets anything for nothing but if the teaching of 12 tone is progressing that's the
important thing. Few men are altruistic in relation to a woman, but
there are a few. If you can receive the flattery and continue your studies
without personal involvement you will indeed have become a woman.

Any man can flatter a woman, but a pretty woman requires no
effort to flatter. I hope you will not be hurt.

Your sense of freedom I understand, for it is a kind of freedom I
like....

... Last night I saw the film 'On The Beach'.[54] If you are at all
depressed don't see it, for if you weren't before you will be after. It
is a film everyone should see at some time, but it is so horrifying I

---

54 The film *On the Beach* (1959), based on Nevil Shute's 1957 novel of the same
name, was a grim, American-made, post-apocalyptic drama depicting the aftermath of a
nuclear war. It starred Gregory Peck, Ava Gardner, Fred Astaire, and Anthony Perkins.

December 1959   185

wouldn't advise it unless a person is well fortified emotionally. Of course I had to see it from the bottom of my well, which did a great job of knocking me down all the way. I've heard that it has been greeted with shocked silence the world over.

Enough.

Know I love you with my whole being. Work hard and we'll be together before you know it –

> Best to Eric –
> Ever, ever –
> your Harry

P.S. Vivienne Stenson was seriously injured in a motor accident last week.[55] Broken bones, internal injuries, facial cuts.

HS TO NB

Monday again –

Dearest:

Before I forget – we got a Christmas Card from the Walshes. Bass Rock Hotel in Kennebunk.[56]

Also got a bill for $2.56 from the 'Jenney Mtg. Co. in Boston and I can't remember for what?

Saw Mario Bernardi on the street.[57] He sends his greetings and apologies for not getting to the party but had just gotten in the door

---

55 Vivienne Stenson (b. 1928?) was born in Wales and in 1951 came to Canada where she worked as a stage manager for Dora Mavor Moore and at the CBC, assisting folklorist Edith Fowke. She later ran two theatre businesses, Vivienne Stenson Concerts and Vivienne Stenson Publicity. In the 1950s, she recorded a collection of nursery rhymes she had learned during her childhood in Wales (*101 Nursery Rhymes*, Folkways Records, 1958). In September 2016, she was the recipient of the inaugural $5,000 Mary Jolliffe Award for Senior Arts Administrators in Ontario.

56 Kennebunk is a small town in York County, Maine, which was an attractive tourist destination during these years, partly due to its sandy beaches. The Bass Rocks Hotel, acquired by the Walsh family in 1912, was one of some ten large hotels there at the time and featured second- and third-floor dormer windows overlooking the sea. This indicates that Beecroft and Somers went farther afield than northern Ontario for holidays. (See chap. 3, n. 55.)

57 Mario Bernardi (1930–2013) was one of Canada's most distinguished musicians and one of its first full-time conductors. Although born in Canada, Bernardi studied piano, organ, and composition in Italy from 1938 until 1945 and then returned to Canada to complete his studies in piano and conducting at the Royal Conservatory of Music in Toronto (1948–51). He made his debut as a conductor during the 1956–57 season with the Canadian Opera Company, and in 1968, he became the first music director of the new National Arts Centre Orchestra in Ottawa.

after arriving from Europe. Too much to do. Tried to phone you later but you had gone.

Your Xmas card arrived, sweetheart, and I <u>will</u> be with you. I cannot enjoy the season, but because I love you I will try a little. My joy lies in thinking of a season a year from now, then we shall make up for lost ones and bad ones with a vengeance!!!

1960 <u>is</u> to bring us close together!!

My plan in more detail is to spend a month with you upon completion of the film – (sometime in February. I will let you know as soon as I know) to return here if Canada Council comes through. Then back to Europe and you in mid-June.

I'm going to try and get airfare to see you on a time payment plan. When I get extra dough I'll pay it off. B.M.I.'s summer stipend will take care of it. The mood I'm in I would sell me old mother's washing machine crutches and bathtub gin to get to you.

The film would pay for it complete but leave little over. Time-payment allows for everything....

... With the Koussevitzky work I get another thousand so there's no worry.

Canada Council's $4000.00 plus fare – of course it has to last awhile, but it is good security.

For a few days I will embarrass you because I want you to drag me, or I'll drag you, to all the 'touristy' things – art galleries, buildings, concert halls – and all those areas that so horrify students! (But not the first days.)

Then I just want to go for walks with you – at dawn, sunset, 4 a.m. – all the magic hours.

How about it, il mió amore? (Is that correct)

I've got one of those 'rapid' systems for Italian. Useful things like 'A che ora incomíncia la prossima attrazione?' 'Balliámo l'ultíma danza, sígnorína?' or 'Dopo le ignezioni, vengi a vedermi di nuovo' – 'Grazíe, dottore.' I've got a million of them!...

---

4 a.m.

... Just back from a gathering at the Wilkins of actors. Forgive me love, but your former amour Ted Fellows was there and I wondered

December 1959 187

how my Normie could have been seduced by such a fool!![58] His girl-friend or wife was there and it just disgusted me. Me, of all people, to be disgusted!!

Such obvious intrigue – George Gowan seduced Jan Webster in the bathroom while her husband knew what was going on!![59] Christ Normie!! She's a bitch who delights in torturing her husband – he must be a masochist and she a sadist!!

It was amusing from the outside but horrifying from the inside....

... The one saving grace was that Norm and Gwen came later and we discussed the possibility [of] the four of us meeting next year in Europe and having a ball together!! I said that you and I would have an apartment in Paris with an extra room for them....

... 3 p.m. (9 p.m. in Rome. I automatically think this way now)

Snowing gently, cold, Christmas crowds. Salvation Army bands all quite colorful but old Don Somers is scraping bottom. Never fear fair Dulcinea, I'm just keeping night vigil in my life and day must come revealing to our hearts the sun.

Just returned from my first French lesson with a Parisian teacher, a rather interesting man of middle years. The lessons with Joan will simply supplement but she and Tony went home to Quebec for Xmas so I didn't want to waste the time.

58 Ted Follows (1926–2016) was a Canadian film, television, and stage actor whose career spanned some seventy years. In the 1940s, he began acting in Hart House theatre productions and started acting professionally in 1945 with Vancouver's Everyman Theatre. He was a founding member in 1948 of Muskoka's Straw Hat Players (a company of students that toured the Muskoka area in the summer months) and later acted with the Neptune Theatre in Halifax. In 1955, he joined the Stratford Festival. Later in his career he had many important television roles. He married the actress Dawn Greenhalgh in 1958 – this was likely the woman referred to in the letter.

59 Like Ted Follows, George McCowan (1927–1995) gained his early stage experience at Hart House Theatre while a student at the University of Toronto and was also one of the original members of the Straw Hat Players. He later worked as an actor and a director with the Ottawa Repertory Theatre, Vineland Theatre in the Niagara area, and the Crest Theatre in Toronto, and in the United States where he directed episodes of *Charlie's Angels*, *S.W.A.T.*, and *Starsky and Hutch* and much else. Jan Webster (née Campbell) was a Scottish-born actress. She was married to the Scottish-born actor Hugh Webster (1927–1986), who was active in the early years of CBC Television and later at the Stratford Festival. Not surprisingly, in view of Somers's observations, the marriage did not last.

188   Between Composers

Discovered that Solesmns is a town 200 miles south of Paris with a population of 240!![60] I don't know if that includes the Monks!

At least it has a post office! Probably the summer months would be the ideal time to go there....

... Oh I'm so sad and lonely for you, dearest! I went to your house, up to your room to get my French book – there was your bed, the mirror that reflected your face, the floor that felt your great big feet (mm) ... Every turn in this city has a reminder of you. Every now and again it hits me full in the heart. All my emotional wind is knocked out of me. I gasp for air, slowly I breathe then get back to work.

I love you so terribly – I embrace you, kiss you, tongue you, make love to you, lie with you, sleep with you – soon, soon, soon!!

It <u>will be</u> a happy new year!

<u>All</u> my heart and love –

Your Harry!

HS to NB
Saturday, Dec. 26/59
Dearest Normie:

It has been a highly charged time emotionally.

Christmas and New Years. Two points in time set aside by a good part of mankind. All mankind sets aside one date or another to signify his mortality, for it does that whether he likes it or not. The earth revolves on its axis and circles the sun in ancient ritual. We dance to strings reaching back to timelessness and we presume in the arrogance of our few moments that we control the strings....

... Yesterday your voice sounded strong, sure, confident and indeed very happy, which in turn made everyone listening very happy. Eric sounded the same as though the two of you have found to some degree your individualities. The dinner must have been great fun, I'm sure, with a lively bunch of good friends.

I believe we had a pleasant time. We had champagne cocktails before dinner. I played practically the whole book of Chopin waltzes to go with the bubbly, we consumed a lovely meal, I played some more, then we finished with some drinks and interesting conversation.

60 Solesmes is a village in the Loire region in west-central France, famous for its Benedictine abbey and its role in the revival of Gregorian chant. It was for the purpose of studying this genre that Somers applied to the Canada Council for a grant to spend a year in France (1960–61). He did, in fact, receive the grant and spent that year in Paris, not with Norma Beecroft, but with his first wife, Cathy.

December 1959   189

In the morning the presents were opened to the oos and ahs of delight. Your mother was thrilled with her gifts.

Ruth was fascinated by the wrapping paper from Rome.[61] She is a very bright woman, extremely alive. She was very happy to be there. I took to her....

... Chris Chapman phoned to-day. The film is in its final state so sometime next week I will get a detailed shot list and start detailed work. It will have to be written in less than a month ... It's an enormous task to write a score which is a complete composition yet complements the film both in general and in particular. However, I've got good material to work with. At times I fragment the row and use a section modally as suits my purpose. Harmonic possibilities are great providing interest and contrast when I want it. At times by substitution and displacement of members of my little army of notes I get wonderful variety....

... I've been realizing more and more lately just how extraordinarily the jazz musician has extended the colour and technical possibilities of his instrument. The lipping, variety of gliss and port, variety of vibrato, of muting, of percussion etc. etc. has created a whole new area of sound. Since their language is so idiomatic the problem is to transfer this to another sphere where musicians are notoriously orthodox in training and execution....

... Normie, the year is running out. I wish that it will be a full, happy year for you. It is a good time for you. May the spark of life show you, as all of us, something of the meaning of life.

        You have all my love –
        Harry

NB to HS
December 27th, 1959 ~
Dearest Harry,

I received your beautiful flowers ~ they were the largest red roses I have ever seen and lasted through Christmas ~ Thank you so much ~ I have even saved the petals ~

---

61 "Ruth" was Dr Ruth Beecroft, the first wife of Norma Beecroft's father's brother Eric. Beecroft writes: "She was an American lady and practiced in public health in the US and was very attached to my mother and to her children (my siblings). Ruth had no children and loved coming to Canada for her visits with her Canadian relatives, and she loved the outdoors. I was quite attached to her, and influenced by her in many ways, wanting to become a doctor. She was quite a character ... She left her estate to my mother." (Norma Beecroft, email to this editor, 24 March 2021.)

I shall not elaborate now about our Christmas here ~ Suffice it to say that I spent perhaps one of the best Christmas' ever, free of family and emotional tension, and that Eric has had a marvellous visit here in Rome and has seen as much in 5 days as I have in a month, thanks to Roberto Savio ~ My friends here have treated him like a prince, and I have given a couple of parties here for him, as well as a real American Christmas dinner for about 8 people, all 'stranieri' with no place to go ~ We had a marvellous time....

... Dearest love, you have written me many letters, so impassioned that you must think my letters are cold ~ You have now posed me a very difficult and delicate problem, which I have found difficult to answer or even think about clearly, and have therefore hesitated writing to you ~ Perhaps even now I am premature in writing but I know that you are waiting for a response to your most recent telephone call and letters ~

I realize full well your sincerity and need and desire in your love for me ~ you do not 'have to prove it' ~ I believe it, that is enough ~ But you have asked me some questions ~ you are now asking me to make firm commitments to you without question after pushing me away ~ I have told you I find it hard to believe now that an ideal life could exist for me, period ~ Perhaps what is more true is that I don't want to think about it for a while ~ for these reasons: a) for the first time in my life I feel freedom, I am not bound by anything but myself ~ and I am growing inside into a very secure female, slowly though ~ I can speak with my friends and acquaintances as an individual, and am respected for my intelligence and individuality and personality....

... b) I am happy here, basically, and that is perhaps what bothers you more than anything, for you may feel if my life is complete I do not need you ~ I don't believe that this is true, but I must be <u>very</u> honest with you at the risk of hurting you a little temporarily, and please forgive me, darling ~ You are a very emotional person, and our life together has been full of ups and downs ~ I am <u>afraid</u>, if you can imagine, of repeating or being caught in emotional explosions again at this time for I am trying to direct my energy to writing music, and I fear if I don't succeed this time in accomplishing self-discipline, I shall not be able to try again easily ~ You see, I <u>want</u> to write music, but somehow have managed to let my will be led astray ... are you asking me to give up my writing really? You <u>want</u> me <u>now</u>, to come back and live with you ~ you must realize what a question this is for me ~ You say you are coming here in February ~ how will it be possible for the two of us to work in one room ~ how will it be possible for me to begin a very heavy course at Santa Cecilia, practice the flute, cook meals, etc. ~ Harry dear, I am so disturbed about the whole thing that I <u>have</u> to write you ~ I want you to come here, but I am worried about the emotional effect on me especially when I am really beginning to work ... It is <u>not</u> a matter of pride with me, you see, ~ I came to Europe to find courage and strength in myself and to work ~ I am <u>now</u> <u>just</u> managing to settle and adjust and I feel secure that I can work as soon as Eric leaves tomorrow....

      Monday AM –

... I stopped writing this letter last night for I was losing the clarity with which I thought I started ~ perhaps just as well, for I have had time to reflect on what I have written ~ It appears as though I am basically terrified ~ terrified of a repetition of my whole life ~ I refuse to fall into the pattern again ~ Helen Weinzweig used to tell me that we repeat the pattern over and over again in our life ~ I guess when we fully realize its dimensions is the only time we can change it ~ This morning I think that maybe I am crazy ~ if you truly understand these things, my darling, then I should have no reason to fear you ~ If you understand my present inability to give <u>all</u>, then you must come here ~ If you understand my true need for liberty, then you must come here ~ and I must have no fear of you, especially you!

I hope this letter has not sounded too strong ~ I am unfortunately or fortunately, obliged to write what I feel to be true ~ Please know my darling, that I want to be with you and want you to come here, but have great fear, mostly of myself ~ This course at Santa Cecilia means much to me, as does my attempts at writing ~ this is [my] primary concern!...

... May I wish you the best of New Years darling, I will be with you even at a distance ~ and may 1960 bring us together with great peace

      Much love

      Normie

HS TO NB

Dec. 28/59

Dearest:

Your letter of Dec. 20 arrived, your happy letter of meeting all sorts of people.

Normie, I'm delighted you're so active, free and so very happy.

Last night I took a girl from India, a girl from New York, a chap from Pittsburgh (Members of a visiting troop of actors), Norm & Gwen up to your house ... We had a fine, gay, conversational evening. Of course your mother was in her element.

These people had been depressed landing in Toronto Christmas with everything closed up, so I was determined to brighten their spirits.

The girl from India was most interesting, Sushma by name, speaking of the attitudes and customs and changes. She is rather appalled at western women's behaviour and attitudes towards them which she feels is lacking in dignity altogether. However, she voiced her views in a quiet manner without offence. A charming person. Her boyfriend, an Indian chap she left in the States for the trip, had asked her not to drink alcohol, so she only drank ginger ale or tea refusing all else....

... You are obviously having the time of your young life – I am happy for you. This is in a sense your 'university' year. Good luck in your studies, good fortune in your friends and good health in your body –

> With all my love – ever –
> Harry

HS to NB
Wednesday – 59
Dearest Normie:
Tragic thing I heard about Donna Scherman, Paul Scherman's wife. She had committed suicide in Paris – sleeping pills. It was a week after she was dead they found her. Evidently two men who were interested in her, and one of whom she had hoped might propose marriage, (either one) both broke with her around the same time. Being unstable anyway it just proved too much for her. She was 41.

Paul is going to be married again in England.

It seems ironic that her life should end there. She had all the material wants satisfied that she could desire, but they meant so little in the long run.

The human comedy.

I was fond of Donna (only as a slight acquaintance.) finding her a sensitive, charming woman. What is one to think of life sometimes? Are we just a bunch of comedians trying to play it straight? Somewhere someone must be laughing at us because it's just too god-damned tragic to endure otherwise. Of course there is always the escape of refusing to be moved or to feel the suffering of others, not that many can anyway....

... Beautiful wintry day of whiteness softening all the hard edges of the city. The air is crisp and stimulating. This is what I miss away from Canada.

I'm on a pretty severe schedule now – I have no choice! It's exhausting but like a severe climate, exhilarating as well. I come truly to life when absorbed in composition.

I'm doing some score analysis of Boulez works with John plus brushing up on John's latest ideas prior to, or anticipation of foreign studies. John is such a subtle person in the truest sense that one must always be extremely aware of everything he says.

Next week I'm going to start a series of shots – vaccination, typhoid, polio, – on the advice of Ruth Beecroft. Of course vaccination is essential for return to Canada.

Also going to phone old MacDonald for a physical checkup.[62] After 14 years since the last one I figure it's time to see what's what....

... There's been a big move for Bailey Bird. He will be head of the Leeds publications in Canada. There will still be an affiliation with B.M.I. but it also ties in with the important serious music publishers the world over. I believe it will make Bailey the most important individual in Canada responsible for publication of educational and serious music. It gives him great freedom and scope and he's completely his own boss. He will be able to publish both C.A.P.A.C. and B.M.I. composers. The next move he wants is to get Canadian composers on commercial recordings – then we'll really start to become international. Everything is moving.

Did I tell you John Reeves won the Prix d'Italia in radio for his 'Beach of Strangers' last year?[63] Over a $3000 prize I believe and

---

62 See chap. 1, n. 13.

63 John Reeves (1926–2022) was a true Renaissance man – a composer, broadcaster, and author, born in Canada but educated at Cambridge. In England he began conducting Gregorian chant and Renaissance polyphony and won a choral scholarship to St John's College, Cambridge. In 1952, he joined CBC radio as a music producer, branching out later into productions of dramas, documentaries, and religious programs. Later, *Beach of Strangers*, a radio play, was published in a book form. (See John Reeves,

194 Between Composers

a trip there to thank the kind gentlemen whoever they were. He's going like hell on Norm's libretto.

————

Is anything up, Normie? I got so little mail from you I'm beginning to wonder. I've no intention of upsetting you anymore but you must, in all fairness, let me know where you stand now – eh love? My telling you of flying to see you seems to have been greeted with silence. Letters are so inadequate – they lead to so much misunderstanding and I don't want more misunderstanding....

... I've got an enormous pile of Boulez, Nono and Stockhausen scores to peruse with John. God, so much work to do.

Normie, I'm a man who loves you so terribly. I have to make decisions for both our lives. You must let me know honestly whether you want me over there in February. In my heart I can understand any way you might feel, so never ever worry about telling me anything you might feel.

A part of me is missing and that part is you, so you see why I am unbalanced without you.

All my love – Harry

NB to HS
December 31st, 1959
Dearest Harry,

There are 24 hours left in 1959, at least on my side of the ocean and I am feeling rather sad and depressed about the passing of another year, especially as it was at this time when we met....

... Tomorrow night I have received two invitations to join a new year's party (parties), one from the Savios, another from a gal who was here for Christmas dinner ~ I have been so sick and miserable with this bloody flu, and so depressed this week that I really don't want to go anywhere, and yet am terrified of staying alone here being aware of all the activities around me ~ Evidently all hell breaks loose

————

Beach of Strangers [Toronto: Oxford, 1961].) The Prix Italia, awarded annually, is an international Italian television, radio-broadcasting, and website award, established in 1948 by RAI (Radiotelevisione Italiana). More than eighty public and private radio and television organizations representing some forty-five countries from the five continents participate in the competition.

here at midnight ~ All the bells and cannons start making noise, and the Italian custom is evidently to throw anything and everything out on the street from windows including old clothes, bottles, wash basins, etc.~ I am told that it is not safe to either drive or walk on the street, and as the street cleaners do not work New Year's Eve, I can imagine what Rome will look like in the morning ~ I guess the best thing for me to do is just let tomorrow look after itself and do what I feel like, including being miserable ~ What are you doing, my love, for the New Year?

Tonight I finished copying the first part of Michael's songs ~ and tomorrow I must submit my application to Santa Cecilia for this course ~ There is an oral exam in January which of course terrifies me, for I a) do not know the type of questions to be asked, b) it is in Italian, and c) there is no definite date set ~ I must be ready at any moment to present my scores and arguments in front of an examining committee of composers ~ Can you imagine this? Maybe my lack of Italian will save me!

After New Year's, health permitting, I am commencing again a heavy schedule of work ~ My new year's resolution ~ I am determined I will enter this ruddy course, if I can get by without a diploma or certificate from an 'authorized musical institution' ~

I spoke this morning to my charming Italian tutor, Cecilia, who told me she could recommend a French teacher here for you, so have no fear ~ This girl evidently speaks excellent French ~ so all is set in that line ~

After Eric left Monday, I was overcome with the first real pang of homesickness ~ I longed for the smell of my house, my room, the Canadian winter, evergreen trees ~ I could see St. George St. and Admiral Rd. all covered with snow ~ you and I walking in one of those crisp, crunchy, nights ~ How nostalgic I am becoming. Perhaps when you and I come together here in February we can dash away to the mountains outside of Rome for a couple of days, time permitting of course ~ I must say I don't like feeling such homesickness ~ Do you know darling that I long to see not only you, but my Mother, if you can imagine ~ Symbol of security, Mothers are, I suppose ~

Today I received a very warm letter from Lilly Barnes who is truly pregnant and has been suffering a great deal[64] ~ She would be about 3 or 4 mos. pregnant now, so perhaps she is a little better ~

64 See chap. 2, n. 8.

Evidently, Milton has been working 16 hr. days for about 3 mos. in his conducting course, so perhaps we will see some progress in both the Barnes ~ It is a nice feeling for me to know that these people are fairly close by, even though they have not been to date really trustworthy friends ~ It gets rather lonely down here ~

Harry love, I am missing you like crazy ~ I am afraid to admit it, but it is so ~ I long for you beside me and for your love which is the most honest thing that I have ever known ~ I am waiting with impatience for your arrival here in Rome, and will hope by that time that I am more secure in this course to have all my fears dissipated ~ Please forgive me if I am a little afraid to believe too much for a while, but also believe that my whole being is longing still to believe in you, and us ~

Please take care of my Mother ~ I don't dare tell her how much I miss her, but you know ~ I guess one needs distance at times for perspective ~

I was also deeply moved by a telegram received at Christmas from Norm and Gwen ~ Please tell them, and give them my love and best wishes for the New Year ~

So much love to you, my sweet
and a great fat kiss and hug
for New Year's 1960
As always
Your Normie

PS. Do you realize this is our 5th New Year ~ and without a battle too!

CHAPTER FIVE

January 1960

NB to HS
January 2nd, 1960
Dear Harry,

How frustrating the telephone is ~ almost impossible to make any conversation at all ~ I wanted to wish you a Happy New Year as it is also a kind of anniversary for you and I, but each call ends and I feel very sad and frustrated ~

I seem to have been weaving back and forth between two extremes lately, one very happy and the other very sad and depressed ~ All my friends here seem to have grave problems, and I am sort of the meeting ground for all ~ It is flattering, but I have really sufficient burden of my own to carry ~ so I think in a week I shall disappear to the sea shore for 2 or 3 days to meditate and ponder ~

I am very troubled off and on about this business of believing ~ I can't explain easily any more, but I wonder if I will ever capture again the ideal I started out with ~ I am constantly observing and comparing the marital problems here in Italy with those of America, and I truly don't know if a true monogamous life exists for any being, and yet I can't condition myself to the type of hypocrisy here, or in America ~ It is all very complicated, and I am terrified of pledging my life to you for fear that it will fall apart by a single mistake on either side ~ Is this silly, or do I have reason?...

... Now ~ pertaining to your trip ~ Yes, I too am very worried about my work at the Accademia in February, but I hope that I shall be sufficiently into the course to not be too easily distracted from my work, and to also know my schedule time-wise ~ I look forward to your trip with much excitement and to being with you again, walking around Rome and exploring together ~ I only hope that my work will permit me some time for this....

... February is the coldest month here, so bring sweaters, and a raincoat for sure ~ A couple of bottles of Crown Royal would be a special treat, and as many cigarettes as you can possibly stow away ~ filter-tip Rothmans or Kents ~ and you can usually buy them on the plane tax-free (I would inquire however)....

... The composers' conference sounds very exciting for Stratford and the League[1] ~ Perhaps I should consider returning to Canada for the summer instead ~ Could you let me know more details ~ when in the summer, for instance, what composers, what countries, etc. I hope they are permitting some experimental music ~ and I am curious to know who will represent Italy ~ Will you tell John W. or Lou that I would be glad to help if there is anything I can do here ~

New Year's here is a very strange one ~ I went over to the Savios to a rather dull party (complete with entertainment organizer) and after midnight went down to Aram's and sat and drank cognac with Aram, the French girl ... Peter, the composer, and an Italian boy called Sandro ~ till about 4:00 in the morning ~ At midnight here they throw monstrous fire crackers, old clothes, bottles, etc., everything and anything, out the window onto the street ... This goes on for about an hour, with some people, all night, and the streets are filled with broken glass ~ I'm not kidding ~ At about 4:00 Peter and Sandro and I left Aram's and came here for coffee....

... Altogether, I neither had a good time or a bad time but rather an uneventful time, missing you very much ~ I have had terrible homesickness since Eric left ... New Year's was just another day ~ So it is gone for another year ~

I am eternally grateful that you are spending so much time with Mother and Linda[2] ~ I am very worried about Mother and feel very uneasy ~ as though any moment I shall have to come home ~ I wish you could convince her to <u>take</u> two weeks and come over here ~ I <u>feel</u> strongly that she needs it....-

... My darling, I wait hungrily for your arrival here and wish you the best of luck with your film score, so that you may be here very soon ~ Very selfish, eh?

1 See chap. 3, n. 50.
2 See chap. 4, n. 49.

January 1960   199

>   Take good care, my strong one
>   Love
>   Normie ~

HS to NB
Mon. Jan 4/60
Dearest Normie

I started to write another letter but tore it up. On the phone you asked me to ignore or take it carefully I must be careful what I say for I have been so deeply hurt before.

It is better just to say that I received your letter and have read and will re-read it carefully.

The repetition cycle you speak of is not the one you think it is, but it is too dangerous for me to go into on paper.[3]

I respect your fears, I respect your freedom, I respect your desire to work, I respect you.

When you have discovered why you are really terrified you will be truly free.

I will pose you no more problems. I have my life to live, my work to write, I have been too deeply affected and for my own equilibrium seem to be righting myself, it is a necessity....

... I'm sorry to have weighted you down with the passion of my feelings at a time when I want you to benefit from your studies and environment. I will endeavour to give you more of this freedom you're enjoying by restraining myself....

... Be confident in my love, but above all be free in it. If it suffocates you too much then it is bad for you, that's all.

Take care, sweet bird of my illusions, and fear nothing from me.

>   Be at peace, my love –
>   Harry

HS to NB
Wednesday evening
Beloved:

... I just spent a most interesting afternoon and early evening at the Weinzweigs, first studying Boulez scores with John, discussing musical composition in general, then a long talk with Helen about you, me, your family and life in general.

---

3 In her letter of 27 December (chap. 4), Beecroft had said: "I am basically terrified ~ terrified of a repetition of my whole life ~ I refuse to fall into the pattern again."

John's views on the present day are so accurate and so perceptive he amazes me. His thinking is at all times clear and he has a great ability for insight and perception which always gets to the essential point. I just ask questions and listen. This spring I want to do a period of concentrated score study with him.

My aim is to become completely conversant with the latest concepts, not that I will necessarily use them, although I intend to write some music using strict 12 tone in the style, but that I may 'stretch' my mind and draw into my creative bloodstream that which I feel will enrich it.

These are the scores I have – Boulez: 'le Marteau sans maître', 'improvisation sur Mallarmé' (2 parts), 'Structures'.

Stockhausen: Kontra-Punkte, No. 5 Zeitmasse, Klavierstücke I–IV

Nono : Il Canto Sospeso, Incontri, la Terra e la Compagna, Varianti.

All their music owes allegiance to Daddy Webern. They are certainly consistent. The refinement of dynamic and duration is extreme coming from the 'colour note' idea which John says was suggested by Schoenberg and applied by Webern. The logical conclusion of this direction strikes me as electronic music where every factor can be perfectly controlled.

It will be fun listening to some of these pieces on record. The search for asymmetrical rhythmic structures interests me. John feels 'Le Marteau sans Maître' to be a good piece of music.

Needless to say my conversation with Helen was long and interesting. She unwittingly helped revive a part of my sanity. She's all right, you know....

———

... Normie, Normie, forgive my nuttiness! I just love you so much I sometimes turn loops trying to get myself untangled. I adore you, girl, and I'm just love sick for you. So please suffer my ups and downs....

... I LOVE YOU I
LOVE YOU!!!!
I LOVE YOU!!!

Harry
(Surely you can hear that across the ocean!)

January 1960   201

HS to NB
Tuesday, Jan 5/60
Normie dear:

I'm working very hard. The film score is progressing with interesting ideas. I think I'm solving the problems in a musical fashion, which pleases me. Tomorrow I fly to Ottawa for another conference.

Last night I was almost killed by a beer bottle dropped from the fourth floor of this building while I was walking by. It missed my head by an inch and glanced off my shoulder. I felt curiously undisturbed but realized in an instant how close a call I had. If one's time is up it's up.

My thoughts of you are at peace. So many things I want you to know and to not be afraid of. I understand your search and needs and I sympathize with them. Be at peace, my love....

... Toronto is in the January month – cold, cold with snow and northern sunsets with that fantastic sense of line and space.

My parents go to Florida on the 24 like migrating birds.

And now I must needs back to work.

My heart and love is yours, they have no wish to burden you or cause you anxiety, they only wish to love you – don't ever be afraid of them.

I hope your work goes well and that you continue in health and happiness.

I am always –
Your Harry

NB to HS
6th January, 1960
Dear Harry,

I write you this letter in reply to a question 'What's up ~why are you not writing?' ~ I shall not write a long letter for it may result in great confusion ~

Suffice it to say only a few things ~ I just want you to realize that I am undoubtedly going through one of the worst periods of my life, and, have been almost ill physically as a result of many tensions ~ of trying to examine myself truly, for perhaps the only time in my life ~ I have announced to all my friends here that I wish to remain undisturbed, but few seem to understand torment, so I am taking off for Ansio Saturday to be alone by the sea for three days[4]....

---

4 Anzio is a town located on the west coast of Italy, about 50 kilometres south of Rome, with an important harbour, serving fishing boats and ferries. It was the scene

Between Composers

... I cannot describe my tensions, but it seems for four months, and perhaps for a life-time, I have been doing everything imaginable to avoid that eternal solitude which is a prerequisite in the life of an artist ~ I am almost paralyzed with the questions I must face, and am not able to write anything ~ I am slowly realizing a few things ~ ie, that I am carrying still my past burdens and worries, which prevent me from having that clear mind for my work ~ that it is not only indolence, but fear of facing such difficult problems in art ~ and yet we are bound by the difficult ~

I must once and for all go into the depths of my being and try to find the answers ~ realizing that answers are not simply there when we need them ~ but at least try to find out if I must write music ~ and once finding this answer, try to live and conduct my life accordingly with no fear, with simply hard work and courage, hoping that some-day the question 'Am I an artist?' will be revealed to me through such a simple procedure ~ all though very difficult....

... I have not discovered real inner strength, dearest Harry, and until this is more certain, I cannot face the decision of marriage, which is equally difficult to me ~ I have been trying to answer all things at the same time, and certainly pertaining to the latter, your letters have been somewhat demanding ~

So I must take all the time that is necessary to find out truths about myself in all directions, which can only be fair to you in the long run....-

... There are few, if any, people other than yourself who can understand this, so I count on your understanding ~ perhaps that knowledge gives me a certain amount of courage ~ I am again taking refuge in Rilke's Letters, which seem to help, and perhaps shall study again a little Eastern philosophy....

... In the worst of crisis, Miss B. always thinks of her stomach ~ and it occurred to me today that a great huge Canadian ham would be marvellous if you could think of some way to bring it over ~ I am so tired of veal and tough beef!

> I think of you often, and long
> for your presence in everyway
> Love
> Normie ~

---

of heavy fighting in the early months of 1944, when Allied forces landed to begin Operation Shingle, which ended with the capture of Rome.

January 1960 203

HS to NB
Wed. 8:30 pm. Jan 6/60
Beloved Normie,

I just returned from Ottawa and was thrilled to find your Dec. 31 letter in which you expressed a complete desire to see me in Rome! My heart is happy, my dearest love, I can't tell you how much!...

... Good luck on your examination for Santa Cecilia. If you succeed, great, if not it doesn't make any difference. I'm with you whatever way it turns out!

Thanks for speaking to your tutor about French.

When I go to Rome we shall dash to the mountains, your studies permitting, if only for a weekend! It is indeed beautiful. I had lunch with the Crawleys in their Gatineau Hills home. My God – the fire, the view of deep snow-covered hills, the wisps and sudden blizzards, the brilliant sky, the air – you can imagine how lonely and nostalgic I feel when I see this!...

... Such a day. I left Toronto at 8:30, worked the day in Ottawa, arrived back 12 hours later. I've got three weeks at the outside to complete the score, and it ain't easy! All sorts of fascinating things can be done on sound tracks. They run two so that if one wishes one can tape a full brass section on one track, a single flute low register on the other and join them so that the flute overrides the brass. All these things have been done in various ways before but it is perfectly natural to this medium. However I don't wish to get gimmicky for its own sake. One spot I want vibes and flute done first ordinarily, then octave or fifth lower, then echoed – a common practice but effective where I want it. The murderous thing is that one writes to a stopwatch to 1/32 of a second. I never dreamed that a second could be so long!

I'm going to drop over to have a drink with Eleanor later. She thinks she's taking care of me and I think I am taking care of her! This way we take care of each other without letting each other know it!

I might be working in your room at Admiral Rd. a good deal.[5] It's like the quartet – I'm too accessible here to phone calls and visits during any hour of the day or night. There are days when there is not so much as a knock, which is ideal for work, but others during

5 Eleanor Beecroft had rented a semi-detached house at 112 Admiral Road, to accommodate her children, who eventually all left their father in Whitby and moved to Toronto.

which I go crazy. How I would love to work and take breaks to have dinner or a drink and some conversation with you as we used to!...

... Yes, the 5th new year – without a battle too. Those crazy battles! Well, there have to be battles before peace. Some of them are riotous in perspective, though at the time they seemed grim. Norm and Gwen have been in histrionics at my account of a few of them – two crazy people on an island – the constipation exercises – chess games – some New Years – my great histrionics – our final scenes – our huffs puffs and such between glorious moments when we touched stars and the roof of the sky!

I just love you with all of me! I want us to love, and live and take life and our likenesses and differences and create between two people the profound experience of giving, taking, sharing – of creating a life through love.

And I send back to you a great fat kiss

and hug for 1960...

... Ever –

Your Harry

NB to HS

January 8, 1960

My dearest love,

Here I am at Anzio, on the sea, a place where the Americans landed during World War II ~ Everything was destroyed here with the exception of one building, so all is new ~

I came by train yesterday, an hour's journey from Rome, and have so enjoyed contemplating the sea, that I will be reluctant to return tomorrow ~ However, a vacation that ends too soon is better than one that continues for a long period ~ and I begin to regain my equilibrium a little, so back to work I go ~

I cannot describe how I miss you these days, particularly when I am near to natural things, such as the sea and how much it would mean to have you walking with me in these surroundings ~ Probably the greatest compliment and truth I can tell you ~ to want to share those things which I consider to be the most beautiful, most profound in the world, with you must surely mean that I care greatly for you (I refrain from using the word 'love' for I begin to re-examine the true meaning of the word ~ it really is so mis-used) ~

January 1960   205

The sea is a constant source of stimulation, relaxation ~ I am growing to love the sea and all things it contains, and someday would love to live 'vicino il mare' ~ It is strange how such surroundings can give you an inner perspective and inner calm ~ I suppose all the world longs for peace, inside each of us, but most people do not know how to begin to seek it out ~

Strangely enough, I am very content to wander with my own thoughts for a while, even though I feel an inner longing for you ~ I guess what is so important about our relationship is that we are able to understand the other's need for solitude, and therefore we are unusual ~ and meant for each other ~ If all the material and transient things didn't sometimes overwhelm us, we could live a rather contented existence together ~

I am also developing a great love for the Italian people ~ they are incredibly warm, and have a phenomenal love for children ~ all children, not just their own ~ The children are most often extremely spoiled, which probably accounts for the type of adult Italians one meets ~ the women spoiled, the men like small boys, also spoiled and not capable of doing anything domestic, as American men are capable ~ They are very beautiful children, and in fact the Italian race is one of the handsomest I have ever seen (this, of course, breeds big egos) ~ I think you might find Italy strange at first, but after a while it is certainly marvellous ~

I am a very definite foreigner to the Italians, for, in the first place, they are unable to understand a female who prefers to be alone, to go away 'da sola' ~ I am a sad person to them ~ I am also not as expansive ~ do not wish to reveal every detail of my life to them, and an a bit of an enigma ~ However, I am smiling at them and with them, am 'simpatica', and find that I usually command respect, and warmth from almost all ~ It is a very pleasant feeling, and I am not so sure I could become used to the reserved, somewhat cold temperaments again ~ Isn't it strange, I never carried any great love or feeling for Italy, but am now doing the reverse, in spite of their dishonesty at times ~ they talk too much, etc. etc. ~ You will find this country indeed a contrast to Canada, and probably even to France ~

Later 12:00 midnight

I suppose today I have walked about 6 miles in all ~ I got properly fatigued physically, but found the sea sufficiently beautiful to compensate for any tiredness ~ A young chap who I met on the train found me wandering along the sea shore, and proceeded to join my explorations ~ which proved to be very interesting to hear information about this whole area ~ He turned out to be a student of medicine at the University in Rome, who[se] father commands some section of the army here at Anzio ... The Italians are indeed a rather aggressive race when it comes to the opposite sex, but ... they are also very polite, and if you objected to their presence strongly enough, they won't quibble with you ... Italy is very much a police state, for here, when one commits an offence, one is guilty until proved innocent, put in jail to await a court trial which conceivably could take three years to come up ~ If the man is proved innocent, he is nonetheless ruined in this hypocritical society, so the police are very important people!

To learn another language is indeed a new life, my love, ~ it is constantly a fascinating experience to chat with all these people, even in my broken Italian ~

Curiously enough my vacation here has taken me through two novels ~ 'On the Beach' a strangely and morbidly depressing story that could in one instant become a reality[6] ~ so terrifying truly, that I truly don't want to consider it too deeply ~ It does indeed sharpen one's awareness of life if nothing else ~

The other book I have just completed – 'Lady Chatterley's Lover'[7] ~ a very moving, sensitive tale ~ There seem to be few writers who have such insight into women (male writers, that is) ~ Maurois is another ~ I cannot understand the righteousness of all those idiots who made such a scream over it ~ The book is not pornographic, or vulgar, but real ~ perhaps that is the thing that horrifies most people ~ they prefer their bloody illusions all the time, and certainly I might react the same way if I were trying to face truly the end of the world as in 'On the Beach' ~

I am finding in many ways that I am a curious mixture of male and female drives ~ I don't know whether reading these books really helps to answer some of the questions which have been giving me mental claustrophobia lately, but it is relaxing to read for hours on end ~ I suppose the greatest part of this sojourn is my communion with nature ~ Dear Harry, I am just a country brat at heart, and when I am in calm surroundings, I am so at peace inside ~ perhaps we shall live in the country someday, somewhere ~

6 See chap. 4, n. 54.
7 See chap. 1, n. 28.

January 1960   207

I leave you now, my love, to sleep ~ I wish you were here beside me ~ Tomorrow I return to Rome and to work ~ Wish me peace of mind, my sweet ~

Your Normie ~

HS to NB
Friday, Jan.8/60
My dearest Normie:
Don't feel badly about the frustration of your New Years' call. The very fact that you phoned thrilled me and came at a time I needed it most. We both know how inadequate the phone is – few moments and click.

Under separate cover you will receive information re: composers conference....

... It's early afternoon. Outside the snow swirls, dances, fills the air with its whiteness. A good day for work. With the deadline I've got every day has to be a good day for work!

---

9 p.m. Taking a break. I've certainly set myself a tough task but if this score comes off it should be quite striking making sense both musically and in support of the film. Timing to the split second drives me crazy at times. Probably good for my wayward musical mind. The pressure's colossal as usual. It would be a pleasant task otherwise.

By the way, congratulations in completing your composition! It must of taken great persistence with all the Christmas commotion. Good girl! A great big hug for you!...

Saturday –
... Just back from my vaccination. That plus typhoid, tetanus and my first polio shot makes a full week of needles. My passport is in Ottawa getting renewed and when I'm certain of the recording date for the film I'll make my air arrangements....

... Normie, there's a blizzard outside. I was looking out the window, figuring out my work when my mind wandered back to another blizzard in the Caledon Hills. It's strange. I was then trying to figure out how I could tell you all the things which have happened to me internally since that time so you would better understand what must seem like a transformation, an inexplicable one almost, to you....

... When I was with you at first I was with you completely, that is to say without concern for anything but the joy of the moment of being together. Then all the sickness of my past came falling in on me and I refused to believe that anything was possible. You were anxious, young and wanted answers ... which only drove me deeper into myself and I more and more closed off, shutting my mind and heart like a trap ... under it all was this bed rock beyond which we could not go. It took dynamite to blast through it and your going away was the dynamite that did it.

Eventually it blew everything in me sky high but after the dust had settled I saw, felt and knew clearly what you meant to me and just how much I really loved you. All the debris is cleared away, not that a few bits aren't lying about, but <u>now</u> I can talk to you of it....

... Night – I get a bit tired. There is no stopping for 'inspired' writing. A movie composer will slam out the expedient thing while a creative composer seeks what is true to himself – a tough thing with a deadline. I refuse to just use a bag of tricks so I sweat it out. Such a noble picture I paint of myself! A battery of natural trumpets with pennants might describe me.

Writing to you in bits like this is like phoning you. Unfortunately it takes so long to reach you on this line – overseas service. It's so far to Rome. Who would have thought two thousand years ago that I would be writing to you from this land beyond the sea. Whoever heard of Toronto? They say it means 'Place or Landing by the Water'. An Indian friend of mine from my youth on a reservation told me it really meant 'Horse Trough'. Can't you just see the Coat of Arms?

January 1960 209

There are others who call it by a cruder name which would require the horse to be viewed from the rear on the pennant.

Toronto, I love thee.

Enough of my nonsense. I must be getting punchy. I shall stagger back to work and send you this missive afore I go completely potto.

Take care sweetheart. Christ, I miss you! I'm feverish for you – just sick sick sick for you –

       All, every bit of my love – I hug you hug you!!

       Crazy Harry

HS to NB
Sunday, Jan. 10/60
My beloved Normie:

More than anything I'm just putting pen to paper that I may touch your lips with my fingers, that I may feel the warmth of your mouth and you the gentleness of my hand.

It is quiet. The snow muffles the city sounds. In the midst of millions I live in solitude holding the thought of you close to me. I hold it dearer than anything else.

———————

Evening – I just spoke to Eleanor and for the same reasons that I stated, she feels it would be impossible for her to go over.

Next week she opens in the new James Reaney play The Killdeer, at the Coach House Theatre....[8]

———————

... Monday – Your letter in which you say you are going to Ansio for a few days arrived. (That of Jan. 6) Ansio – wasn't that one

---

8 The Killdeer, the first play written by Canadian poet and playwright James Reaney (1926–2008), was put on at the Coach House Theatre in Toronto by the University Alumnae Dramatic Club, beginning on 13 January, and directed by Pamela Terry. Eleanor Beecroft played a minor character, the jailer's wife. The play deals with various aspects of life in small-town Ontario and is unified, in part, by the image of the bird, the killdeer. The drama critic of the Toronto Daily Star, Nathan Cohen, wrote that it was "a desperately bad play, which only someone of talent could write." (Toronto Daily Star, 14 January, 35.) Nevertheless, the play went on to win an award at the Canadian Drama Festival that year. In 1962 Reaney was awarded his third Governor General's award for the publication of The Killdeer and Other Plays.

of the American beachheads where so many were killed during the landing?

My love, you are so disturbed.

I understand all your questioning. I understand you.

I apologize if my letters have been demanding. Please feel that I'm not 'crowding' you for answers. Don't feel you have to face a decision relative to marriage or anything else with me. You are having enough struggles, yet all are related....

... We can only know just so much about ourselves, time can only reveal the rest. Some uncertainties are always with us. It is a condition of living. I believe part of our inner strength comes only when we know our weaknesses. We cannot have it all ways and maturing comes in accepting this. It is <u>not</u> to be confused with compromise.

Barbara Pentland is a happy woman now. It took years....[9]

... Just don't set yourself too big a task. It takes a lifetime to find some answers, though we are impatient....

... In some ways you are probably on a similar search as Jane's – to find what is true for you. In the Beecroft children it is extremely complicated because so many factors are involved.

You know where I stand now and to a certain extent, what I am....

... I have never really proposed marriage to anyone else in my life before you.[10] Please put that pressure aside – if necessary forget it so that you may better face what you must unhampered.

9 Somers had known the composer Barbara Pentland (1912–2000) since the late 1940s, when she was living in Toronto, and he had performed an entire recital of her piano music on 20 March 1948 at the Royal Conservatory of Music, a week after giving a recital entirely of his own music. This recital of his own music was extremely unusual at the time and is an important part of the appearance of modern music in Toronto in those years. In this letter, he was probably referring to the fact that she had, in October 1958, married John Huberman, an industrial psychologist, and that the marriage was a happy one. In 1956, Pentland had had a bitter dispute with the Canadian League of Composers (CLC) over the performance of her String Quartet No. 2 at the 1956 ISCM (International Society for Contemporary Music) Festival in Sweden. The CLC could not afford the performance expenses demanded by the ISCM Festival and withdrew from the organization. Pentland's Quartet was, nevertheless, performed at the festival.

10 This is a strange statement, coming as it does from a man who had already been married (in October 1949) to Catherine Mackie and was still married to her. If he didn't actually propose to Catherine, perhaps the marriage came about through some kind of unspoken understanding between them, possibly with much encouragement (management?) from Ruth Somers (Somers's mother), who was very fond of Catherine, and also very close to her son.

January 1960   211

Heaven and hell are surely within us. You are going through the inferno and purgatory. May you emerge to Paradiso!

I shall bring over the largest ham I know, – 'myself', and if possible a smaller one.

Remember, if for any reason it would just be too much to have me in Rome, just let me know darling, I will understand. This crossing of letters is like a teeter tottor [*sic*]!

Take courage, my dearest, from me. 'No man is an island unto himself'. And that goes for ladies too!

Don't worry that I will misunderstand what you say.

> Take care, dear one
> I love you with all my heart –
> Your Harry

HS to NB
Monday, Jan 11/60
Evening
My darling Normie:

I'm boiling along in the rapids heading for Lake St. John![11] The timp and brass are beating, punctuating, the strings rush on, the rhythm is insistent. I've got to make the dam by midnight then I'm in electricity. High strings: wds. 'Stingers' from brass and perc. Never stopping. Relentless flow.

Sitting on the shore a moment I think and feel so deeply for you. Wishing you peace, yet knowing it only comes through great trial....

... The clock chimes the hour calling me back to my labours.

Think of going to Florence with me for a couple of days, will you? An Italian once told me of all the cities he would like to live in in Italy it would be Florence. (Well why didn't he? Hm.) Then we could spend a day or two in the Alps....

Midnight -

... And I feel thoroughly depressed about my work. How the devil am I going to get through this mountain of writing in two weeks?

11 Lac Saint-Jean is a large lake in south-central Quebec. The Saguenay River originates from this lake at Alma. It has two channels: La Petite Décharge and La Grande Décharge, where the Ile Maligne hydroelectric plant was built.

Writing, scoring, getting it to the copyist in time and keep up a standard!! God Damn it! The music is always left to the last. They want a masterpiece knocked off in a few weeks! And I've got another miserable cold to boot. Shit! Sorry Normie. Just blowing off steam. Ah what the hell, there are times I just get fed up – don't we all!

Back to work.

———

Wed. 2.30 a.m.
To bed after an 18 hr. workday. It's the only way I'll ever get it done. Oh well. Might as well make up my mind. I won't see daylight for a few weeks.

Outside ice coats everything creating a magical crystal palace of this town....

———

Wed. afternoon Jan 13
... Just heard that there's a good chance the 2nd Piano Concerto might be done in New York on March 18 at a concert called 'Music in the Making'. It seems they want the work, Reg is available so we'll see. (He's worried about a good page turner!) Coincidentally Reg is in town at the right time. However they're only putting out feelers at present so I won't know for sure for awhile.[12]

I'm writing frantically – page after page after page but the end seems always out of sight no matter how much I write. Whew. Its mad. It's ridiculous!

My heart goes out to you, sweetheart, I do hope you're feeling a little better. I love you so much. Don't worry or bother about writing, or me, please, I understand.

With all my love and feelings –
Harry

———

12 Reginald Godden had played the solo piano part in the 1956 CBC premiere of the work. In fact, it was the Passacaglia and Fugue for Orchestra, which was performed at the New York concert on 18 March 1960.

NB to HS
January 13th, 1960
My dear Harry,

The seashore vacation ended all too soon, and I returned to a very cold and rainy Rome ~ My apartment was like an ice-box so I had to take refuge in a friend's house for a few hours to get warm ~ However, the two days seemed to do what I wanted ~ namely, escape from the telephone, door, people, etc., and the next day I began to work ~ practically no one knew that I had returned ~ for I telephoned no one ~ it is the only way ~

Sometimes even creative people don't understand, or forget, that in order to create, one must endure, and contemplate in absolute solitude ~ It's easy for me to say 'Sure, come on over' for I at times prefer to have people around ~ Such a life this is ~ I am back into Michael's songs again, determined to finish them once and for all[13] ~ I do feel rather badly that I haven't telephoned Petrassi for about a month now (not quite), but figure that I will undoubtedly see enough of him if I go into the course ~ (When a teacher of his stature gives you lessons for nuttin', one feels that one should take advantage of it) ~

I am delighted to hear that you will again use my room at Admiral Road to work in ~ Tell me how the house looks?

I am beginning to find my equilibrium again, and now begin to wonder just what all the internal fuss was about ~ It occurs to me that I perhaps work better, or would work better if you were around all the time ~ why do I worry so much, my love? In retrospect, I certainly wonder....

... I sent a letter to Michael Fram requesting urgently the remainder of the words to his song that I am working on (he made some cuts, and I would like these words if possible) ~ and information about the estate money, for I need some soon! ~ I have not heard from him at all, and this was a month ago ~ could Mother call him ~ please! (I suppose I should have written her really about these things, but would you mind very much relaying the contents of this page, darling??)

Please wish your parents a very happy trip and sunny weather (I will miss their house this year!) and tell your Mom I am truly sorry not to have written before, but will soon ~

13 See chap. 3, n. 20.

Between Composers

Very best luck and speed with your film score, darling ~ Waiting impatiently for your arrival here ~

Love, love ~

Normie

PS. Have you made your plane reservation? Any chance of borrowing a camera?

PPS. I thank you muchly for the information about the composers' conference ~ I wrote John offering my services from abroad if I can do anything ~ Perhaps this is the summer we <u>should</u> be in Canada ~ I am very excited over the whole thing, and asked to be informed, as I am doing a little ambassadorial work here!!

N~~

HS TO NB

Thursday afternoon, Jan. 14/60

My dearest Normie:

You see, now I'm working day and night I don't see a soul so that these breaks are with you, (As I regard them.) makes you my only company, which is the only way I would have it.

My feelings for you are muted strings and low register flute. (Sounds suggestive.) They change to every instrument in the orchestra, and some not even heard of.

The deadline is murderous....

———————

Suppertime:

... Bought all the Papers to see the reviews of the Killdeer. It seems unanimous that as a playwright Reaney is a good poet. Your mother fared well in her small part.

I hate the papers with their headlines of doom and impending H bomb disaster over our heads. It seems now Russia has missiles, super bombs and secret weapons enough to cut her army, air force and navy and to blow us all to a premature eternity, should she wish. One day some idiot will press a button and all our trivial poor earth will be finished. No problem. No thing.

I simply don't buy papers as a rule. If we are to dissolve then I don't want to know when so that I can live whatever time is left in peace, search, learning and creating, because when the end comes it will be final. I'm convinced mankind is simply too immature to

January 1960   215

survive, or too stupid. His greatest enemy is himself and that he doesn't know how to cope with.

Sorry to sound this depressing but it's the damn newspapers and I don't know how much time is left for the earth.

No matter what happens I have to get back to work!...

Midnight –

... How I long for a quiet walk with you, not saying anything in particular, just absorbing the air, the sounds, the infinite small things to see, a word every now and again like 'look!' and there would be the first bud on a tree or a dead leaf in a puddle or the moon or a cat or the shadow of a tree....

Saturday –

... Your Ansio letter arrived. The sea has been [a] tonic for you I am happy for you – a chance to contemplate your 'navel' if you'll excuse the expression.

You are happy with the Italian people, and that is good....

... You will understand one day that to care is to love in its way.

Be calm, be at peace. I hope you are well by now, Normie, and able to work. Dearest love, take care –

Ever,
Your Harry

HS TO NB
Saturday evening
Jan 16/60
Darling:

I told Helen McNamara about the beer bottle almost killing me and she broke into such a fit of laughter she could hardly stop. Helen immediately visualized the headlines 'Great Canadian Composer Dies From Beer Bottle'. She said it would be an appropriate death. Of all the ridiculous ways to go!

---

216   Between Composers

Midnight – A Clear Midnight.[14]
This is thy hour, oh soul, thy free flight into the wordless, away from books, away from art, the day erased, the lesson done, thee fully forth emerging, silent, gazing, pondering the themes thou lovest best, night, sleep, death and the stars.
(Thanks to Walt Whitman.)

———

The night continues on and on and I write and write – some completely wild ideas. There's so much to do. It's ok coach, I'm ready for the next quarter.

———

And o'er fields hidden in mist I wander seeing shadows dancing against the pattern of my thoughts. All is mystery never touched, never known, wherein is hidden secrets in themselves shadows. Land of desolation, world without end fashioned from the fantasy of some unknown and the refrain keeps returning. There – behind, in front, look around and about the Bog told Peer but he had to always return to himself and the dance never stops like an endless sea, ebb and flow from nothing into nothing go the ghosts for a moment screaming a sound from their throats mistaken in the night for singing. I hear it from water, from currents of air, from the sound of birds into a moment of shape renewing childhood vision for a moment, or is it the sound of tinkling brass or shimmer of a softly struck cymbal symbol reverberating through endless corridors of the mind. The ancient gods are dispelled with a whisper. Only a murmur is left to ripple through time until without a moment between dies into the endless sea. Mists of sound conjuring mists into dying shapes of feeling. A moment of blinding light is enough to illuminate an eternity of darkness. You see, it is four a.m.[15]

14 "A Clear Midnight" is the final poem in the section "From Noon to Starry Night" in the seventh edition of Whitman's *Leaves of Grass* (1881). This poem was the text for the third of Somers's early set of songs, Three Songs, which he completed in May 1946.
15 All of this appears to be a reference to Henrik Ibsen's *Peer Gynt*, a five-act play in verse published in 1867. In the play, the character Somers refers to as "the Bog" is called "the Bøyg" ("one who can be bent") – a creature/troll found in Norwegian folklore but who has no real description and is merely an all-surrounding voice. Somers's

January 1960 217

Now it's dawn. The great sphere revolves. Good morning, Good night, Good afternoon dear Normie.

Sunday – My mind is a restless traveller seeking every corner of feeling and thought.

We are all strangers, but there is no greater stranger than ourselves.

It's curious the love I have for the shaping of sound. It would be a great pity should composers, like insurance companies, only use computers and gadgets. Nothing can equal the thrill of writing a dot on paper which is translated into vibrations through an instrument set in motion by another human being who will always vary it, humans being so variable. It is the human element – the communion of people performing and listening – which is the greatness of music. I know the beauty of music listened to over a radio or in solitude. But even if there are only a few listening and performing the air can be transformed. It is that moment of truth that exists in no other way.

But I so love sound! Chamber music was one of my first loves. The infinite subtlety of solo instruments in concert – all the quartet literature, Lieder, woodwind, Mozart violin sonatas etc. How can one explain it? One can't, it's foolish to try. It just is, like the comprehension of beauty, of subtlety, sense of taste. So few in this world possess it, but those that do possess the treasures of this world.

'What is beauty?' It's an empty question, for like jazz, if you know what it is you don't ask, you just know.

In short, I'm looking forward to the recording date for the film, in spite of the pressure. I will never get over the excitement of putting dots all over paper and hearing them transformed into a reality. All the years, hours, minutes, seconds of work, study, setbacks, endless endless struggle within to achieve craft, to evolve, to have something to say – all melt into a moment of listening and there is no question.

---

imagery may be partly based on memories of Ibsen's play but is largely in tune with his own imagination, especially "shadows dancing," as in his own 1944 poem "Fantasy." (See chap. 4, n. 6.)

Christ, how I go on. Sorry old duck! I'm awfully full of bull shit sometimes. No offence. Get carried away y'know how it is. Da da, da da da da, boom!

B.D.

... A few more thoughts about my coming over. Normie, I can respect all your feelings. Should you wish it, I can stay at a hotel or some other accommodation, and I would understand....

... I'm coming over to visit you, <u>not</u> to burden you. You know I dislike people to feel they have to entertain or amuse or do anything for me. I've bashed about the world a bit and have yet to find a place in which I'm not at home – for you see I am at home in myself. I enjoy just taking things as they come.

So just relax at my visit, will you darling? I'm placing absolutely no demands on your busy life. It is enough for me to see you and talk with you and find out all the things you've discovered, or else just enjoy a few silences with you. All right?! Just take it cool, baby.

I give you my love – in fact <u>all</u> of it.

Harry

NB to HS
January 16th, 1960
Dear Harry,

Last night I went to hear Julian Bream ~ for some reason I expected an older, less energetic man ~ and was naturally very surprised ~ He was performing with an Italian string quartet ~ the Carmirelli quartet[16] ~ and I went back and introduced myself to Bream before the concert ~ He seemed very pleased as I discovered he speaks only English and knows no one here in Rome ~

So at the end of a very fine concert ~ Bream played both the lute and

---

16 The Carmirelli Quartet was founded in 1954 by the distinguished Italian violinist Pina Carmirelli (1914–1993) and lasted as an ensemble until sometime in the 1960s. It included her husband, the cellist Arturo Bonucci (1894–1964).

January 1960   219

guitar beautifully, and the quartet were 'simpatico' ~ I and another student of Gazzelloni's who I met at the concert, waited patiently to chat with him ~ adjourned to one of Rome's many bars for a drink ~Later we went to a greasy joint for supper where Gazzelloni joined us ~ It turns out that Bream knows Nono well, as does Gazzelloni, and Nono is planning to write a work for them, so I thought that, as Gazzelloni is easy to talk with, I asked him to join us ~ It was a very funny evening for me acting as translator, and Bream's enthusiasm sort of amazed me ~ The usual conversation ensued, you can imagine ~ Both gents will be teaching this summer in Dartington, England, where is an active summer school in August, and this year Berio and Maderna will be there I am told as well as other interesting composers....[17]

... Bream said he was working on your guitar sonata and was enjoying it tremendously ~ If he had been here for a longer time (he is doing a frantic tour and only had one day here in Rome) perhaps I might have heard your work ~ He gave me news of Thea Musgrave, and the English world of music....

... As far as I am concerned, nothing much to report ~ I have been lent, temporarily, a flute (Selmer), and I am much happier with this instrument ~ I am buying a second-hand radio which will take away some of those feelings of complete solitude as well as help me with my Italian ~ I am patiently awaiting my appearance before the examining committee at Santa Cecilia ~ should be any day now ~ trying to do some work (It is very difficult, believe me) ~ The weather here has been freezing, and so have I in 'casa mia' ~ we had a hail storm the other day ~

I wait for your arrival, my love ~ please let me know when ~ and how your work is going ~

Much love
Normie

---

17 Dartington International Summer School began in 1947 as Bryanston Summer School at Bryanston School, Dorset but moved in 1953 to Dartington Hall, an arts and education centre near Totnes, Devon. It offers musicians (including composers) instruction by distinguished figures as well as concerts each summer. Beecroft went to Dartington in the summer of 1961, acting as translator for both Severino Gazzelloni and Bruno Maderna. It was at Dartington that she was first introduced to Maderna's "magic squares," a method of organizing musical material.

220   Between Composers

HS to NB
Sunday evening, Jan.17/60
My dearest love:

Jane was happy and extremely well. It was good to chat with her....

... We spoke of experience, of faith, of the paths to truth. We spoke of the artists' struggle within, of the nature of reality, of much.

It is my belief that Jane has gone through great inner struggle to arrive at her present calm. She is truly happy in her faith and it is unshakable. Her external life centres on the convent, her inner life is to be one with God as she believes it....

... The walk from the end of the bus line to the convent was unbelievable!! Toronto for weeks has been coated with ice which makes trees and bushes into magic glittering crystal. I've been quite awed by the beauty of it and can't ever recall it ever lasting for this long. The reflection from sunlight or moonlight turns the air into shimmering vibrations of light. It is some childhood fairyland filled with tiny creatures of glitter. Fantastic really. The air so clear and just cold enough....

... Late, late. A couple of hours with a stunned brain. Well, that means I must sleep.

Dear girl, I do miss you like hell, my sweet mad soul-searching love. This world, this time is Through the Looking-Glass – we have to go in the opposite direction to get where we're going.[18] I'm quite as though I'm drunk yet I haven't touched a drop. The simplest things are so complex. Crazy world, crazy Harry, crazy White Knight, crazy Don Quixote – the last of the Romantics, the last with the illusions, the last idealists but it gives depth to shallowness shadows to a light bulb....

... Mind not this man out of time who loves you in a way which is out of another age. I suppose it is 'my misfortune and none of your own'.[19] Normie, I love you — these words need no qualification,

18 *Through the Looking-Glass, and What Alice Found There* by Lewis Carroll was published in 1871 as a sequel to *Alice's Adventures in Wonderland*. In the world beyond the mirror, everything is reversed. In chapter 8, the White Knight comes to Alice's rescue, escorting her through the forest and reciting his poem "Haddocks' Eyes."
19 This quotation is likely from the popular cowboy ballad "Git Along, Little Dogies,"

January 1960   221

they just are. You, dear one, are the dream giving shape to my longing. Sleep well and at peace, always.

———

Your Harry

HS to NB
Monday 18 of Jan/60
Dearest Normie:
   A great blizzard rages outside and here I am up the Saguenay in
the middle of summer. Every now and again I look at the clock and
say 'It's 8 p.m in Rome' or 'she must be asleep or getting up' etc. Is
there any scent like cedar or pine? Is there any sound like the brushing of wind through pine trees? Resphigi wrote of the Pines of Rome
so they must be about there.[20]
   'O joy of my spirit – it is uncaged – it darts like lightning! It is not
enough to have this globe or a certain time, I will have thousands of
globes and all time!...'[21]

———

   Evening —
   ... My thoughts are of this human condition. How we are swayed
and turned by a million small things around us. How the 'still small
voice' must be found in the silence....
   ... As usual, dear Normie, I stand in awe before such a vast mystery and feel truth within myself and seek a frame of sound for that
which I feel. I feel a compassion for all that lives and wonder if it is
the echo of something beyond my immediate ken....

---

believed to be a variation of an Irish ballad and recorded many times from 1929 on
(which may explain how Somers knew of it). The line quoted comes from the following
verse: "Whoopee ti yi yo, git along little dogies, / It's your misfortune, and none of my
own / Whoopee ti yi yo, git along little dogies, / For you know Wyoming will be your
new home."
20 *Pines of Rome* (1924) is a four-movement symphonic poem for large orchestra by
the Italian composer Ottorino Respighi. The piece depicts pine trees in four locations in
Rome at different times of the day and is the second of Respighi's trilogy of tone poems
based on Rome. The others are *Fountains of Rome* (1917) and *Roman Festivals* (1928).
21 This is another quotation from a poem of Walt Whitman, this time the poem "A
Song of Joys." ("O to make the most jubilant song! / Full of music – full of manhood,
womanhood, infancy!")

... I work so much alone, yet am not alone. From the length of my solitude I draw my inner strength. For twenty-one years I've been writing music in endless solitude peopled with countless struggles, ideas, – the silent sounds. I think perhaps I might be fortunate in time to write something of real and lasting worth. If not, then it is not to be.

If so, then it is to be....

... These last months without you have been a time of the most intense inner experiences of my life. I embrace such suffering for it has revealed to me the reality and verity of existence. We never know what trials await us. Through them we find the measure of our love and strength. We discover what is worthwhile and what is only passing, yet the final answer is never known. We live, we seek, we suffer and we know moments of joy....

... 4 a.m. My God, it's the story of my life! I lie down to sleep but ideas keep shaping and I have to jump up to write them down! Mad mad! There's little rest when I'm in the middle of a work.

By the way. Since you've seen me I've lost close to 20 lbs, so I look more craggy, gaunt and generally thinner. Imagine more what I looked like when you first knew me so you won't be too surprised. My hair's long again as well.

Back to work....

... Tuesday – Isn't it ironic – the recording session for the film is to be in the Victor Studio on Mutual Street – remember when we first met that was where the orchestral rehearsals were for the New Years show.[22] Being in such places I find the toughest on my sentimental constitution.

---

22 In 1947, CHUM Radio set up a studio in what was known as the Fulpart Building at 225 Mutual Street. When CHUM relocated to Yonge Street a few years later, RCA Records established a recording studio in the building. Over some fifty years, major entertainers such as Rosemary Clooney, Mel Tormé, Chubby Checker, Wilson Pickett, James Brown, Steve Winwood, and Mark Knopfler, and famous Canadian performers, such as Gordon Lightfoot, Anne Murray, Bachman-Turner Overdrive, and Rush, all made records here. The studio also provided recordings for numerous CBC Television programs. In 1979, McClear Place Studios purchased the studio space from RCA and recording sessions continued there until 2005. In 2010, the building was demolished to make way for a parking lot.

Beloved —

Your letter of return from your holiday arrived. I rush up with the letter, slam my door, rip open the envelope and devour the contents.

You sound so well I'm delighted – Your house looks the same – your room hasn't been touched, everything is as it was....

... The moment my work clears I'll make my plane reservation. I'm thinking of jet — New York to Paris, then to Rome. If there were only a direct flight! Everything in between 'till I see you is a waste of time.

Likely leave 'round 15th February....

... <u>One more thing</u>. For myself I hate to say this, and it would be a serious and grave sacrifice emotionally, but should you not receive money from the estate I would forego the trip and send you the money instead so that you could pursue your studies. I believe in you as a person, I love you as a man loves a woman, and I would see that you have every opportunity to complete whatever studies you wish to....

... Take care, work hard, be at peace, fear nothing – and don't eat <u>too</u> much or you'll look like many Italian men and women do as they get older – not that I wouldn't love you just the same fat, thin, gray or anything I love you just as you are!

My dearest one – all my love is yours –

Love love love —

Harry

HS to NB
Tuesday evening,
Jan. 19/60
Beloved Normie:

Old Symonds just called. He and Gwen have just returned from Montreal. They were driving back, quite drunk, in a blinding snow storm and drove into a snow plough from the rear! The car was smashed up but they fortunately escaped only shaken up a bit. Norm swears he's learned his lesson. He recalls the mad journey of he and I stoned to the ear drums driving back at 80 on the wrong side of the road and off it. Remember? You fed us an omelette when we got in town. He and I have no business being alive, really.[23] It's funny to look back on in a horrifying sort of way. I've had so many close calls I look back in wonder (My latest play.)[24]

Now the north wind blusters and howls. I'll never forget when I was completing the 2nd piano concerto I spent a couple of weeks in the winter at Reg's place in Ancaster because I needed the solitude his place offered.[25] One fierce winter day I walked along to the escarpment overlooking Hamilton. On the way I walked across a field under those great hydro-electric wires. What I heard I could hardly comprehend at first. It was like the vibrations of some enormous double bass string with a 'thwummm~~~~' coming from a string possibly 200 or more feet in length. The wind was setting in motion the most fantastic music.

I was half frozen to death but I loved it and was so invigorated by such a surprise. All about us is the world of natural sound outside the cities' mechanical noise – though the cities' sounds are also fascinating. The world is full of so much to see and hear and so few people are aware of what is right around them. And the wind must be Orpheus, though the Gods of the north have a breath in it.

I tell ye lass, 'tis wondrous fair.

Listened to Nathan Cohen talking with Norman Mailer – 'Naked and the Dead'.[26] You know something – an awful lot of well-known

---

23 Driving while inebriated seems to have been a regular occurrence in Somers's life; there would be a number of "close calls" in the years after 1960.

24 This is probably a reference to John Osborne's 1956 play, *Look Back in Anger*. See chap. 3, n. 61.

25 This would have been the winter of 1955–56, since Somers completed the Piano Concerto No. 2 in January of 1956. In 1954, Reginald Godden and his family had moved into a large house in the historic village of Ancaster, located on the Niagara Escarpment.

26 This conversation took place on 17 January 1960 on the CBC television program *Fighting Words*, hosted by the Toronto theatre critic Nathan Cohen (1923–1971). The program ran from 1952 until 1962, with brief interruptions and changes of format. Usually four panellists would try to identify the authorship of three quotations during the half-hour and then discuss each of these but on a few occasions (such as this) the

January 1960   225

names in this world are full of shit – bull shit. One wouldn't listen to two minutes of this nonsense talk if one didn't know the name. They get so used to sounding off to idiots and hero worshippers they can't shut up.

An extraordinary interview in its way. As you know, I am very fond of most Americans, but there is such a streak of something adolescent in their creative and philosophical thinking that it shocks me at times.

Mailer is following, supposedly, the creed of the 'hip' or 'hipster.' He presented such a jumble of contradictions, unqualified generalities, naïve promises that he began to sound like a freshman college student. He was hardly fair game for Nathan who got Mailer so tongue tied he had to leap off in every other direction but answer a direct question....

... There are points here and there which are good but which he just couldn't follow through on. The American tends to think in the puritan tradition of black and white, good and evil, the good guys and the bad guys. Everything is a 'western' in its way. They still have the illusion of the 'west' in many different forms. A land of cults, of one extreme or the other, of amazing self-consciousness....

———

Wed. 20 – (I lose track.)

... 'Morning. The Chinese saying that, 'A journey of 10,000 miles begins with one step' entered my head for some reason.[27] Meditating on't.

If this performance in N.Y. went through, Howard Shanet would conduct.[28] Reg. tells me Shanet met us at Lukas Foss's in Tanglewood. These concerts get wide critical coverage but rehearsal time is short, so I have me doubts. Reg, God bless him, would do it for practically nothing....

---

program consisted of a one-to-one interview. This program can be found in the CBC Archives: https://www.cbc.ca/player/play/1872030671. Mailer's novel *The Naked and the Dead* was published in 1948.

27 "A journey of a thousand Chinese miles (li) starts beneath one's feet" is a common saying that originated from a Chinese proverb.

28 Howard Shanet (1918–2007), a conductor and composer, started his career as a cellist, then studied composition after the war with Bohuslav Martinů and Aaron Copland. In 1953, he joined Columbia University's faculty as professor of music and was chair of its music department from 1972 to 1978.

... If not the concerto they want to do the symphony. That would be even worse. The only people who could hope to read it on short rehearsal in North America is the C.B.C. symphony. This much I know....

———————

... Your red card table is a Godsend here. I've set up my viewer and reels of the film on one end and the rest I use for my composition with these enormous orchestration pads I use and my twenty-stave conductor's short score (divided into 5 staves a section) I have to write out as well. Man it's tense work. Lose one second in your calculations and you're 24 frames of film out! 12 to 1/2 sec, 6 to 1/4 sec, 2 to 1/12. You can just imagine what it is to be writing music continuous and logical in itself yet written to coincide at exact melodic, rhythmic, harmonic points to points in the film – to a single frame! That means I have to be exact to 1/24th of a second/
And the score is 20 minutes long without break!
They gave me a full orchestra that I wanted of 27 men with 2 perc. men who can cover every perc. instrument you can name. So I've no cause for complaint that way. The best studio men in town will be in it which makes me quite happy.
In those sections where I'm using 12-tone I've a series of enormous 12-note chords which should give a hell of a wack when I want it. These chords come close to solving a problem of virtual tone-clusters which I wanted to arrive at logically and which I will extend in the Koussevitzky work. (With apologies to Cage, of course.)

———————

Asking Norm about perc. He gave me terrific ideas about the alternation of the heavy and light end of a snare stick on bongos and tom-tom, use of hard, soft, medium mallets, pressure of hand on drum etc. etc. The jazz field has extended colour possibilities so extraordinarily I'm just digging into the grab bag. Their mistake is when they have colour, rhythm and little else – exciting for the first while then it starts to pall.
They have a new cymbal with small metal weights loosely fastened on top of cymbal which greatly scintillates and extends the vibration.

January 1960

You can get a steady series of rim shots any speed on s[nare] d[rum]. Vibes, of course can use 4 mallets of different weight and the use of vibrator electrically can change (by use of foot bar) the speed of any given pitch into slow pulses like waves or fast or any degree between or acceleration.

The use of brass and wd. glisses, port. etc. and the number of mutes for brass and the wide variety of vibrato – (Everything to the wide head vibrato of Harris used on trombone for years) gives a range of colour the 'square' musician is hardly aware of. Even such a simple thing as a tight cup mute can change the whole character....

... Just discovered from Fen Watkin trombones can do flutter tongue growl![29] Such news! I'm having tromb.'s answer tpts. in one section in this manner. It'll shake the poor old exec.'s at Alcoa Aluminum. Ho ho! But what an idea the fluttergrowl is for this bit!

... there are times I feel 100 or more years old. Like 'Here I am, an old man in a dry month, being read to by a boy, waiting for rain.' by our friend T.S. when he was young.[30] 'In the room the women come and go talking of Michelangelo'. Or Burnt Norton or oh well or his cutting 'Portrait of a Lady' – portrait of her platitudes on romance, on art, on friendship, on life. Poor T.S. Well since conversion he's happier but a bloody preacher.[31]

29 Fen Watkin (1922–2019) was a Canadian musician – a trombonist, conductor, pianist, and arranger – who had played trombone with the Toronto Symphony Orchestra for three seasons (1955–58) but had also worked on a number of CBC television variety shows (such as General Electric's Showtime) as an arranger and copyist. That is probably how Somers had come to know him (i.e., through his own music copying for various shows). In 1965, Watkin began conducting at the Charlottetown Summer Festival and conducted *Anne of Green Gables* there every summer for forty years.

30 This is the opening of "Gerontion," a poem by T.S. Eliot that appeared in 1920 in *Ara Vos Prec*. The Greek title means "little old man," and the poem is a dramatic monologue relating the opinions and impressions of an elderly man.

31 Eliot had converted to Anglicanism from Unitarianism in June 1927.

228   Between Composers

Mario Prizak did an excellent production of the 'Cocktail Party' awhile back.[32] I must say the dialogue and wit of T.S. is brilliant at points....

...Wonderful sound on the street – clip clop clip clop of horses' hoofs. Takes me back to childhood – dawn in late spring – sneaking out to view the great mystery of night into day – milk wagon horse-drawn – clippety clop clippety clop in the empty otherwise silent street – the fabulous sweet earth smell of dawn – and I a child a manifestation of nature's desire to see itself becoming one with myself, such wonders to behold – I would stand and stare atop the hill opposite our house then with joy run down the hill laughing singing hopping tumbling back.

Friday – Saw the Reaney play last night – without a doubt the craziest most uncoordinated stuck together play I've ever seen – mad mad – the last act fell apart like some crazy Marx Brothers film.[33] I found it hilarious in its most tragic moments and couldn't suppress great guffaws. It was a big bag of haggis.

Interesting conversation with Bailey yesterday – Weldon and Lois on 7 months tour – she a fabulous success in Moscow recently.[34] Maureen Forrester regarded as one of the greatest contraltos of the day[35] – many concerts with Bruno Walter etc. Wonderful gal –

---

32 Mario Prizek (1923–2012) was the director and producer of many shows on CBC Television from 1951 until 1985, including *Eye Opener* and *Bamboula*. His production of *The Cocktail Party* was taped in Toronto on 12 December 1959 for broadcast in early January 1960 on "Ford Startime."

33 See chap. 5, n. 8.

34 This refers to the renowned Canadian soprano Lois Marshall (1924–1997) and pianist/vocal coach Weldon Kilburn (1906–1986), her accompanist and, briefly, her husband. They had gone on a second tour of the Soviet Union in January 1960; Lois Marshall was rapturously received, as had been Glenn Gould on *his* first visit there in May 1957.

35 By the late 1950s, Maureen Forrester (1930–2010) had performed successfully in international centres such as New York, Berlin, and London, including a performance of Mahler's Symphony No. 2 (the *Resurrection*) with the New York Philharmonic under Bruno Walter in 1957. In 1956, she had premiered Somers's *Five Songs for Dark Voice*

January 1960   229

3 kids, works like a Trojan – absolutely no pretention or conceit – a complete human being – always did like old Maureen and success ain't spoiled her a bit. Crazy Glenn Gould cancelled a European tour 'cause someone slapped him on the back and he thinks he's ill.[36] (He is, but not in the back.)

I'm taking time off for a while this evening and going to a costume party with Donnica.[37] (Now now – <u>absolutely no</u> need for jealousy upset or anxiety.) Feel it would do me some good away from my hermitage for a bit, 'though I'll have to leave early to get back to work.

This is a long rambling letter. I contemplated throwing it out but instead I'll wrap the whole mess up and send it to you....

... Dear love, always, always, I hold you close and dear to my thoughts and heart – you are my love, my one and only love, you are my woman —

Your Harry

NB to HS
20th January, 1960 ~
Dearest Harry,

Once in a while we all have to let off steam, and will you please forgive me if I tell you of my irritation first ~ Yesterday I received my notice for this exam ~ Monday the 25th at 9:30 I go before the committee ~ On this little notice, it stated that I would not be admitted to the exam without my documents ~ I am so bloody angry with two people, one Michael Fram for not having sent me the words to his bloody song which I requested over a month ago, and the other perhaps more important, John Weinzweig ~ I wrote him a letter on 31st December to request some kind of certification that I had studied x number of subjects with him, and to ask his advice on whether this letter perhaps should come from Mazzoleni (sounds all very confusing) but as you know, I have no diploma or certificate to present to Santa Cecilia, and the secretary of the Accademy told me

---

at the Stratford Festival, a work commissioned especially for her. She had married the violinist Eugene Kash (1912–2004) in 1957 with whom she had five children.
36 On a visit to Steinway Hall in New York in 1959, the chief piano technician, William Hupfer, slapped Gould on the back by way of greeting him. As a result, Gould complained of aching, lack of coordination, and fatigue and even explored the possibility of suing Steinway & Sons if his apparent injuries proved to be long-lasting.
37 This was probably Danica d'Hondt. See chap. 3, n. 101.

230 Between Composers

that a letter (as above) would suffice[38] ~ Now not having this letter, I don't know whether I will be admitted to the exam, and I am angry with John because I have heard nothing at all, and I had informed him that it was relatively urgent....

... I have pondered what you say about coming here, and the living arrangements ~ My only concern, dear Harry, is that we <u>both</u> have the freedom and space for our work ~ Do not contemplate a hotel, for you will be broke in no time ~ remember, <u>nothing</u> is cheap here! But, do you wish me to inquire about studios, or perhaps a pensione situation where you could rent a piano, or do you wish to wait until you arrive and worry later? If I knew precisely when you were coming, I could find the type of place and book it, if you wish...

... It occurs to me, when will you receive payment for your film work ~ this could hold you up somewhat, if they don't pay immediately, in your plans to come here....

<u>Friday</u> AM
... My darling, my thoughts seem to be totally involved with this forthcoming exam on Monday, so I dare not write you anything too intelligible ~ I suppose, not only am I concerned because I haven't received John's letter, but that the exam is in Italian and I have no idea the form it will take ~ I am going over to the Accademia now to pay my examination tax, so perhaps I shall inquire ~?...

... Thank you darling, for your marvellous letters ~ and your offer to bail me out of difficulties financially ~ To date it is not necessary, and I have just received from Mother (and Michael) some encouraging words re the estate[39] ~

Keep your toes crossed for me that I may enter the course ~
So much love ~
Normie ~

38 Ettore Mazzoleni (1905–1968), a Swiss-born conductor and teacher who had come to Canada in 1929 to teach music and English at Upper Canada College, was principal of the Royal Conservatory of Music of Toronto from 1945 until his death. He was also director (from 1952 until 1966) of the Royal Conservatory Opera School. During the 1950s and 1960s, he conducted many important opera productions in Toronto as well as for some of Canada's leading orchestras, including the CBC Symphony Orchestra and the Toronto Symphony Orchestra, of which he was associate conductor from 1942 until 1948.
39 Michael Fram was handling the legal matters for her inheritance.

January 1960

NB to HS

January 23rd, 1960

Dearest Harry,

I have just returned from another concert of the radio orchestra where a beautiful work for 3 string orchestras by Gabrieli was performed, and Petrassi's 5th Concerto for orchestra ~ During the Gabrieli, I kept thinking that if I had only been born a few hundred years ago I would in some ways be happier ~ And then listening to Petrassi's work thoroughly depressed me ~ this work was commissioned by the Boston S.O. and the Koussevitzky foundation, and undoubtedly was written after the death of Koussevitzky, for it is of funereal quality ~ extremely sad, but well-written composition, with a great knowledge of the orchestral medium[40] ~

But I felt so sad, truly ~ this music is not of our time in a sense, a thought which plagues the hell out of me ~ I can no longer even listen to Bartok very often without getting restless, and perhaps bored even ~ I fear the future ~ I cannot understand the avant-garde music of today as music, and other things written in the past 50 years are not expressing to me what I want to express ~ I wonder sometimes if I really will ever answer securely these enormous, paralysing questions ~

Oh well, I am in a low state of mind tonight ~ so these thoughts will pass, I am sure ~ a least for a while ~

I chatted with Petrassi a bit, and told him of my problem regarding the letter that hasn't arrived ~ He looked rather dubious as to whether I will be admitted to the exam on Monday ~ Christ, Harry, why hasn't John responded to my request ~ After deciding that I want this course ~ to be stopped for lack of certification would be the last straw....

~ ~

---

40 In his review of the recordings of the eight Petrassi Concerti for Orchestra (STR33700), Richard Whitehouse writes that "By this time [1955], Petrassi was at the height of his success as a composer. The Fifth Concerto, composed in 1955 for the Boston Symphony and Charles Munch, is the biggest of the cycle in terms of length and impact. The five-movement 'arch' form is used for maximum contrast, with the limpid expression of the central Andantino offset by the rhythmic onslaught on either side, and given perspective by the fatalistic mood of the framing slow movements – resulting in a brooding and anguished utterance." www.classicalsource.com/cd/goffredo-petrassi-concertos-for-orchestra-tamayo/.

Sunday Afternoon

... A somewhat better day, but the great worry of tomorrow morning hangs heavily in the air ~ Harry dear, if someone were to ask me tomorrow whether I really wanted to write music, what could I truthfully answer? External me says 'Why bother ~ it is so difficult, the problems at your stage of the game and in your time are enormous' to the extent that I would like to crawl under the sand for a few years and let someone else figure it out ~ But something inside pushes me on and on, and try as I may to stand still, I can't ~ Is that an answer for an examining committee?

I think somehow that it must have been easier about 10 or 15 years ago, immediately following the war where there was a period of intense reaction and undoubtedly great activity ~ But today we are in a transient stage which is affecting even older generations of artists ~ They, however, are having perhaps a little easier time of it for they have a good 10, 20 or 30 years of solid writing behind them and perhaps cannot be as easily uprooted ~ I recall Gazzelloni telling a group of us a story of a concert either in Paris or Poland, I'm not sure, attended by Shostakovitch, and the program consisted of 2 of his works and the music of the avant-garde school (a strange program indeed) ~ His works received little enthusiasm and polite applause, and the new music received cheers and a thundering ovation ~ Gazillion said it was indeed very sad to see a man such as Shostakovitch almost in tears....

... It appears that many, almost all I have met, composers are fighting this gigantic problem internally ~ and even though we may know the final answer, we cannot help but be affected by this ~ Petrassi has solid views, thank heaven ~

By the way, I was told that this course was originally conducted by Pizzetti, and no one applied for entrance[41] ~ This will be Petrassi's first year in the lead, and it should be interesting ~ Strangely enough there are no Americans, but 2 applicants from Argentina, 1 from Spain, 4 from Italy, and other countries which I don't remember....

---

41 Ildebrando Pizzetti (1880–1968) was an Italian composer, musicologist, and music critic. He was a contemporary of Ottorino Respighi, Gian Francesco Malipiero, and Alfredo Casella, all of whose work was centred in genres other than opera, whereas Pizzetti wrote some twenty operas as well as music to some of Gabriele d'Annunzio's plays. He taught at the Academy of St Cecilia in Rome from 1936 to 1958.

January 1960   233

... Now, darling, I must return to work and worry ~ Hope you are managing well with your work, and that you are happy with it ~ I know you will make your deadline ~

              Much love,
                Normie

NB to HS
25th Gennaio, 1960
Dear Harry,

I normally get myself worked up to something which turns out to be very easy in the long run ~ Needless to say, I was accepted into the course with four others, one from Spain, Portugal, Holland and Italy ~ a class of five ~ I am very happy because it was senza documenti for me ~

This is just a short letter to let you know of my joy at the moment ~ We did not even see the examining committee ~ they looked at scores submitted ~ that's all, I am happy to say, that I was not accepted as a female, but on the basis of my work ~ Ain't that great ~!!

Classes begin on Wednesday morning, so we're off immediately ~

I am too elated to write much now, so I make this letter very brief ~ I still must have the letter from John as soon as possible, so I shall write him later today ~

There is a scholarship connected with this course as well but I do not know how much ~

         Wish me buon lavoro, darling
            Love
             Normie ~

HS to NB
Jan.27/60
Darling darling Normie!!

I'm thrilled!! Absolutely!! At your confidence, security in self and development! ...

... You see, before, you leaned far too much on me, on excuses etc. I was disappointed in you because it seemed you were more interested in the 'idea' of becoming a composer than being one and doing the work....

... I am proud of you! – but a caution – beware of depending or relating criticism to approval. The lack of criticism could do more harm and you learn less than having it. Remember, we all want

234   Between Composers

approval, we all want to shine to be brilliant in the light – but it can obscure learning essentials – you should invite criticism. The teacher becomes a father image. Which is fine – but only by being absolutely ruthless in appraisal do we learn....

... But girl – all the best – ole Harry here is thrilled beyond words at what's happened to you!! Harry is with you all the way.

When you were excusing yourself previously I was actually hurt, now I'm so happy. My girl, I _am_ _indeed_ _proud_ of you. You are proving that you have the guts and courage I believed you had to become an individual, a composer.

I'm glad the flowers arrived – yes. I do share your excitement! The importance of a thing is always measured by the significance to each one of us individually – nothing else matters!

My love, my girl, my woman, my composer friend – stick with it as you will – it's just the beginning so take a deep breath so as to go a long way!...

... Your love who is happy and proud of you —
Har.

NB to HS
27th Gennaio, 1960
Darling ~
The first day of the class, and I feel rather exhilarated even though somewhat ill ~ I woke up this AM at 1:00 with practically a closed throat, a situation which I begin to accept as my normal state of health ~ Undoubtedly I am being hit again by this bloody flu epidemic....

... At 8:45 I commenced to practice the flute in spite of cold ~ and then after a long wait, to send a parcel to my brother Charles, in the post office, I ran to the class ~

We sat and analysed one composers work for about 1 1/2 hrs., Petrassi being also sick with a cold ~ However his comments on orchestration are quite excellent, so the course began slowly but well ~ Friday morning they will attack my songs ~ even though incomplete ~ and in spite of the fact that I am nervous showing my work in front of a new class for the first time, I very much need a criticism from Petrassi ~ The chap from Holland did not appear as he had the flu, but I discovered that he knows Rudi Van Dyck fairly well[42] ~

---

42 Rudi Martinus van Dijk (1932–2003) was a Dutch-born composer of orchestral, chamber, and vocal music. Because he had studied oboe, in 1953 he joined the Canadian

January 1960 235

It turns out that the Spaniard is not from Spain but from Buenos Aires, and knows Mario Davidovsky (you remember the tall, clever, string-bean composer who won the Koussevitsky prize in Tanglewood?) who is now evidently in the US now[43] ~ It is a very small world isn't it!

We have an Israeli in the class as an addition, so we number 6 in total ~ I look forward to the pressure imposed by three classes per week ~ It will keep me very busy ~

Darling, I am feeling very happy now, and certainly more secure ~ This course has taken on great significance to me ~

However, I have had some disturbing thoughts lately about 'my other life' ~ The more deeply involved I become in music, the less I wish for a domestic life ~ This is rather shattering for one who so loved to cook and look after a man called Harry ~ Maybe this is pure reaction, but it worries me a little ...We shall talk about these things when you come here in detail....

... I am happy to hear that Michael is finally sending the words to his poem ~ When Petrassi heard that I had not received them, his comment was 'he must be a little poet' ~ otherwise one without much ego....

... By the way, who is Donnica?[44] I am afraid that my absence has brought many women into your life who must love me with open arms! At times, I am consumed with the most frightening jealousy, remembering all the incidents of the past which hurt ~ and then have to tell myself 'Remember, old girl, you are not exactly innocent either'! I wonder if I shall ever be able to forget these things ~ You know Harry, (and I realize that I am placing the responsibility for

---

Grenadier Guards Band as an oboist and moved to Canada, where he composed background music for educational programs but also played piano on radio for the CBC (which is likely how he came to know Beecroft and Somers). From 1966 until 1972, he taught piano at the Royal Conservatory of Music in Toronto but left Canada in 1972 to take up a teaching position at Indiana University, although he continued to have performances of his music in Canada.

43 Mario Davidovsky (1934–2019) was born in Argentina, but in 1960 emigrated to the United States, where he spent the remainder of his life. Beecroft had met him at Tanglewood in 1958, where he was studying with Aaron Copland and met Milton Babbitt. As a result of meeting Babbitt, he developed an interest in electronic music and worked at the Columbia-Princeton Electronic Music Center for many years, serving as director from 1981 until 1993. He is best known for his series of compositions called "Synchronisms," which include both acoustic instruments and electronically produced sounds.

44 Danica d'Hondt. See chap. 3, n. 101.

my actions entirely on your shoulders) but I don't think I would ever have eyes for someone else but you, if you had allowed me to trust you ~ You see, I am still somewhat jealous, because I can only see what happened, and hear your blank refusal to confide anything to me in my ears, in the past years ~ We have done somewhat of a switch, I think now ~ for now I am the one without belief and riddled with fear ~ The only difference is that I am single....

... I hope that you are happy with your work and you will have a little time now to rest, and eat, and put back some of those lost pounds ~ Come to Italy to get fat ~ I have put on about 10–12 pounds, I discovered – Old fatty!

> I wait for your letters as always
> Love
> Normie ~

NB to HS
29th Gennaio, 1960
Dear Harry,

What a marvellous feeling to begin to find oneself and the inner security it brings ~ to know that you can stand alone and on your own feet for even a certain period of time ~

Even though I have been relatively ill the last two days ... I managed to make it to the second class this morning for Petrassi's criticism of my songs ~ For some strange reason, I was not mortified to show this work to him or the class, and I begin to feel a sense of direction ~ His criticisms were very few, be that good or bad ~ I feel it very good, in this particular case, for I feel I have the beginnings of a sense of judgement with regard to my own work ~ A marvellous feeling, I might say... His criticisms were things that had previously been bothering me for the most part ~

But the most exciting part of the day is the feeling that I know there is a certain path I must take, and I begin to see what it is ~ I am afraid every day I become more committed to composition ~ and this also makes me happy ~ Whether my independence is good for you in the long run is a serious story, but I am surely finding Norma Beecroft ~

The class of 6 is a trifle strange, and I again feel like a senior thinker, as I did in Tanglewood ~ There are 2, perhaps 3 composers who find it impossible to write anything for the very reason that the music of today is paralysing them ~ I do hope that Petrassi can free them somewhat ... for really the first time in my life I am starting to relax the internal muscles and am feeling like a reasonable sure human being ~ There are sure to be endless moments of doubt, but not right now ~

I am told by well-informed people that it is really a feather in my cap to be accepted into this class ~ the Corso di Perfezionamento, and that this diploma will carry me a long way in my profession ... Petrassi intends to spend practically all the time on critical analysis of our work, and on little else ~ so in essence, it is a course in composition, and similar to a private lesson only the entire class gets the benefit from the other's mistakes....

... Tomorrow, I think I will have the opportunity to meet Maderna, which should be interesting[45] ~ so I will finish then ~

Buona notte, caro mio ~

<u>Sunday</u> <u>Afternoon</u>:

Well my love, naturally enough Maderna did not show up which was rather disappointing, but I suppose one can understand if an Italian, <u>and</u> a composer, doesn't quite appear ~

However, what did appear today were some beautiful red roses from you ~ How very pleased, –sad I felt ~ and how very thoughtful of you darling ~ Thank you so much for thinking of me in this way....

... I have just finished this morning reading 'Dr. Zhivago', and this tragic tale of human life, coupled with my own illness these days probably accounts for my feeling of sadness at the arrival of the flowers[46] ~ I have been in bed off and on with the flu which manifests

---

45 Bruno Maderna (1920–1973) was one of the leading Italian composers of the avantgarde during the 1950s and 1960s and an important conductor as well. With Luciano Berio, he founded the Studio di Fonologia Musicale of the RAI in 1955. This provided them with the facilities they needed to develop electronic music. They also founded *Incontri Musicali*, a periodical (overseen by Berio) and an ensemble (founded and directed by Maderna). Maderna was also an important teacher, giving, for instance, an introductory course on twelve-note composition at the Milan Conservatory in 1957 and 1958. See also chap. 5, n.16.

46 *Doctor Zhivago*, by Boris Pasternak, was first published in 1957 in Italy. Its protagonist, Yuri Zhivago, is a physician and poet, and the plot extends over several decades, between the Russian Revolution of 1905 and the Second World War. Due to his critical attitude toward the Bolshevik revolution and the novel's concern with the welfare of the individual, the USSR would not allow it to be published; the manuscript was smuggled out of the USSR and published in Milan. In 1958, Pasternak was awarded the Nobel Prize for Literature.

238   Between Composers

itself in my chest strangely enough ~ God, it would be nice to feel well, for once ~!

Needless to say, I was very moved by the whole of the famous book, but found the writing at first rather difficult to get into ~ It is indeed Russian in character, but so much dwelling on historical details of the revolution rather tires me, not being a person who enjoys reading history in this moment ~ For some reason I would rather have facts, and the novel (the story of the doctor's struggle against this background) separately ~ Meanwhile, Pasternak beautifully weaves his characters, and leaves much to the imagination of the reader, which is fascinating ~ Actually, I find the book rather like an ever-changing painting, characters passing and meeting and parting and re-meeting, against a background of human tragedy....

... We have had about 5 days of late spring weather here ~ tomorrow it is liable to freeze, but meanwhile it is very beautiful ~ Taking advantage of this weather, with flu and all, I went yesterday to visit Ostia antica – the old port of Rome at the mouth of the Tiber ~ They have excavated a whole city, which I am told probably held 50,000 people 1,000 years ago or more ~ There stands the remains of temples, endless houses, schools, outdoor 'johns' ~ there remains a 24-holer made of marble, if you can imagine ~ Everything seems incredibly modern ~ You must see this place when you're here ~

I think of you finishing your work love, and hope the deadline was met ~ Please write soon and let me know your plans ~

Love

Normie

Thank you so much for the flowers ~

HS to NB
Saturday/ Jan 30/60
My beloved Normie:

Just another note to say again how happy I am for you. Norm S. sends his congrats and best wishes.

Working in a small class is excellent for you can learn from the criticism given the others as well as yourself. The only danger is that of competition and comparison, which is inevitable I suppose – a virtue and a vice for it can make one more concerned with what the others think of your work rather than treating it as problems posed, answered successfully or not but always learned from....

January 1960

... My score's almost done. A lot of approaches I've never used before have emerged backed by much I have. I'm getting closer and closer to the realization of concepts I've had for over ten years but required much time to mature and grow.

Heard a brilliant work of Gunther Schuller's from N.Y. Phil. called Spectra.[47] All colour tone technic revealing a complete mastery of instruments and technic. Orch. divided in 7 parts. (Any composer to be anybody nowadays must have his own seating arrangement, my dear.) I feel the basic enjoyment for such a tour de force is one of sensation, (re: senses) intellect. You just get your kicks like, but not a wiff of healthy human B.O. I suppose it would be just too vulgar. However that ain't the way to dig this must. The guy handles brass like no one I've heard. You'd swear half the sounds were electronic. He uses the whole range of contemporary verbiage – broken row all over the place, short spurts, dramatic contrast, extreme registers, dovetailing crescendos, levels, dynamic extremes etc. etc.

And doll, if you have two notes of equal length follow each other, you're dead! (This is my teaching method.)

Exciting stuff, but after a while a certain monotony sets in, the bane of artists. You can write anything you want, but you can't be a bore. However my messy radio could have contributed. (Hey.)

Enough, enough!! What am I doing! One day left to finish the score! (I got the last shot list yesterday!)....

... but I send the most love – a great enormous shipment of it – bigger than the Queen Mary – bigger than a whole city – a whole country – a whole continent – a whole world – a whole universe even!!!!

A great sweltering hug for you – now get in there Rocky and come out swingin!!

Your ever lovin admirin ole Harry!!

---

47 *Spectra* was written in 1958. The orchestra is divided into seven smaller groups, five of which are of chamber-ensemble size. The emphasis is on texture and colour, the latter breaking up timbres into various colours, similar to the way a prism breaks up light. Due to the unusual seating arrangement, the sounds can give the impression of moving among the various ensembles, giving rise to "stereophonic" effects. It is possible that this piece was somewhat of an influence in Somers's own orchestra piece of 1962–63, *Stereophony*, written for the Toronto Symphony Orchestra to be performed in Massey Hall. In this piece, musicians are distributed throughout the hall but the emphasis is instead on texture and colour (in contrast to Somers's earlier orchestral music). In *Spectra*, the effect of "electronic" sounds may be due to "sound masses" scored for different combinations moving between one group and another. A similar effect can be found in Somers's *Stereophony*.

240   Between Composers

HS to NB
Again Saturday
My darling Normie:

You see what you will be answering to me now. That is that you will want me because of want, <u>not</u> need, in the objective sense. That it will be <u>me</u> you want and not just something that I represent that you could get anywhere. I want you to make your decision, in other words, not when you're blue or discouraged or any other thing ... but when you are fairly poised and secure, when life seems good....

... I cannot live without you, Normie, I do so want to marry you and make a life together – isn't that wild for me to talk this way?! I find it absolutely empty without you. I'm being dragged across a bed of broken glass. You are my love and I'm being tortured by my feelings – wondering what you're doing, how you really feel, how you will answer, how I will react, I imagine every conceivable thing you might answer and I feel so fearful.

'She's like the swallow that flies so high'[48]
or I sing to myself – 'I'm sad and I'm lonely' with the last verse 'I'm troubled, yes, I'm troubled, I'm troubled in my mind, If this trouble don't kill me, I'll live a long time.'[49] Sing along with Mitch Somers.

I don't joke any more when I hear the phrase, 'My heart bleeds.'
        I love you so terribly much,
            Harry

48 Somers may have heard the well-known Newfoundland folk song "She's like the swallow" on a 1959 Jupiter recording ("The Jupiter Book of Ballads"), performed by the British harpist Osian Ellis, but by 1960 he may have encountered other arrangements. The song had been published in Volume II of *Folk Songs from Newfoundland* (London: Oxford University Press, 1934). It was also included in Kenneth Peacock's 1965 publication *Songs of the Newfoundland Outports* (3 vols, Ottawa: National Museum of Man, Bulletin 197). It was from the latter version of "She's like the swallow" that Somers based his arrangement, one of the *Five Songs from the Newfoundland Outports*, a CBC commission written in 1968 for the Festival Singers of Canada. This set of songs became one of his most performed and successful pieces.
49 I'm sad and I'm lonely, my heart it will break / My sweetheart loves another, Lord, I wish I was dead!... I'm troubled, I'm troubled, I'm troubled in mind / If trouble don't kill me, I'll live a long time. See Carl Sandburg, *The American Songbag*, 243–5.

CHAPTER SIX

February 1960

HS to NB
Feb 1st/60
Darling Normie:

Look!!! Do you think I give a good god-damn about all the petty little worries of whether our fears will do this or that! I'm a man not a child! You're my woman and I love you. All the rest means nothing.

Donnica is nothing!! Nothing! I've lived as a bloody celibate because I love you and I don't want other women even if they attract me....

... There is only one question for you, and one only – do you love me?

If not, I'll be out of your life in a twinkling. If yes, then just try to get rid of me. It's the only question that interests me.

So you're in a class, so you're in a routine, so it makes you feel secure for now, so you've got a thousand male admirers to pamper madame – so what else is new?

Baby, if you want that kind of life above all else then wail and au revoir. You [go] your way and I mine....

... My work's finished – I met the deadline – I'm fuckin' invincible!! A giant in a world of bugs and beetles – a great bloody colossus striding seas and oceans over worlds of dried-up little brains concerned with their little boops and bips who can't see the space and strength and great curving arcs through the sky!! Normie, Normie, enough of smallness! Let's open our arms to each other and keep all these strangers out!!...

... I've spent the whole week at 112 Admiral. Your mother has been tremendous – seeing there was food in the ice-box, bringing up trays of food after midnight, cooking on occasion and leaving me alone. I might not have made it without her help – she's all mother-woman-warm-giving human being. In short – a doll.

Day and night merged so that I didn't know which was which nor did it matter. And in the midst of it the nature of the Koussevitsky work jelled!...

... Take care, old worry wart – a fat worry wart at that, and they worry the most, you know. They get soggy and spongy soaking up great quantities of alcohol and pills. Work hard – and ... don't fear anything, particularly me....

... Frere Harry

HS to NB
Monday evening/Feb 1/60
2nd letter
Dearest:

I've had a few hours sleep so feel a bit alive or almost human. The first letter was written after 48 hrs no sleep....

... Of course you don't feel like a domestic life when you're active and happy. So why worry. I'm certainly not. You get so up or down with each passing thing.

You must understand one thing – in loving you I am not in any way presuming you should live a life alien to your needs or inclinations. You must do what you do because you believe in it – what's the point otherwise?

Dearest, don't get upset at whatever you feel. All of us go through many transitions during a day and many periods in our lives. You learn eventually to sort out the real from the unreal.

Petrassi's statement re: Michael is somewhat shallow. It's the little poets and people who are prompt, who push, who remember. The little people have great egos all right, it's their mark.

Your statement in relation to Donnica and 'other women' in my life somewhat amazed me in light of the truth – 1) I went with Donnica to the party and left by <u>myself</u> bloody early to get back to an exhausting night and continuation of my work. 2) I told you of her in a previous letter – she's only company to the odd gathering. 3) It was the <u>only</u> time I've been out in <u>a month</u>....

... Let me not to the marriage of true minds
Admit impediments, love is not love

Which alters when it alteration finds,
Or bends with the remover to remove,
O no, it is an ever-fixed mark
That looks on tempest and is never shaken;
It is the star to every wand'ring bark,
Whose worth's unknown, although his height be taken,
Love's not Time's fool, though rosy lips and cheeks
Within his bending sickle's compass come,
Love alters not with his brief hours and weeks,
But bears it out even to the edge of doom:
 If this be error and upon me proved,
 I never writ, nor no man ever loved.[1]

Be at peace, my dearest and only love –
Harry
P.S. Now a long session with the conductor, then to-morrow the fatiguing recording session. I'll inquire of Gordy Day about a Powell closed hole flute for you.[2]

I'm dead – down to 155 lbs – must somehow get some sleep and eat.

HS to NB
Tuesday Feb 2/60
Oh my Normie love!!

Wow! Did it come off! It has some of the most brilliant writing I've ever done!! Everything I conceived in my head was realized in actual sound.

The sections in which I used pointillist technic with solo vibes, harp, glock, piano, violin harmonics sound so well it seemed almost too easy to write. (Also added solo wds.)

My 'colour tone' writing worked perfectly.

My rhythmic and dynamic concepts – many new – were as exciting as hell.

---

1 Shakespeare's Sonnet 116. The punctuation varies, depending on which publication one uses.

2 Gordon Day (1914–1962) was one of Canada's leading flutists for more than twenty years. After playing with Horace Lapp's orchestra in the 1930s, he served as principal flute in the Promenade Symphony Concerts, in the Toronto Symphony Orchestra (1941–48), and in the CBC Symphony Orchestra (1953–62). He was also a member of the CBC Woodwind Quintet and in 1955 a founder of the Toronto Woodwind Quintet.

244 Between Composers

There wasn't a flaw in my scoring and I took some wild chances. The twelve-tone chords had terrific impact – three and four part harmony produced by superimposition of intervals was fresh and distinctive and when they dovetailed produced magical results.

The film will be distributed in theatres throughout Europe and America and South America eventually and should be wonderful to hear from a 30 mm. track!

All Norm's suggestions re: perc. brass, wds were strikingly successful –everything 'tells.'

I achieved assirhythmical [sic] results by the simplest means possible with the result the musicians could virtually sight read it!!

I'm starved, no sleep – (We went over the score 'till 3 a.m. Rehearsal started 7.45 a.m.) dying – but on top of the world. I'm on the threshold of some wondrous writing – this score has intimations of my new world – girl, girl, I want to share so much with you – what I do – what you do – there is so much we have to share together!!

A six hour session of intense concentration and I'm flying, baby!!

Gordy Day says he could get a Powell flute for you but it would likely take six months to a year and cost $400 to $500 dollars. He hasn't heard of anyone using a closed hole flute for thirty years or more – he wonders if you simply meant closed G#?

He says a Haines would be almost, if not as good as a Powell and he could get one in about a month.[3] It would cost around the same as a Powell – maybe $350 to $450. Let me know immediately.

Girl – I'm a God damn genius!! <u>Anything</u> I can conceive in my head I can realize on paper!! Such a feeling – such rarified air to breathe! From now on I'm really taking off! – such things to write!! I feel that everything up to now is just training for what's to come!! But then that's one's whole life!

They announced the Koussevitsky commission in the N.Y. Times.[4] It's like a prodding reminder to get to work immediately – which I'm

3 The Wm. S. Haynes Company of Boston has been making flutes since 1888.
4 The Koussevitzky commission for Somers (which became his orchestra work *Lyric*) had been awarded in 1958. The other eleven composers commissioned that year were Ross Lee Finney, William J. Russo, Easley Blackwood, Alberto Ginastera, Héctor Tosar, Gian Carlo Menotti, Edgard Varèse, Frank Martin, Sir William Walton, Yehudi Wyner, and Pierre Boulez. Of these, the works by Finney, Russo, and Blackwood had been completed and the works by Ginastera, Somers, and Tosar had been promised in time for the Inter-American Music Festival to be held in Washington in April 1961. Somers met this deadline. See Ross Parmenter, "World of Music: Koussevitzky Foundation: Its Seven Latest Commissions Bring Its Tally of Ordered Works to 109," *New York Times*, 31 January 1960.

February 1960   245

going to do. Oh my blood is rich my language strong!!

By the way – ye olde Pass. & Fugue was done in Liverpool last week. Ain't heard wha' happened.

The sun sings in my veins, the sky streams from my eyes and I have worlds to tell of in my music.

To-day is a spring-winter day, truly. Those days of snow yet mild air.

My spirit sings – of thee I sing, Baby!![5]

I know – I know what is true! – do you realize!!

Dear love, since you are not here I shall celebrate by starting on my next work. It's just as well – you would have difficulty containing my enthusiasm – I would overwhelm you with it!

I'm strong, I can sing with the Gods, I <u>know</u> you are my love and I am happy. You can't protest – it's like stemming the St. Lawrence river or the ocean tide – even King someone or other couldn't do <u>that</u>!!...

... Good God – take courage and life in your hands and accept my fantastic love for you!!

Just got a call from Stratford – Douglas Campbell would like me to do the music for 'A Midsummer Night's Dream'.[6] Me and Mendelssohn! – though by God his score is a gem. So will discuss it Friday. It's interesting to contemplate that beautiful scherzoish play – hmm – a few wds. Stg q'tet, bit of perc – could be....

... I'm seeing a travel agent to-day or to-morrow – aiming for a couple of weeks from this date....

... I see or go with no one – I couldn't care less – you are the one and don't give me that "well I can't forget that you – "etc. bit. I'm yours yours yours!!! Live anew with me – I'll show you how my sweetheart –
           Love – buckets bathtubs full of the stuff
Just that — Mad about you sad about you glad about you Bharry!!![7]

5 This may be a reference to the Broadway musical *Of Thee I Sing*, with a score by George Gershwin, lyrics by Ira Gershwin, and book by George S. Kaufman and Morrie Ryskind. The successful original production opened in 1931 and ran for 441 performances.

6 Born in Scotland, Douglas Campbell (1922–2009) became one of the leading actors in Canada in the second half of the twentieth century. In the first season of the Stratford Festival in 1953, he played Hastings in the production of Richard III, after being invited by Tyrone Guthrie. Campbell remained active with the Festival for many years and in 1960 directed *A Midsummer Night's Dream*.

7 A reference to the song "Mad About Him, Sad About Him, How Can I Be Glad About Him Blues" recorded in 1942 by Dinah Shore. Music and lyrics by Larry Markes and Dick Charles.

246   Between Composers

HS to NB

Wed. Feb. 3/60

Dear heart:

... I leave Toronto 3 p.m. Tuesday, Feb 16 –

Arrive Rome 10.10 a.m. Wed. Feb 17. by T.W.A. jet from New York which has a short stop-over in Paris.

Normie, if it would interfere with your classes to meet me, write me so immediately and I shall take the airport bus directly into Rome and taxi thence to your pad. If I know airport transportation it would likely take 1 hr into the city, and then a ride to 99. (An interesting number!)

No fuss, no worry – eh girl – just as long as I know what's up and what to expect.

Reading Tyrone Guthrie's intro to Midsummer Night's Dream is stimulating my mind. He feels Mendleson's music (Mendelssohn) has given a false conception to the play. He feels that the speeches of Oberon, Titania and Puck do not agree at all with Mendelssohns's music.

It is an artificial comedy of contrast. The Fairies 'a serious reminder in a predominantly frivolous work that, even in gentle loveliness of a moonlit summer night, there are elements abroad which just cannot be accounted for in terms of reason and common sense. The play will lose a great deal of its meaning if it is robbed of a magic which springs, not from the glittering tip of a department store wand, but from the earth, the trees, the stones, the very air of the wood, and a magic which is not merely pretty, but dark and dangerous.'[8]

Great stuff, eh? This is where I would definitely apply pointillist and colour tone technic. You can't imagine how well it came off in the film.

My mind's just electric with ideas....

... Must go, me love, got a million things to do. Let's worry about a studio when I get there. I definitely want one but we can work out our times so that when you are out at class or things you have to do I can use your place....

... don't ever worry about kicking me out when you've got study or work to do.

---

8 Since this passage is in quotation marks, it must have been copied from Tyrone Guthrie's introduction to the play but it was not possible to find which edition contained this introduction.

February 1960 247

See you soon –
All my love
Har.

HS TO NB
Thursday, Feb. 4/60
My dearest love:

Before I see you I want you to understand a few things about me. When I level it's all the way, just as previously you knew where you stood with me because I always gave it to you straight, now it's the same way – you know I love you and want you completely and when I say that, it's total faith and committing of myself to you.

In the truest sense of the word I have never deceived you and never will.

Normie, in all fairness, your letters doth protest too much, enough to make it evident to me that there is a 'cause behind the cause.' In short, as a woman you have your reasons, but they aren't the ones you're giving me. (Now you'll get a bit mad – but understand I <u>do not</u> say this with any malicious intent – only a desire to clarify.)

This business about Donnica I found extraordinary when you are at total liberty to enjoy the company of any male you've mentioned in your letters, and likely many you haven't, yet you come 'on' so strongly – almost as if you were salving your own conscience....

... I feel the final answer must come for you for you know where I stand, and if you don't by now then you are indulging yourself – do these sound like tough or hard words? They are just an attempt to be direct.

If one eternally brings up the past in a negative fashion, then it begins to sound awfully like an excuse for the present....

... You are an honest person, but also a complete woman – and I love you for both reasons. I would not be such a humourless male as to not enjoy your womanly deceptions and conceits. But I would also not be such a stupid male as to not acknowledge that they exist. It is the particular charm of a woman, like the various ways she says 'no.'

There were some things you never would call by their proper names which revealed a delightful coyness to me, really. You often pretend to be such a straightforward person when you're all woman inside – and consider <u>that</u> a compliment.

248   Between Composers

Now this is the difference with the French from anyone else – they have no illusions about human behavior. Their writers cut with a surgeon's scalpel into the human makeup and condition. They value individuality above all else. (A bad thing for governments.) They insist on clarity in the presentation of ideas and do not think profound that which is simply obscure. They have the most stimulating intellectuals in the world. They have a sense of taste and a dislike of the vulgar – or common – unequalled elsewhere. They enjoy artifice in life, and artificial play between people, but they don't kid themselves what it's all about ever. In this way no one could ever call the French hypocrites – they are far too proud as individuals to descend to that level.

I go to this length because from time to time you've made casual reference to the French and I've felt the need to elucidate....

... Normie, sweet wondrous fair, I'm totally in love with you – but as a man, not a boy ... that's really what I've said in this letter.

Take care. I hope your work goes well – no doubt the usual ups and downs – but persist through both conditions.

           Your man who loves you like nobody's
               loved you –
               Harry

NB to HS
6 February 1960
Dear Harry,

Congratulations on finishing your work and being so pleased with the realization of your ideas ~ You must indeed be floating on a cloud ~ I hope some time to have the pleasure of hearing this score for it sounds fascinating, all your ideas and sonorities ~

I am pleased my Mother and our house again took part in your last minute activity ~ She's not bad, is she, my grey-haired Mammy ~ Bless her soul ~!

You have probably heard that I have been ill again from Mother which was very discouraging ~ I went nowhere for 4 days, and felt very badly about missing two classes ~ However, I am now better, a little weak and despondent perhaps, but managed to make class this morning ~

However, before leaving this AM, I received four letters from H. S., all long and all different ~ Naturally I realize that there was probably a great explosion at the completion of your work, but with all this knowledge, I cannot help but be disturbed by your explosions concerning me ~ I am really so tired of trying to sort out feelings by letter, my dear that I sometimes feel I have no feelings at all ~ and I feel incapacitated to even try to write my own reactions ~ So probably better I say nothing ~ but the usual Beecroft can't keep her mouth shut about everything!

Sure I am a person of ups and downs – thank God! Do you wish that I level a bit and tread the straight and narrow path? Do you know Harry that I don't even care to feel responsible for my actions or words these days, that I don't want to have to face anything but problems pertaining to my work ~ What you write to me has often great truth and maturity, but I don't want to listen to reason very much ~ I think that when you come here you will be able to understand better for we will be able to chat at length ~

I know that I am still stinging from a hard slap ~ and will continue to smart until I choose or am able to believe ~ You must have changed a great deal, as indeed I have too, and whether we can really commence again will have to be seen and felt when we meet ~

I welcome your visit to Rome, for we cannot continue writing these letters forever ~

Saturday AM

I had to stop writing yesterday as I found myself getting too confused to continue ~ Suffice it to say that I am tired and not too well, and do not wish to answer any questions ~ and I feel too much pressure ~ So no more said on this subject for the time being ~

Re the flute: thanks for contacting Gordon Day, but he is wrong about the closed hole flute ~ my maestro here plays a gold closed-hole (that is closed key) flute made by Powell not too long ago, and the other players here used closed-hole flutes as well as Americans ~ It seems that there is no distinct advantage in have an open-keyed instrument....

... Tonight I am going to the best RAI orchestra concert of the season[9] ~ they are doing a Schoenberg-Webern-Berg program, and my maestro is playing ~ It promises to be excellent, and is quite an occasion here for the opportunities to hear contemporary music are few in Rome ~

9 The orchestra of Radiotelevisione italiana (RAI), the national public broadcasting organization.

250 Between Composers

I can say nothing more about your arrival expecting to hear any day from you ~ Harry, please understand if I am a little afraid of you – please!
         Love
         Normie

HS to NB
Sunday, Feb. 7/60
My dearest Normie:
  For a long while I have pondered whether I should say anything to you or not re: Petrassi's statement re: Shostakovitch – and that concert he told you of where the avant-garde was cheered and poor old Shostakovitch was given a cool reception and wasn't it sad.[10]

As a person who loves you I have hesitated to speak because I realize a teacher becomes a father-God image and everything is sacred – and as a woman (You'll hate this but it's nevertheless true) you will tend to take it personally.

But as a <u>composer</u> I <u>must</u> take issue, no matter what the consequences, with a statement which has the most superficial implications in its attitude towards creative art that I've encountered since student days.

I'm sure that Petrassi is an excellent teacher and a fine composer, but do you realize the question he raises? It's right back to style and fashion – the attitude of the commercial artist – you do a thing because of audience reaction – to be favourable with a certain group or clique – it 'sells' – etc. etc. – for every conceivable expedient reason outside of the important one. Is that why Petrassi takes up certain technics? I'm amazed. Surely one writes from <u>inner</u> conviction that evolves its own technic and which, being true to itself, <u>cannot</u> be concerned with either favour or disfavour but <u>only</u> the search for truth.

I'm no 'fan' of Shosakovitch, but my God what difference what the reaction of the audience is?! Fashions come and go, each generation must speak against the previous one etc. but so what – this has nothing to do with the raison d'être of serious art – it has only

---

10 This criticism of Petrassi is rather strange, since in her letter of 23 January Beecroft says that the story about the reception of Shostakovich's music was related by Gazzelloni, not Petrassi. There are no comments from Petrassi about this story in any of her subsequent letters.

February 1960 251

something to do with surface – Broadway, and evidently a good part of European thinking.

One must write from conviction and not intimidation. If a lot of external things are primary factors one is nothing, at the most the centre of notoriety for the day....

... As far as fashion, people who are concerned with it I pity because it passes so quickly and by its very nature must or it wouldn't be fashion. Krenek is an example of this – he writes as a consummate craftsman who has been so concerned with trends he has no voice of his own. Who knows – Shostakovitch (God help us!) could be the only composer to remain after another hundred years. It has happened you know. But how foolish to even have this a small part of ones' consideration!

By the way, if the concert was in Poland, the Poles hate Russians and anything Russian. The reaction would be ethnic – political anyway....

... I would do you a dishonour were I not to speak openly and frankly. At all times it is essential for me to keep my thinking straight for there are so many traps to fall into....

... I love you dearly and hope that you will feel free to be as direct as I have been in discussing these things and to contradict directly anything I've said which you feel to be wrong or false.

Har.

NB to HS
8 Febbraio, 1960
7:00 P.M
Dear Harry,

I just received your third letter today ~ My dear love, I try to be calm and read calmly and think calmly, but damn it, I can't ~ Don't you understand what I write ~ Why do I have to answer to anything right now ~ You feel very able and strong, because your life is clear after many hazy years, so you want clarification from me ~ Well, I can't! and certainly not in a letter ~

I am sorry about questioning you re Donnica ~ It should prove that I care enough to be jealous ~ As far as salving my own conscience, I truly feel, why do I have to justify anything, past or present ~

Harry, you are making me feel guilty and trapped and I frankly can't stand it ~ You surely must know that feeling, for you told me this is what I inflicted on you for x number of years ~

As far as you not having deceived me ever ~ we can question the meaning of deceit ~ Are you aware that what you <u>didn't</u> say caused all the damage inside of me, and that is what is bothering you right now ~ because of what I am not saying, you are disturbed ~ Please don't feel so righteous ~

I am saying nothing because I know nothing for certain ~ I know neither what I want in personal life and am afraid to ask myself, for fear that the answer will present insurmountable problems at this time ~ I am rather content to move from day to day doing some work and study, and fighting with the problems of composition ~ I can say no more ~ You have been through this period, and you should understand ~ It is a reaction of course, and I hope that I shall not take the length of time to move out of it that you did....

... I am sorry to write so strongly ~ But you want me to level with you ~ you want answers ~ Maybe you will find them when you see me here, or maybe not ~ I asked you in an earlier letter if you had the patience to wait, which you never replied to ~ Have you?

You told me to move around ~ to live some more ~ that I needed it ~ Remember? Well, here I am ~ if you love me, please don't trap me, for I don't know what the reaction might be ~

I can only say ~ I think that I still love you, but I am afraid of you truly....

Tuesday morning

Action and reaction always ~ I suffered through the night with dreams, neuralgia, swollen glands and another sore throat ~ You really cannot win ~ the weather here changes every day and so does my physical condition ~

However, last night I managed to put in some good hours of work ~ I am almost finished the second part of Michael's songs, having yesterday received the complete words, and am barreling ahead on the third part ~

I also started to write a set of songs for flute, piano and contralto voice, on those Yeats poems which I extracted a couple of years ago ~ I am finding it extraordinarily difficult to write for solo piano ~ I don't know whether I am too inhibited by my father to think clearly about the instrument, or what cooks ~

In any case, I await your arrival here ~ If I don't finish these letters and send them you may never receive them – so with haste I finish

Much love

Normie ~

February 1960
253

HS to NB
Tuesday, Feb 9/60
Beloved:

I suppose it was bound to happen I've been flying so high from my work. This morning I woke in black depression [with] the image of seeing the death throes of that grey cat in front of your house. A grey flame quivering, the spark that gives life to everything in the universe, going out. And God said let there be light and there it was held in a moment before my eyes. You know Normie, I was overwhelmed. If I could have cried I would have, for it was the dying of the innocent, a creature asking nothing of existence, a child of creation – but death does not distinguish one from the other.

And I placed the dead creature at the foot of the great tree before your house. Gently I placed it there. And the snow covered it and companion to the earth, air, to the tree – protected their own.

Eventually the snow melted, the earth softened to receive the moisture....

... But the animal was dead. And the mists of spring were as tears and my heart and being would burst with so much feeling. I sometimes dread my capacity to feel to react to love – love – to love.

And as the spring flooded the whole world of life men and women somewhere were in prisons, held by walls and bars and death and in hospitals and in solitude – the whole great suffering mass denied what they were created for or forgetting.

'And it was only a cat' they would say.

Just heard the commission from the Pittsburgh Wind Ensemble is definite. (It's a whole orchestra of wds. brass and perc.)

Good Lord I've got work to do!! That's three commissions to be completed in the next few months!

Stratford, Koussevitsky, Pittsburgh. I hope I get a chance to see you when I arrive!

I was quite despondent for a while yesterday. The bank which handles air loans wouldn't take me as a risk without a guarantor. I thought for a bit I would have to cancel the trip. Everything started to appear hopeless. Ominous dark clouds of doubt appeared on the horizon – countless letters in which you've indicated many things

254 Between Composers

clutched my throat. I felt the great fatigue of life of only death as the only thing I could count on – a friend. Very poetic, you see, but hard as hell on the emotional system....

... And so you see – I'm mortgaging me earthly things and coming over to be with you awhile, the only one I love. I'm no god-damn weakling whose love is made of alcohol and outer show and circumstance and surroundings! It's made of all my sinews and convictions and beliefs...

... Why is it I feel death's touch on my shoulder? Is it just romantic or just a sense of what is always there – the ice-man, the man in the white sheet ... I felt it so this morning. So truly alone – not sad loneliness or complaining loneliness – just – – alone.

Enough!!! This will pass in an hour a day. What a dreadful letter to send just before my arrival! But it will get rid of it so that when I see you I will be on the upswing. Really, Normie, I suppose it's just the bottom after the top – always has to swing.

I love you beyond belief. Old Don Quixote charges forth on the wings of a bird arriving Rome 10.10 am (your time) T.W.A. jet New York stopping for a moment in Paris, Wed. Feb. 17. This is likely me last missel (misile?) before I see you.[11] It seems impossible! But I'll keep writing anyway. Might even write a letter to myself! Hah! Every letter I'll let you know the time. Girl, girl – I love you, just understand that and you will understand everything!!

Your Don Harry!!

HS to NB
Later Tuesday afternoon.
Feb.9/60
Darling:

Now the soft afternoon light complexions my thoughts.

From top to bottom and now somewhere in between. All the gloom of my earlier letter is just murk in the distance now, a receding shadow barely discernable.

But awakening this morning was like awakening with a nightmare for some strange reason, and all the evil spirits that fly about crowded my thoughts.

---

11 Somers was undoubtedly thinking of the word "missive" but in his attempt to spell it correctly, it nearly ended up as the word "missile" (missing only an "s"). Beecroft might well have experienced some of his letters to her as emotionally powerful, "epistolary" missiles, as can be seen in her last few letters to him.

Now I feel that wonderful perception as after a fever. How old Harry is torn and tattered by himself so often! Ah, but he's started into the Koussevitsky work and will speak with strength in his mural for this world needs affirmation.

Sean O'Casey speaks so wonderfully in an article which he heads 'Not Waiting for Godot' where he speaks to young people at a university telling them that he has fought his fight and they must take over and choose their sides[12] – whether to affirm or deny – whether Beckett et company or Beethoven, Shakespeare and all the rest. He speaks strongly, affirmatively and with all the joy and verve he has, even in his seventies, for life.

God bless the Irish – even dear Beckett – their voice has created such riches in the lyric vein....

... I bumped into Jack Nichols other day.[13] We had coffee and chatted. Jack misses Paris incredibly. It seems the city was conducive to work for him and the atmosphere congenial. In many ways Jack is a most unhappy fella but I'm fond of the guy. I hope one day he will find an inner peace to match his inner artistic assurance. He wanted me to send his regards to you and wish you well.

Your mother's sweet. She's having a little going away party for me Sunday – all the gang – Harvey Hart, Theda, Norm, Gwen, Linda, old Doc MacDonald if he can make it (as usual) – then Pam & John Beckwith, Bob Gill, the Youngs, David Gardner and girl and maybe Eli & Naomi.[14] Should be a lively and interesting group. Naturally

12 This essay is published in Sean O'Casey, "Not Waiting for Godot," in *Blasts and Benedictions: Articles and Stories*, ed. Sean O'Casey (London: Macmillan; NY: St Martin's Press, 1967), 51–2. Part of the text reads: "Beckett? I have nothing to do with Beckett. He isn't in me; nor am I in him. I am not waiting for Godot to bring me life; I am out after life myself, even at the age I've reached ... That Beckett is a clever writer, and that he has written a rotting and remarkable play, there is no doubt; but his philosophy isn't my philosophy, for within him there is no hazard for hope; no desire for it; nothing in it but a lust for despair, and a crying of woe, not in a wilderness, but in a garden."

13 See chap. 2, n. 27.

14 Robert Gill (1911–1974) was an American-trained theatre and opera director and teacher who served as director of the Hart House Theatre at the University of Toronto from 1946 until 1965. In this role, he trained the generation of actors and directors

256   Between Composers

much theatre talk and art talk and fast talk. Always enjoy Bob and the good old Doc. Also John & Helen.

Sorry about the Frams. It's just they make it so difficult [and] I don't know. They really give so little of themselves yet are such witty intelligent people, particularly Michael when he gets going. I doubt if Michael ever sees himself as others see him. But then who does?

My relationship with them is a strange story and I'm truly sorry about it.[15] I was always happy to see them. There are a lot of people who are easy to be with but who haven't a stimulating or interesting idea in their heads. Well, the Frams are difficult to be with but their thinking is original, learned and stimulating. Personalities always get in the way. It's too bad.

———

Wednesday – in one week I'll be seeing Poop! I can't believe it.

Last night attended the Con. Concert and a Magnificat of Hovannes then a small party afterwards at the Royal York given by a Walter Heindrickson, American representative for Peters.[16] Bailey,

---

who launched postwar professional theatre in Canada. This included Barbara Chilcott, Murray and Donald Davis, Ted Follows, Barbara Hamilton, Donald Harron, Eric House, William Hutt, Charmion King, Kate Reid, and Donald Sutherland. David Gardner (1928–2020) was a Toronto-born actor, director, and educator who played a major role in the development of Canadian theatre. In addition to playing numerous roles on stage, radio, film, and television, and directing for stage and television, he taught at the University of Toronto and at York University. In 1960, he was chair of the committee that founded the National Theatre School of Canada. "Old Doc McDonald" was Ian Bruce MacDonald who had removed a cyst from Beecroft's spine some years earlier. (See chap. 1, n. 13). It was not possible to discover who "Theda" was.

15 See ch. 1, n. 31. Michel Fram had originally been a friend of Catherine Mackie's, Somers's first wife, but after she and Somers returned from France in 1950, Fram was introduced to Somers and both he and his wife, Isabel, became friends with them.

16 The correct name of the American representative of the music publisher C.F. Peters was Walter Hinrichsen (1907–1969), one of the sons of Henri Hinrichsen (1868–1942), who had been director of the company in Leipzig since 1900 and who was murdered at Auschwitz in September 1942. Walter Hinrichsen had left Germany in 1936 and fought in the US army during the war, becoming an American citizen. In 1948, he established the C.F. Peters Corporation in New York. The firm strongly supported contemporary composers and presumably Hinrichsen was in Toronto to attend the Toronto premiere of the American-Armenian composer Alan Hovhaness's *Magnificat* (1958). The program also included Delius's *Sea Drift*. (See Blaik Kirby, "It's Modern Music – And 'Listenable,'" *Toronto Daily Star*, 10 February 1960.)

Irene, John J. Mazz. Healey Willan and wife, Gibbs, Boyd Neil etc. were there.[17] A pleasant gathering, no fuss or trouble, small enough that one could talk to people.

Heindrickson is somehow connected with the Pittsburgh commission. He was saying they play on a barge during the summer which travels up and down some large river playing to towns each night with audiences of 10,000 listening on the river bank.

1.15 p.m. here, 7.15 your time. I've just put a call through to Rome. Lines are all busy. Now I wait. It's crazy but I wanted to confirm by phone just to make sure. God damn instrument is so frustrating but at least you get the information.

I've gotten over my nightmare and try to figure what it's all about. This distance and letter writing are so bad for understanding. All the subterranean things slither about trying to poison the mind....

... I must apologize for all my kookiness in many letters but my reason needs no apology – that I'm crazy about you. It's just I regret having disturbed you, if I have, at a time of great inner searching of yourself. But then again perhaps it forced you to see yourself as you would not otherwise. I don't know. It's been the maddest winter of my life in terms of feeling, self-discovery, upset and downset, solitude and all through it some of the best writing I've ever done. It sure makes me wonder and wonder. I've discovered much about others through myself. It has given me an understanding of people in spite of all the wildness and in moments of calm a sense of inner depth and beauty of this soap opera on earth....

... It was Josh White who said 'You've got to stop hating yourself before you can love'....[18]

---

17 The people mentioned are Bailey and Irene Bird, John Weinzweig, Ettore Mazzoleni, Healey Willan and his wife, Gladys, Terence Gibbs, and Boyd Neel. Healey Willan (1880–1968), the distinguished composer, organist, and teacher at the University of Toronto, had probably attended the concert to hear Delius's *Sea Drift*, since he was not exactly a fan of contemporary music, even though Blaik Kirby had thought the Hovhaness piece quite "listenable." Terence Gibbs was a CBC music producer. Boyd Neel (1905–1981), the British conductor, had come to Canada in 1952 to become dean of the Royal Conservatory of Music of Toronto (which was divided into the School of Music and the Faculty of Music). After his arrival in Canada, he founded the Hart House Orchestra. The others in this list have been identified in earlier chapters.

18 Joshua Daniel White (1914–1969), a singer, guitarist, songwriter, actor, and civil rights activist, was one of the most important and influential Black American musicians, from the late 1930s on.

... 2.35 p.m.

It was so great to hear your voice – sure, calm – it makes me happy pet!

This nutty world – a voice in Rome next door!

This is absolutely and finally my

LAST LETTER

Arrivederci. A presto, Baby
It's love love love – Harry Bonkers CoCo

NB to HS
8 [?] Febbraio, 1960[19]
Dear Harry,

How very marvellous flying jet to Rome ~ I hear that it is absolutely fantastic ~ Do you know that either in March or April you will be able to fly directly from Canada to Italy ~ This is a big thing here, so perhaps for the return trip you could inquire ~

I beg you to not pay too much attention to parts of my previous letter, for I was pretty dully-headed and depressed at that time ~ I am a little better now, but still have a cough and a runny nose ~ To find a studio for you may be a problem here but I shall inquire at the Accademia on Wednesday ~

At the moment we are having classes Mondays, Wednesdays, and Fridays, commencing at 10:30 AM until roughly 12:30 or 1:00 PM ~ This would naturally prohibit me from going to the airport to meet you, but I will leave the key to my apartment with the portiere who will show you where I live ~ She knows you are coming ~ A little advice ~ take the airport bus in, for a taxi would cost you about $8 - $10 ~ The trip is about 1/2 hour and you would be left at Termini station ~ From there take a taxi, but beware, the drivers will

19 Beecroft's final letter is dated 8 February but the previous letter is also dated 8 February, written around 7:00 p.m.. There are no instances in her correspondence of writing a second letter the same day, let alone another letter later the same evening. It may be that this letter was written the following day, 9 February, a Tuesday, since she says that she has to prepare to present her work on Wednesday (which would have been the following day).

February 1960

259

try to take you for everything ~ the <u>fare</u> should cost no more than 500 lire, and they charge you a rate of 50 (or 100, I can't remember) for suitcase (one) ~ Tip no more than <u>100</u> lire, and make sure you have change ~ One other thing, the less you look like a tourist, the more direct will your trip be in the taxi ~ otherwise you will be driven round and round, for Rome is full of one-way streets ~ Also, watch your briefcase and pocket book at all times ~

In the event that our class schedule changes I will try to get to the airport ~ Otherwise, carry on as above, and I will personally welcome you at 1:00 ~ I enclose a map of Rome, if you can see the pencil marks, you will perhaps get your bearings ~

I have many new problems coming up ~ one perhaps, changing apartments at the end of March, but before deciding anything ~ I shall wait for your arrival and advice ~

There will be some interesting concerts during your stay here, and perhaps we can arrange a few soirées with composers, etc. You will find the musical atmosphere quite different, but I hope you like Rome as much as I do for what it does have to offer ~

Don't worry too much about the language problem, for when you arrive you will only realize how little you do know ~ I am delighted to serve as your translator, and will gladly help you with it here, but your French will serve you reasonably well, with the educated class ~

Must away to work now, as Wednesday is my day to present work in class ~

Have a marvelous trip over, and welcome, my love ~ See you soon
Love
Normie

Epilogue

17 February 1960: Harry Somers arrives at Norma Beecroft's apartment in Rome:

Harry decided to make the journey to Rome ... but completely lost control of himself when confronted with the actual person called Normie. I had made arrangements that [he] would be admitted to my apartment while I was attending a class at Santa Cecilia, as his flight would arrive early in the morning. I came home to find him, and he immediately started the attack on everything that I was about or striving to achieve. That included not only my person, but my studies with Petrassi, Petrassi himself, the fact that I was a female in a male dominated world of composers, and so on. It was strange coming from this person who had been so encouraging to me in my desire to pursue composition, that it seemed everything I thought about Harry Somers turned about to be a lie, a falsehood, that he had no respect for me as a potential composer, and that he was simply trying to control me. He was extremely hurtful in his attack, as only someone who knows you well can hurt. The fact that he was on the edge of being violent was scary, to say the least. I had never seen this side of this man who I had cared for deeply for a number of years. He eventually calmed down, but any chance of renewing our relationship was gone, and he knew it. In the hours that followed, we were both civilized, but he knew he was not welcome and realized he needed to make arrangements to return to Canada. After he left, I recall being taken out to supper at a seashore restaurant,

Epilogue 261

and watching the sun sink into the horizon caused me a great deal of anxiety, like a slow death – it was a black thought – the ending. I did recover from such a mood however.
– Email from Norma Beecroft to this editor, 4 May 2021.

As the letter above indicates, Somers's visit to Rome did not go well. Upon his arrival at Norma's apartment on the morning of 17 February 1960, he appears to have lost control of his emotions and launched an angry and emotional attack on what she was doing, calling into question all that she had accomplished since arriving in Rome, even questioning whether she, as a woman, could realistically expect to succeed as a composer. This outburst brought an abrupt end to their personal relationship and made it impossible for him to remain in Rome for an extended period, as originally planned. Within a few days, he returned to Toronto and resumed his regular life. In the following years, they remained colleagues through CBC work and other professional activities, maintaining a cordial but formal relationship.

The account of Somers's visit in the communication quoted above, based on Beecroft's recollections of it over sixty years later, corresponds closely with Norma's account of it in a letter to her mother, Eleanor, written nearly two weeks after the incident in Rome:

It seemed in retrospect that Harry, upon seeing me, lost complete control of his emotions, and as a result, proceeded to attack me in every sense, as only a person who knows you well can do ~ Although I understand and forgive him, I could not help but see a picture of my father who tried to destroy everything that <u>you</u> lived for, that <u>was</u> you, out of jealousy of possession ~ This is the first time I have seen this in Harry, and as I have said, I understand the reasons but he committed one grave error ~ he attacked my music, through Petrassi, my friends here, the dangers for a woman working in the field of art, etc. ~ I guess to me, this was the biggest and most serious blow, for when he left, I was psychologically a wreck … It is a hard blow to take when the person you most trust in the world attacks you with such force in the things you believe in ~ I guess if I survive this one I may emerge as a composer, for I now feel completely alone in my struggle ~[1]

262   Between Composers

The last part of the above excerpt makes it clear that Somers's behavior not only profoundly shook Beecroft's confidence in her studies and her compositional aspirations but also made her reappraise the possibility of any permanent relationship between them, such as marriage:

> Harry has posed some difficult questions which will require so
> much time to answer ~ He wanted to know if I love him ~ Well,
> I have been thinking so hard about this word 'love' and I don't
> know any more really what it means ~ how can I answer that? I
> have been trying to contemplate a life with him, and after seeing
> what an influence he has over me this time – that he could destroy
> me in an instant – I am more afraid than ever of trying to answer
> that ~ This man has a powerful hold over me, but I cannot marry
> him for the wrong reasons ... just know this – that it is very hard
> for me to stay here now, that for the first time in my life I am
> afraid for my life, that spirit and body are on rock bottom ~ and
> I am trying to find my strength ~ Harry has done some serious
> damage, and I am trying not to run away, in other words.[2]

As pointed out in the introduction to this correspondence, it is clear from Beecroft's last few letters to Somers, before he arrived in Rome, that she was becoming exasperated by his constant pressure to commit to a permanent relationship with him. Her correspondence with her mother during the months in Rome before Somers's arrival in February 1960 indicates that she was initially puzzled and more than a little uneasy about Somers's passionate declarations of love and his desire to marry her. In an early letter, written not long after her arrival in Rome, she wrote that she couldn't tell Eleanor how "upset" she felt, that after wanting a decision (about marriage) for three years, now that it had finally come, she was "terrified." She even wrote that she had tried to protect herself by reconciling herself to "a new life without him."[3]

By the middle of November, she was still trying to sort out her feelings for him but beginning to get a glimmer of an idea of some kind of independence for herself:

> You are quite right in saying that it will take me some time to
> re-consider a life with him, but I still miss his conversations and all
> the battles, and his understanding, and music, etc. etc. His letters

Epilogue 263

have sounded at times rather desperate which led me to telephone the other night, but such short calls are so unsuccessful ~ Although I feel my answer to him will be affirmative, and is now, I can only say that I am, for the most part, beginning just now to enjoy my freedom from personal tensions, my freedom to live independently, to think independently, to find out what I am ~ even though there are the blackest moments ~ to date very few ~ and I know the longer I live this way, the less I will want to change it … it is possible for me to live alone and to know I have values underneath, or a sense of values, which can't be shaken.[4]

The beginning of this excerpt clearly shows Beecroft's dilemma: she missed certain aspects of their relationship but needed to achieve some kind of personal and artistic independence. She still cared deeply enough about Somers to worry about his state of mind, even to the point of making transAtlantic telephone calls – expensive and often of poor quality in those days.

By early January 1960 she clearly felt that Somers's letters were contradictory:

… for his letters are sometimes encouraging to work, and the next one demands answers, and me, and completely negates the last letter … one minute I feel Harry is giving me freedom to be a composer, and the next moment he is chaining me to him … it is now too late to contemplate sudden marriage."[5]

Norma's final two letters to her mother, before Somers's arrival in Rome, written during the early weeks of her composition course with Petrassi, indicate that she was enjoying her classes and about to begin work on an orchestra piece, which would either be played at a concert or read by the Santa Cecilia Orchestra. She declared that she would not be able to provide any answers to questions of matrimony, that she was "content to avoid answering these things right now" and that she wanted to solve her "work problems somewhat more [than marrying]." She was, therefore, not willing to commit herself to him in any permanent way and, as she stated in her letter of 16 February, quoted in the introduction, not willing to marry someone she didn't love. It may have been the stark realization of this that set off Somers's explosive behaviour upon seeing her again on the morning of 17 February in Rome.

During the course of the next two-and-a-half months, Somers wrote ten further letters to her, beginning on 26 February with a letter assuring her that the "madman is back in his cage and quite calm again." Despite this initial admission that his behaviour in Rome had been inappropriate, he went on to justify it, saying that it was "impossible for a man who is as passionately in love with you as I am to be removed from the one he loves for a long period of time and not go a little berserk when he sees her."[6] In this letter, he thanked her for being honest with him in revealing her situation to him and assured her that he would no longer "force or push" her to marry him – he would wait for her *if* she wanted him to. Yet he then seemed to blame her for the collapse of their relationship, since she wasn't "woman enough" to accept his love: "I believe one day you will be big enough and woman enough to accept and return a complete love which hides nothing, offers everything and doesn't play games with you."[7]

Most of his subsequent letters to her during this period were fairly impersonal – reassurance that she would get over her reaction to his visit and be able to work again, news about common friends, performances of Stravinsky ballet scores in Toronto, tax information for her, and his plans for the coming summer and fall. (He had been invited to spend that summer at the Stratford Festival, providing music for its production of *A Midsummer Night's Dream* and playing guitar on stage in the production. He then planned to travel to Paris for an extended stay, with the aid of a Canada Council Senior Arts Fellowship.)

In a letter he wrote near the beginning of April, he again returned to the Rome incident:

Upon my return it was essential that I free myself from the obsessive emotions which were strangling judgement. It was extremely difficult but gradually I regained some clarity, strength and balance. It was necessary to face the facts of your situation, feelings and attitudes – to accept them and rebuild my personal life and emotional stability from there. Rightly or wrongly I had built my personal and emotional life around the idea that you and I would one day live together in love and companionship with all its attendant ups and downs ... It took a long time to arrive at this decisive step in my life, as you know, and much inner conflict. I possess an inner cynicism born of experience. At times I feel that

Epilogue 265

life, myself and humankind are just too absurd to take seriously.
I had to fight this to attempt to rid myself of it – to get beyond it.
Consequently I arrived in Rome at a peak of emotional tension,
rather exhausted from months of combatting inner doubts, of
emerging with a desire to finally settle my life with someone I
loved ... I had misunderstood you and had expected something
which was really only of my own imagination. In the state I was
in I was in no condition to reason such things out.[8]

Here he seemed to have actually realized that he had built up in
his mind some imaginary future relationship to Beecroft that was
the result of his own fantasies and was out of touch with her current aspirations and desires. He was encountering a different Norma
Beecroft than the one who had left Toronto some five-and-a-half
months earlier.

The last in this series of ten final letters written to Beecroft, begun
on 5 May but not completed until 16 May, is a gigantic affair,
seventeen pages long. It is a kind of "summing up" and "termi-
nation of the relationship." It is not unlike a lengthy letter Somers
sent to his wife Cathy at the end of the previous November, when
he was considering divorcing her so he could be free to marry
Norma. He declared, after a lengthy preamble about certain basic
differences between men and women, that he had come to the conclusion that "it would be impossible for us to live together anyway."
This was partly because he must constantly make sacrifices (with
respect to things of "flesh and sense" i.e., most material things) to
pursue his art (which does not provide the means to acquire things
of "flesh and sense"). He was "more and more concerned with a
search for truth and honesty," whereas Norma (he asserted) could
not live without the "luxuries of life," they represented "an inner
need" to her. If there was a "choice between composition or luxury," he would "always drop the luxury" and "will never change."
He seemed, however, to also have realized that there was also the
difficulty of "two people pursuing the same thing living together" –
Norma needed, he declared, to fulfill the needs of her own ego and
not in him. But he then assumed, unjustly, that if they lived together
she would "inevitably" become jealous of him and "seek attention"
whichever way she could get it. This implied that he, as the senior
and recognized composer, would continue to be successful, whereas
she would always be the lesser figure. Because she was younger?

Because she was a woman? This kind of thinking indicates that there was little expectation on his part that Beecroft could succeed as a composer and would (as a woman) seek attention to compensate for this. Such remarks make one wonder whether his frequent words of encouragement to her over these months were a kind of automatic reassurance, going through the formal and expected motions, while not really meaning any of it.

Regardless of this, he came to the same conclusion that Norma Beecroft had already come to several months earlier when she encountered him in Rome: that their relationship was finished. They must go their separate ways, he wrote, "call it quits" so they could both "be free to accept a partner on open terms." Toward the end of the letter he declared that he was undecided about a possible future relationship with someone: "At this point I don't know whether I'll go back to my wife, who, God help her, still loves me after all these years of hell, whether I'll go it alone ... or seek another permanent relationship ... I want a deep and enduring life with a woman." In the end, he chose to get back together with his wife, Cathy – a puzzling sequel to his relationship with Norma Beecroft.

For Cathy Somers, unfortunately, this did not turn out to be a "deep and enduring life." Sometime in 1962 or early in 1963, she learned that Somers was having an affair with the actress Barbara Chilcott. After years of separation, then reconciliation, this was too painful for her to endure. In May 1963, she committed suicide. Somers went on to marry Barbara Chilcott in 1967 and remained married to her until his death in 1999.

In 1969, Norma Beecroft married a Toronto lawyer, John Wright, but they were divorced five years later, largely due to his alcoholism. In 1978, she met a plastic surgeon from Sudbury, Dr Ronald Turner, and eventually married him in 1990. Unfortunately, by the time she married him he had some serious health problems, but the marriage was generally a happy one and she looked after him faithfully until his death in 2005.

Notes

INTRODUCTION

1 There was also the problem that Somers had never been divorced from his first wife, Catherine, from whom he had been separated since about 1954.
2 Norma Beecroft, "A Life Worth Living" (unpublished autobiography, 2021), 20.
3 Email message to the editor, 9 July 2019.
4 Email message to the editor, 15 July 2021.
5 Benita Wolters-Fredlund, "A 'League Against Willan'? The Early Years of the Canadian League of Composers, 1951–1960," *Journal of the Society for American Music* V, no. 4 (2011), 462.
6 Ibid., 462. Weinzweig had been making some use of twelve-tone organization with respect to pitch since the early 1940s, but his music did not reflect the developments taking place internationally in those years – it was basically neoclassical and essentially lyrical.
7 NB to HS, 27 November 1959.
8 NB to HS, 24 November 1959.
9 NB to HS, 23 January 1960.
10 NB to HS, 27 December 1959.
11 NB to HS, 25 January 1960.
12 NB to HS, 29 January, 1960.
13 The National Film Board film *Rehearsal* (1953) featured the Montreal harpist Marie Iösch-Lorcini, with Paul Scherman conducting the orchestra. Paul Scherman is mentioned toward the end of the Beecroft-Somers correspondence.
14 HS to NB, 25 January 1959.
15 NB to Eleanor Beecroft, 28 October 1959.

268   Notes to pages 18–30

16   NB to HS, 13 October 1959.

17   HS to NB, 29 October 1959.

18   NB to HS, 19 November 1959.

19   NB to HS, 6 November 1959.

20   NB to Eleanor Beecroft, 29 November 1959.

21   NB to HS, 15 December 1959.

22   Ibid.

23   NB to HS, 27 December 1959.

24   Ibid.

25   NB to HS, 27 December 1959.

26   NB to Eleanor Beecroft, 10 February 1960.

27   NB to Eleanor Beecroft, 16 February 1960.

28   HS to NB, 23 September 1959 (but this part of the letter is dated 26 September).

29   HS to NB, 29 October 1959.

30   HS to NB, 1 February 1960.

31   See footnote 13.

32   HS to NB, 22 September 1959.

33   HS to NB, 10 December 1959.

34   HS to NB, 23 September 1959 (but this part of the letter is dated 28 September).

35   HS to NB, 3 October 1959.

36   In his letter of 20 November 1959, Somers writes about the connection between the Canadian landscape and his music: "Forgive me, I'll sound like those documentary orators, but Normie, it is in my blood and I want some day that some of my music will speak for the strength, wildness, ruggedness, beauty of what I feel about this country outside the cities. Land of rocks lakes forest trees, sky."

37   HS to NB, 19 April 1957. There is no envelope or signature in this letter, which may mean that it was never actually posted.

38   HS to NB, 9 February 1960.

39   HS to Cathy Somers, 19 July 1954.

40   It turned out that Somers enjoyed the luxuries of life as much as anyone else did. In marrying the actress Barbara Chilcott in 1967 he also married into considerable family wealth and did not seem to object to the luxuries that went along with a fine house in Toronto's Rosedale district or a separate rented studio.

41   HS to NB, 18 January 1960.

42   HS to NB, 16 January 1960.

43   HS to NB, 1 December 1959.

Notes to pages 31–265 269

44 See, for instance, HS to NB, 3 December 1959.
45 Neoclassicism (from about 1920 to 1950) can be found in such composers as Stravinsky and Hindemith. They employed many characteristics of the Baroque and Classical periods, especially the use of tonal centres, traditional forms (such as sonata-allegro), contrapuntal textures, and a rhythmic language similar to that of the Baroque period. In Somers's case, this is most evident in his frequent use of contrapuntal textures, such as fugue.
46 The use of varying degrees of chance, beginning with American composer John Cage in the early 1950s.

EPILOGUE

1 NB to Eleanor Beecroft, 29 February 1960.
2 Ibid.
3 NB to Eleanor Beecroft, 28 October 1959.
4 NB to Eleanor Beecroft, 15 November 1959.
5 NB to Eleanor Beecroft, 4 January 1960. Later in this letter she admitted that she had always been conflicted between "a creative career and a home life" and was tired of fighting with herself and "what seems to be the rest of the world."
6 HS to NB, 26 February 1960. Later in the letter, he appeared to be justifying his behaviour: "When I'm short tempered and sometimes brutal it is also a way of protecting the softness of my heart."
7 Ibid.
8 HS to NB, 8 April 1960.

Index

Abbado, Claudio, 6, 181

Accademia Nazionale di Santa Cecilia. *See* National Academy of Santa Cecilia course

Adaskin, Murray, 99

Allan, Andrew, 144

American Academy (Rome), 67–8

American Wind Symphony Orchestra, commission from, 85, 122–3, 253, 257

Applebaum, Louis, 113–14, 198

avant-garde, 12, 23, 97n23, 101n30, 152, 232, 237n45, 250

Baboukian, Aram, 115, 170, 198

Backhaus, Wilhelm, 82

ballets, 40, 93, 177

Barker, Lex, 76, 174

Barnes, Lilly, 56–7, 195–6

Barnes, Milton, 56–7, 196

Bartók, Béla, 9, 12, 108

Beaudet, Jean-Marie, 99, 142

Beckwith, John, 83n5, 85n11, 99

Beecroft, Carolyn (NB's sister), 156, 161, 162, 179

Beecroft, Charles (NB's brother), 156, 161, 162, 179

Beecroft, Eleanor Norton (NB's mother): acting career, 5, 29, 37n6, 42, 209, 214; divorce, 156, 161, 162; HS spends time with, 37, 42, 90, 91, 171, 178, 179, 189, 203, 241–2, 255; on NB, 37–8, 90; in NB's letters, 41, 67, 83, 195, 196, 198, 213, 230, 248; NB's letters to, 17, 19, 22, 261–3

Beecroft, Eric (NB's brother): career overview, 38; NB's autumn visit with, 39–40, 41, 44, 49–50, 53, 74; NB's Christmas visit with, 104, 162, 173, 174, 181, 190, 195

Beecroft, Jane (NB's sister), 151, 210, 220

Beecroft, Julian Balfour (NB's father), 5, 37n6, 156n18, 178, 184, 252, 261

Beecroft, Norma: career after Rome, 32–3; desire to write music, 20–1, 117, 136–7, 190–1; editor's visit with, 3–4; feelings of unhappiness and search for self, 86–7, 145–6, 154, 155,

194–5, 201–2, 210, 213, 231, 261–2; financial situation, 19, 61, 87, 100, 106, 223, 230; growing confidence of, 12–13, 20–1, 79, 116, 117, 136, 236–7, 262–3; health problems, 34–5, 41n13, 75, 234, 237–8, 248, 252, 258; on Italian people, 61, 205; language barrier in Rome, 63, 64, 75, 94, 95, 181, 195; living arrangements, 60, 63, 75, 76–7, 82–3; marriages, 266; ocean voyage, 34–7, 39, 42; social life in Rome, 75, 102, 105, 111, 124, 154–5, 170, 180, 181; travels in Europe, 44, 50–2, 53, 55–7; trip to Anzio, 201, 204–6, 213; trip to London, 39–41, 43–4, 49–50, 53, 74; writing style of, xiii, xiv. *See also* Beecroft-Somers relationship; compositions (NB); flute lessons (NB); National Academy of Santa Cecilia course; Petrassi's private lessons; Rome, NB on

Beecroft, Ruth (NB's aunt), 189, 193

Beecroft-Somers relationship: from 1955 to fall 1959, 7, 8–9, 16, 31; conversation on 27 October 1959, 18–19, 75–6, 77, 97; editor's research into, 3; end of, 22, 31, 260–1, 265–6; expressions of loneliness and missing one another, 43–4, 47, 51–2, 62, 104, 136, 204; first meeting, 6–7; HS supports and advises NB, 38, 46, 64, 123, 124–5, 137, 162, 179, 223, 233–4, 263, 266; HS's bad behaviour, 16–17, 91,

173, 184, 252, 260–2, 263–4, 265, 269n6; HS's declarations of love, xiv, 18, 31, 81, 89, 120, 159, 182–3, 200, 262; HS's influence on NB's musical development, 8–9, 23; HS's jealousy and lack of trust, 18, 78, 87, 90, 241, 247; HS's plans to visit Rome, 22, 27, 182, 186, 190–1, 197–8, 218, 223, 230, 246; HS's reasons for not joining NB in Europe, 58, 144, 148, 161, 182, 230; HS's thoughts on marriage, 17, 31, 72, 90, 91, 240, 262, 264; HS's visit to Rome, 258–61, 263, 264, 265; NB's desire for HS to join her in Europe, 57, 63, 87, 145, 180; NB's doubts about, 19–23, 165, 173, 190–1, 199, 249, 250, 251–2; NB's jealousy and lack of trust, 31, 69, 130–1, 136, 143–4, 235–6, 242, 247, 251, 265–6; NB's thoughts on marriage, 17–19, 21–3, 72–3, 96, 197, 202, 210, 242, 262, 263

Berio, Luciano, 219, 237n45
Bernand, Ron, 169
Bird, Bailey, 98, 193, 228
Blake, Katharine, 43
BMI (Broadcast Music, Inc.), 14, 57, 58, 67n30, 98n25, 186, 193
Bochner, Lloyd, 43, 167n35
Bochner, Ruth Roher, 43
books: HS on, 7, 45, 46, 54, 58, 63–4, 85, 118n57, 123n62, 255; NB on, 36, 44, 69, 73, 74, 129, 139, 202, 206, 237–8
Boulez, Pierre: Gazzelloni plays music of, 103; HS and, 23, 85,

Index

142, 193, 194, 199, 200; NB and, 20, 115, 130, 139

Bream, Julian, 95, 101, 119, 218–19

Cable, Howard, 6, 48, 71, 168n38

Campbell, Douglas, 113n49, 126n69, 245

Canada Council: concerts sponsored by, 128n75; encourages new Canadian music, 14; established, 85; HS applies to, 148, 161, 186, 188n60, 264; HS on importance of, 107n42; NB applies to, 117, 137, 171; NB obtains grant from, 13; Senior Arts Fellowships at, 109n45, 264

Canadian League of Composers, 7, 9, 14, 83, 99n27, 144n100, 198, 210n9

Canadian Music Centre, 14, 99n28

Canadian Music Journal, 81, 84

Carmen (opera), 54

Carmirelli quartet, 218–19

Casey, Len, 70–1

CBC: *The Crucible* on, 42n15, 126; *Fighting Words* on, 224n26; HS and NB's first meeting at, 6–7, 78, 92; HS's work at, 29, 70, 85n11, 98, 113n48, 212n12, 240n48; interest in composers, 14; NB's work at, 5–6, 13, 32, 54n4, 65n22, 261; politics at, 70–1

CBC Symphony Orchestra, 14, 83n5, 226, 230n38, 243n2

C.F. Peters (music publisher), 256

Chapman, Christopher, 108, 112, 113, 133, 168

Chevalier, Dr Paul, 74–5, 110

Chilcott, Barbara (HS's wife), 30, 41, 157n22, 266, 268n40

Chinni, Peter, 180

Chrisòfides, Peter: education, 11, 129; helps NB with compositions, 103, 104–5, 129, 139; NB first meets, 96; NB socializes with, 97, 174, 181, 198

Clayton, Wilbur Dorsey "Buck," 74

Cohen, Nathan, 127n71, 209n8, 224–5

Collier, Ron, 64, 71, 121

Columbia-Princeton Electronic Music Center, 32, 235n43

composers' conference (Stratford), 113, 198, 214

compositions (HS): in 1960s, 32, 269n45; ballet scores, 177; influence of physical surroundings on, 27, 112–13; *Louis Riel,* 32, 41n14, 158n24; for *A Midsummer Night's Dream,* 31, 245, 246, 264; *North Country,* 14, 113n48; other guitar pieces, 120; performances of, 10, 78, 81n2, 85–6, 89n13, 127–8, 210n9, 212, 225–6, 228n35, 240n48, 245; Pittsburgh commission, 85, 122–3, 253, 257; *Serinette,* 29; Sonata No. 2, 89n13; *Stereophony,* 23, 32, 239; String Quartet No. 3, 81, 88, 105, 127–8, 165; Symphony, 15, 59n16; Three Songs, 216n14; twelve-tone fugues, 67. See also *Five Songs for Dark Voice; Guitar Sonata* (HS); *Lyric* (HS); Passacaglia and Fugue for Orchestra (HS); Piano Concerto

274 Index

No. 2 (HS); *Saguenay* (film), score for

compositions (NB): avant-garde's influence on, 23; chamber orchestra project, 11, 94, 103–4, 115–16, 128–9, 138; commissioned, 32; early works, 5–6; *Fantasy for Strings,* 6, 9, 56n8; Fram's songs, 11, 12–13, 94, 110, 115, 171, 174, 195, 213, 229, 235, 252; *Movement for Woodwinds and Brass,* 6, 9, 106n39; Tre Pezzi Brevi, 13; twelve-tone piece for piano (four row forms), 174; twelve-tone piece for piano (original row form only), 11, 138, 139, 155, 165, 171

concerts: in Canada, 9–10, 65–6, 83, 101, 148, 256; in Europe, 140; on ocean voyage, 36–7; in Rome, 11–12, 74, 82, 93, 97, 154–5, 218–19, 231, 249; of Shostakovitch compositions, 232, 250, 251. *See also* compositions (HS): performances of; music festivals; Tanglewood Festival

Copland, Aaron, 49n35, 96

Coughtry, Graham, 127, 140, 147–8

Couture, Jean-Papineau, 99

Crawley, Frank Radford "Budge," 131–2, 133, 160, 203

Crawley, Judith, 131–2, 133, 160, 203

Crawley Films, 27, 113, 131

The Crucible (play), 42, 126, 162–3

Dallapiccolo, Luigi, 103

Darmstadt music festival, 11, 13, 20, 102–3, 117, 130, 155, 171

Dartington International Summer School, 13, 219

Davidovsky, Mario, 32, 235

Davis, Donald (HS's brother-in-law), 30, 41n12, 157n22

Davis, Murray (HS's brother-in-law), 30, 41n12, 157n22

Day, Gordon, 243, 244, 249

Debussy, Claude, 92

d'Hondt, Danica, 144, 229, 235, 241, 242, 247, 251

Diamente, Edward, 118

Díaz, Alirio, 128, 135, 137, 141

Dijk, Rudi Martinus van, 234

Dolin, Samuel, 144

Eaton, John, 68

electroacoustic music, 23, 132n84, 235n43, 237n45

electronic music, 32–3, 97, 108, 109, 117, 200

Electronic Music Studio, University of Toronto, 32, 109n44, 149

Eliot, T.S., 5, 227–8

Fairfax, Joan, 70

Feldbrill, Vic, 85–6

Ferry, Joan, 143, 144, 157, 176, 187

Ferry, Tony, 143, 157, 158, 176, 187

films: HS on, 168, 172, 184–5; NB on, 35–6, 50, 154; *Rehearsal,* 25, 86n12, 267n13. See also *Saguenay* (film), score for

Five Songs for Dark Voice (HS), 15, 47n31, 71n41, 104, 118, 228n35

Index
275

flute lessons (NB): content, 75, 164; cost, 68; NB cancels, 174; need for new flute, 146, 155, 171, 219, 243, 244, 249

Follows, Ted, 186–7

Forrester, Maureen, 47n31, 228–9

Foss, Lukas, 6, 8, 49n35, 96

Fram, Michael, 7, 47n31, 88, 230, 235, 242, 256. *See also* compositions (NB): Fram's songs

Franchetti, Arnold, 107, 114, 124, 139

Gazzelloni, Severino: Franchetti *vs.*, 114; gives NB information and introductions, 11, 95, 102, 117, 154, 180; NB socializes with, 219; on Petrassi, 103; tells story of Shostakovitch concert, 232, 250n10. *See also* flute lessons (NB)

gender roles, 4, 23, 117, 137, 180–1, 192, 269n5

Ghedini, Giorgio Federico, 155

Gillespie, Dizzy, 74

Giuffre, James Peter, 142, 148

Godden, Reginald, 14, 38n7, 82, 168n36, 212, 224, 225

Gould, Glenn, 228n34, 229

Gowan, George, 187

Grudeff, Marian, 89

Guitar Society of Toronto, 44n23, 46n26, 65, 128

Guitar Sonata (HS): Bream's work on, 101, 219; choice of name, 122; commissioned, 65n24; HS's frustrations with, 46, 47, 119; HS's success with, 58; Segovia and, 158, 165–6; technical aspects, 70

Guthrie, Tyrone, 245n6, 246

Gwen (Symonds's girlfriend), 65, 91, 168, 187, 223

Hall, James, 142

Hart, Harvey, 126, 162–3

Hindemith, Paul, 108

Hinrichsen, Walter, 256–7

"The Hollow Men" (Eliot), 5

Honegger, Arthur, 14, 59n16

Ives, Charles, 9, 26–7, 149

Ivy, Robie, 144

Jacobson, Berthe Poncy, 25, 34–5

Jarrett, Charles, 43

jazz, 30, 38n7, 39, 53, 55, 74, 189, 226–7

Jones, Linda, 178, 198

Kane, Jack, 71

Kassner, Eli: career overview, 44n23; Díaz and, 128, 135, 137; HS's Guitar Sonata and, 158; at Royal Conservatory, 67; studies with Segovia, 51n41, 66, 70

Kassner, Noémi, 51, 66, 67, 137

Kilburn, Weldon, 168n36, 228

The Killdeer (play), 209, 214, 228

Koussevitzky, Serge, 84n7, 231

Koussevitzky work. See *Lyric* (HS)

Kraemer, Franz, 41, 44, 45, 46, 54n4

Krenek, Ernst, 119, 251

Lamb, Marguerita, 154, 170, 174, 181

Index

letters: editing of, xiii–xiv; given to editor by NB, 3–4; overview of HS's, 24–32; before fall 1959, 7–8; trajectory of, 4–5. *See also* Beecroft, Norma; Beecroft-Somers relationship; Somers, Harry

Little, George, 85, 127

Littlewood, Joan, 43n18, 46, 176n45

Lombardo, Roberto, 106

Lopez, Gustavo, 65–6

Lyric (HS), 47n29, 84n7, 153, 161, 186, 226, 244

MacDonald, Ian Bruce, 41, 193

Mackie, Catherine. *See* Somers, Catherine Mackie

MacMillan, Sir Ernest, 116

Maderna, Bruno, 12, 13, 219, 237

Mailer, Norman, 224–5

Major, Leon, 158

Malloch, William F., 40–1, 49

Marcello, Benedetto, 164

Marlene (HS's friend), 121, 130, 143, 147–8

Marshall, Lois, 228

Mazzoleni, Ettore, 229, 230n38

McNamara, Helen, 65, 91, 144, 215

Mehta, Zubin, 56–7

Mendelssohn, Felix, 245, 246

A Midsummer Night's Dream (play), 31, 245, 246, 264

Milhaud, Darius, 15, 59n16, 96

Montand, Yves, 148

Monteux, Pierre, 93

Musgrave, Thea, 49, 95

music festivals, 13, 78, 81n2, 99, 106–8, 118, 219. *See also*

concerts; Darmstadt music festival; Tanglewood Festival

National Academy of Santa Cecilia course: applicants, 232; content and other students, 233, 234–5, 236–7; HS's visit to Rome and, 197, 258; institution established, 93n18; NB accepted into, 12–13, 233–4; NB enjoys, 263; NB seeks information on, 110–1, 115, 138; NB's entrance examination for, 195, 203, 229–30, 231; NB's submission to, 11, 20, 181; Petrassi encourages NB to apply to, 94, 138, 174; social opportunities of, 139

New Music Concerts, 32–3

Nichols, Jack, 65–6, 127, 140, 255

Nono, Luigi, 101, 194, 200, 219

Norton, Eleanor. *See* Beecroft, Eleanor Norton

Olnick, Harvey, 109, 149

operas, 15, 29, 32, 41n14, 54, 158n24

Paris (France): HS in, 14–15, 31, 59, 85nn8–9, 142, 188n60, 264; NB in, 50–1, 53

Passacaglia and Fugue for Orchestra (HS), 15, 85, 93, 142, 212n10, 226, 245

Pentland, Barbara, 10, 23, 210

Petrassi, Goffredo: Abbado and, 6; career overview, 61; compositions performed, 231; on Fram, 235, 242; Franchetti on, 124, 139; Gazzelloni on, 103; HS criticizes, 250, 260, 261. *See also*

National Academy of Santa
Cecilia course
Petrassi's private lessons (NB):
assignments, 11, 138, 155, 174;
cost, 68, 87, 213; discussion on
state of music, 139; HS on, 178,
184; language barrier, 94, 95; NB
awaits Petrassi's return, 61, 75,
84; NB meets Petrassi, 19, 93–4;
NB's frustrations and fears, 111,
171; score study, 129
Piano Concerto No. 2 (HS), 15,
82n3, 142, 212, 224, 226
Pizzetti, Ildebrando, 232
plays. *See* theatre and plays
poems: quoted or alluded to by HS,
60, 91, 165, 216, 221, 227,
242–3; written by HS, 150n6,
216n15
Porena, Boris, 130
Prizak, Mario, 228
Putsché, Thomas, 106–7

Reaney, James, 29, 209, 214,
228
Reeves, John, 193–4
Rehearsal (film), 25, 86n12,
267n13
Respighi, Ottorino, 93, 221
Ritt, Morey, 36–7
Rochberg, George, 105, 118–19,
129, 139–40
Rome, NB on: beauty, 61, 95;
birds, 170; food, 63; gender
roles, 180–1; high cost of living,
19, 68–9, 76; New Year's Eve
celebrations, 195, 198; shopping,
83
Rosenfeldt (patron of music), 111,
115, 124

Royal Conservatory of Music, 6,
14, 44n23, 210n9
Rushing, James Andrew, 74

Saguenay (film), score for: commissioned, 113; description of film,
112; fee, 27, 133, 160, 186; HS
agrees to work on, 159; HS's
complaints about, 211–12, 214;
HS's elation with, 243–4; HS's
responsibilities on, 132; HS's trip
to Rome and, 161, 182, 230;
HS's work with Chapman on,
108, 168; technical aspects, 23,
152–3, 163, 189, 203, 207, 211,
226, 227
Saturday Review (magazine), 116,
140
Savio, Carla, 63, 95, 97
Savio, Roberto, 170, 190
Savio, Signora, 63
Savio family, 60, 86, 97, 194, 198
Scherman, Donna, 172, 192
Scherman, Paul, 172, 192, 267n13
Schmitz, E. Robert, 125n63, 168
Schoenberg, Arnold, 119, 129, 200
Schott (music publisher), 57, 58
Schuller, Gunther, 57, 58, 239
Segovia, Andrés, 66, 70, 158,
165–6
Serge Koussevitzky Music
Foundation, 47n29, 84n7, 231,
244n4
serialism. *See* twelve-tone technique
Serinette (opera), 29
Shadbolt, Ted, 70–1, 141
Shanet, Howard, 225
Shostakovitch, Dmitri, 232, 250, 251
"Showtime" (TV program), 6,
70n39, 71

278 Index

Somers, Catherine Mackie ("Cathy," HS's wife), 28, 88, 256n15, 266. *See also* Somers-Mackie marriage

Somers, Harry: awareness of his physical environment, 26–7, 59, 63, 71, 98, 131, 156–7, 220, 224, 228; on composition, 28–9, 149, 151–2, 175, 250–1; copying by, 6, 8, 15, 27, 29, 70, 98; earlier book on, 3; education, 14–15, 59n16, 82n3, 125, 168, 188n60; extramarital affairs, 16, 30–1, 130n82, 266; feelings of elation, 15, 25, 108, 174–5, 241, 243–5; feelings of sadness, 24–5, 27, 98, 150, 253–4; financial situation, 27, 77, 108, 125, 186; living arrangements, 27, 47, 59; marriage to Barbara Chilcott, 41n12, 266, 268n40; in the military, 24, 133; overview of letters written by, 24–32; self-portrayal as an artist, 28, 92, 114, 208, 265; sense of humour, 25–6, 48, 60, 118, 153–4, 186, 208–9; writing style, xiii–xiv. *See also* Beecroft-Somers relationship; compositions (HS); Somers-Mackie marriage

Somers, Russell (HS's father), 163n28, 201

Somers, Ruth (HS's mother), 48, 83, 91, 163n28, 201, 210n10

Somers-Mackie marriage: divorce, 27, 99, 108, 109, 141, 161, 265, 267n1; HS's elated letter to Cathy, 15, 25; proposal, 210; reconciliation, 17, 31, 266;

separation, 15–16; year in Paris, 14, 31, 59n16, 188n60

Spectra (Schuller), 239

Stenson, Vivienne, 185

Stockhausen, Karlheinz, 194, 200

Strate, Grant, 177

Stratford Festival: conference of composers at, 113, 198, 214; HS's work for, 31, 47n31, 228n35, 245, 246, 264

Stravinsky, Igor, 54, 85, 92, 101n29, 113n49

Symonds, Norman: admires HS's work, 142; advises HS on *Saguenay* score, 226, 244; on Beecroft-Somers relationship, 91, 166; broken leg, 134; dislikes Schuller, 58; drunk driving of, 223–4; at G.M. party, 168–9; interest in jazz, 30, 38, 39; interest in writing for the theatre, 102; trip to Europe, 187

Tanglewood Festival: NB's compositions played at, 6, 8, 9, 106n39; NB's work on Cantata at, 94; other students and people NB met at, 40, 49n35, 56n9, 68, 181n52, 225, 235; Santa Cecilia course and, 236; teachers at, 77

Terry, Pamela, 99, 209n8

theatre and plays: in Austrian mountain, 56; *The Crucible*, 42, 126, 162–3; HS on other plays, 46, 113, 126–7, 157, 158, 176, 177–8, 193, 216n15, 228; *The Killdeer*, 209, 214, 228; NB on, 40, 43, 50, 102. *See also* Stratford Festival

Index

279

Theodore Presser (music publisher), 105, 129

Tudor, David, 11, 97

Turner, Ronald (NB's husband), 266

twelve-tone technique: HS and, 67, 108, 137, 200, 226, 244; J. Weinzweig's use of, 7, 10–1, 267n6; NB's use of, 12, 129, 142, 174 (*see also* compositions (NB): twelve-tone piece for piano [original row form only]); Petrassi's use of, 103, 139, 184; Rochberg's use of, 105n37, 118–19, 139

Universal Edition of Vienna (music publisher), 13, 57

University of Toronto, 7, 32, 44n23, 109n44, 149

Walter, Arnold, 109n44, 149

Webern, Anton, 10, 108, 129, 130n81, 149, 160, 200

Webster, Jan, 187

Weinzweig, Helen, 7, 83, 175–6, 191, 199, 200

Weinzweig, John: career overview, 6–7, 267n6; composers' conference and, 198, 214; compositions performed, 10, 78, 83, 106; founder of Canadian League of Composers, 144n100; as HS's teacher and friend, 7, 14, 84, 137; letter for NB's course and, 229–30, 231, 233; in the military, 133n85; as NB's teacher, 5–7, 8–9, 10, 129, 137; score analysis with HS, 193, 194, 199–200; twelve-tone technique used by, 7, 10–1, 267n6

Winters, Kenneth, 81

Wright, John (NB's husband), 266

Yeats, W.B., 13, 252